Risk of Death

in Canada

What We Know and How We Know It

Risk of Death

in Canada

What We Know and How We Know It

Simon P. Thomas & Steve E. Hrudey

University of Alberta Press

Published by
    The University of Alberta Press
    141 Athabasca Hall
    Edmonton, Alberta
    Canada T6G 2E8
in association with the Eco-Research Chair in Environmental Risk Management at the University of Alberta.

Printed in Canada 5 4 3 2 1

Canadian Cataloguing in Publication Data

Thomas, Simon, 1970–
    Risk of death in Canada

    Includes bibliographical references.
    ISBN 0-88864-299-7

    1. Mortality—Canada—Statistical methods. 2. Mortality—Canada—Statistics. 3. Health risk assessment—Canada. 4. Canada—Statistics, Vital. 5. Death—Causes—Statistics. I. Hrudey, S. E. (Steve E.) II. Title.
        HB1359.T46 1997   304.6'4571'0727   C97-910437-8

Printed and bound by Hignell Book Printing Ltd, Winnipeg, Canada.

Printed on acid-free paper.

The University of Alberta Press gratefully acknowledges the support received for its publishing program from the Canada Council for the Arts, the Department of Canadian Heritage, and the Alberta Foundation for the Arts.

COMMITTED TO THE DEVELOPMENT OF CULTURE AND THE ARTS

THE CANADA COUNCIL | LE CONSEIL DES ARTS
FOR THE ARTS | DU CANADA
SINCE 1957 | DEPUIS 1957

Contents

1. Introduction   1
    Categories of Health Risk Information   2
    Health Risk Evidence and Inference   4
    Numerical Data Information   15

Part One: Direct Evidence

2. Background Mortality Information   23
    Evidence Source   23
    Population Evidence   25
    Rates   31

3. The Death Certificate   37
    Total Registered Death Evidence   40
    Evidence of Sex Differences   42
    Evidence on Age   44
    Evidence on Marital Status   54
    Evidence on Usual Residence   56

4. Cause of Death Evidence   59
    International Classification of Diseases (ICD)   59
    Detailed 1994 Evidence   64
    Major Causes of Death   67
    Uncertainty in the Reported Cause of Death   102

5. Other Ways of Accounting for Mortality   105
    Potential Years of Life Lost (PYLL)   105
    Loss of Life Expectancy (LLE)   111

Part Two: Indirect Evidence and Inference

6. Epidemiology   119
    Measurement   119
    Types of Epidemiological Study   122
    Causal Inference   124
    Uncertainty   127

7. Major Individual Risk Factors   131
    Biological Risk Factors   132
    Lifestyle/Behavioural Risk Factors   135
    Societal Risk Factors   148
    Environmental Risk Factors   155

8. Risk Factors by Cause of Death   161
    Infectious Diseases   161
    Cancer   162
    Cardiovascular Disease   166
    Respiratory Disease   166
    External Causes   167

Part Three: Predictive Inference

9. Risk Assessment   175
    Four Stages of Risk Assessment   175
    Toxicology   178
    Quantitative Interpretation of Cancer Data   186
    Exposure Assessment   190
    Risk Estimates   191
    Uncertainty   200

Part Four: Discussion and Summary Observations

10. Discussion   203
    Comparisons Between Categories   203
    Summary of Health Risk Evidence and Inference   209
    Summary of Uncertainty   218

11. Summary Observations   221
    Direct Evidence   221
    Epidemiology (Indirect Evidence and Inference)   222
    Quantitative Risk Assessment (Predictive Inference)   223
    General Observations   224

12. Additional Information Sources   225
    Popular Literature   225
    Governmental and Non-Profit Health Agencies   226
    Textbooks   226
    Scientific Journal Articles   227
    Government Publications   227
    Contacts   228

Appendixes

Appendix One Detailed Causes of Death, 1994   233
Appendix Two Causes of Death by Age, 1994   245
Appendix Three Cause of Death, 1991–1994   253
Appendix Four Morbidity and Mortality Risk Factors   259

Glossary

263

References

265

List of Figures

Figure 1.1   Disability versus Impairment   5
Figure 1.2   Causal Chain Model for Environmental Health Risks   11
Figure 1.3   Health Risk Evidence, Inference and the Uncertainty Hierarchy   12
              for Adverse Outcomes
Figure 1.4   Log Scale Example   16
Figure 1.5   Normal Scale Example   16

Figure 2.1   Population, 1930–1990   27
Figure 2.2   Population Age Distributions, 1930–1990   28

Figure 3.1   Death Registration Form   38
Figure 3.2   Population, Deaths, and Crude Death Rates, 1930–1990   41
Figure 3.3   Total Deaths by Sex, 1930–1990   43
Figure 3.4   Crude Death Rate by Sex, 1930–1990   43
Figure 3.5   Total Deaths by Age, 1994   45
Figure 3.6   Death Rate by Age, 1994   45
Figure 3.7   Total Deaths by Age, 1930–1990   47
Figure 3.8   Death Rate by Age, 1930–1990   47
Figure 3.9   Crude and Age-Standardized Death Rates, 1930–1990   48
Figure 3.10   Total Infant Deaths, 1930–1990   49
Figure 3.11   Infant Death Rate, 1930–1990   49
Figure 3.12   Cumulative Percentage of Deaths by Age, 1930–1990   52
Figure 3.13   Median Age at Death, 1930–1990   52
Figure 3.14   Remaining Life Expectancy at Selected Ages, Males, 1930–1990   53
Figure 3.15   Remaining Life Expectancy at Selected Ages, Females, 1930–1990   53
Figure 3.16   Death Rate by Marital Status, Males, 1990   55
Figure 3.17   Death Rate by Marital Status, Females, 1990   55
Figure 3.18   Total Deaths by Province, 1994   57
Figure 3.19   Age-Standardized Death Rate by Province, 1994   57

Figure 4.1   Cause of Death by Age, Males, 1994   66
Figure 4.2   Cause of Death by Age, Females, 1994   66
Figure 4.3   Major Causes of Death, Males, 1994   68
Figure 4.4   Major Causes of Death, Females, 1994   68
Figure 4.5   Major Causes Death Rate, Males, 1930–1990   69
Figure 4.6   Major Causes Death Rate, Females, 1930–1990   69
Figure 4.7   Infectious Deaths by Age, Males, 1994   75
Figure 4.8   Infectious Death Rate by Age, Males, 1994   75
Figure 4.9   Infectious Deaths by Age, Females, 1994   76
Figure 4.10   Infectious Death Rate by Age, Females, 1994   76
Figure 4.11   Infectious Death Rate, 1930–1990   77

Figure 4.12	Infectious Death Rate by Age, Both, 1930–1990	77
Figure 4.13	Cancer Deaths by Age, Males, 1994	80
Figure 4.14	Cancer Death Rate by Age, Males, 1994	80
Figure 4.15	Cancer Deaths by Age, Females, 1994	81
Figure 4.16	Cancer Death Rate by Age, Females, 1994	81
Figure 4.17	Cancer Death Rate, 1930–1990	82
Figure 4.18	Cancer Death Rate by Age, Both, 1930–1990	82
Figure 4.19	Age-Standardized Incidence Rates (ASIR) for Selected Cancer Sites, Males, Canada, 1969–1996	84
Figure 4.20	Age-Standardized Mortality Rates (ASMR) for Selected Cancer Sites, Males, Canada, 1969–1996	85
Figure 4.21	Age-Standardized Incidence Rates (ASIR) for Selected Cancer Sites, Females, Canada, 1969–1996	86
Figure 4.22	Age-Standardized Mortality Rates (ASMR) for Selected Cancer Sites, Females, Canada, 1969–1996	87
Figure 4.23	Cardiovascular Deaths by Age, Males, 1994	89
Figure 4.24	Cardiovascular Death Rate by Age, Males, 1994	89
Figure 4.25	Cardiovascular Deaths by Age, Females, 1994	90
Figure 4.26	Cardiovascular Death Rate by Age, Females, 1994	90
Figure 4.27	Cardiovascular Death Rate, 1930–1990	91
Figure 4.28	Cardiovascular Death Rate by Age, Both, 1930–1990	91
Figure 4.29	Respiratory Deaths by Age, Males, 1994	93
Figure 4.30	Respiratory Death Rate by Age, Males, 1994	93
Figure 4.31	Respiratory Deaths by Age, Females, 1994	94
Figure 4.32	Respiratory Death Rate by Age, Females, 1994	94
Figure 4.33	Respiratory Death Rate, 1930–1990	95
Figure 4.34	Respiratory Death Rate by Age, Both, 1930–1990	95
Figure 4.35	External Deaths by Age, Males, 1994	97
Figure 4.36	External Death Rate by Age, Males, 1994	97
Figure 4.37	External Deaths by Age, Females, 1994	98
Figure 4.38	External Death Rate by Age, Females, 1994	98
Figure 4.39	External Death Rate, 1930–1990	99
Figure 4.40	External Death Rate by Age, Both, 1930–1990	99
Figure 4.41	Total Maternal Deaths, 1930–1990	101
Figure 4.42	Maternal Death Rate, 1930–1990	101

List of Tables

Table 1.1	Three Categories of Health Risk Evidence and Inference	3
Table 2.1	1994 Evidence	24
Table 2.2	1930–1990 Trend Evidence	24
Table 2.3	Population by Age Categories, 1994	26
Table 2.4	Changes in Population Age Distribution, 1930–1990	31
Table 2.5A	Crude Death Rate Example, 1930 and 1990	33
Table 2.5B	Infant Mortality Rate Example, 1930 and 1990	33
Table 2.5C	Cause Specific Death Rate Example, 1994	33
Table 2.5D	Age-Specific Death Rate Example, 1994	33
Table 2.6	Crude and Age-Standardized Death Rates, 1930 and 1990	35
Table 3.1	Vital Statistics, 1994	37
Table 3.2	Death Certificate Sections Related to Direct Evidence	39
Table 4.1	Identifying the Underlying Cause of Death	61
Table 4.2	Major Categories and Shortened Names of Causes of Death	62
Table 4.3	Example of Four-Digit ICD-9 Coding	63
Table 4.4	Mortality by Major Category, 1994	65
Table 4.5	Changes to the Classification System, 1930–1990	71
Table 5.1	Percentage of Total Deaths vs the PYLL, Males, 1994	108
Table 5.2	Percentage of Total Deaths vs the PYLL, Females, 1994	109
Table 5.3	Percentage of All Deaths Considered by Three Age Cutoffs, 1994	110
Table 5.4	Comparison of Male and Female Total PYLL, 1994	110
Table 5.5	Life Table, Males, 1994	112
Table 5.6	Total Deaths and the LLE, Males, 1994	114
Table 5.7	Total Deaths and the LLE, Females, 1994	115
Table 6.1	Exposure vs Disease	120
Table 6.2	Types of Epidemiological Study	123
Table 6.3	Comparison of Observational Study Designs	128
Table 7.1	Individual Risk Factors Relating to Health	132
Table 7.2	Smoking-Attributable Mortality (SAM) by Disease Category, Canada, 1991	137
Table 7.3	Estimated Deaths Attributed to Smoking in Canada	138
Table 7.4	Estimated Effects of Dietary Actions on Reducing Cancer Incidence	143
Table 7.5	Summary of RRs for Lifestyle Variables Found to be Statistically Significant for Affecting 44 Health Conditions	147
Table 7.6	Age-Standardized Mortality Rates for Combinations of Lifestyle Variables	147

Table 7.7	Occupational Mortality, 1993	152
Table 7.8	Risk by Various Modes of Transportation	154
Table 7.9	Risks Associated with Various Recreational Activities	154
Table 7.10	Chemicals and Exposures Associated with Human Cancer	157
Table 7.11	Risks Associated with Various Natural Disasters	159
Table 7.12	Worst Tornadoes in Canada	159
Table 8.1	Estimated Proportion of Cancer Deaths Attributed to Various Factors	164
Table 8.2	Estimated Causes of Cancer Deaths in Canada	164
Table 8.3	Estimates of Potential Effects of Prevention or Early Detection on Cancer Incidence	165
Table 8.4	Risk Factors for Motor Vehicle Accidents	169
Table 9.1	Summary of CEPA Chemicals for Toxicity, Carcinogenicity, and Exposure Data	193
Table 9.2	Estimated Daily Food Intake (μg/kg.bw/day) by Age Categories	194
Table 9.3	Exposure Values	194
Table 9.4	Carcinogen Slope Factors and Unit Risk Factors	197
Table 9.5	Basis for Carcinogen Slope Factors	198
Table 9.6	Estimated Lifetime Cancer Risk	199
Table 9.7	Maximum Plausible Annual Number of Predicted Cancers	199
Table 10.1	Comparison of Epidemiology and Toxicological Risk Assessment	205
Table 10.2	Comparison of the Quantitative Capabilities of Human Epidemiological Studies with Toxicological Risk Assessment Predictive Levels	206
Table 10.3	Annual Cancer Mortality Associated with Environmental Exposures	208
Table 10.4	Summary of Statistics Related to Mortality, 1994	208
Table 10.5	Summary of Major Causes of Death, 1994	208
Table 10.6	Causes of Death, 1994	210
Table 10.7	Annual Risk of Dying by Age and Sex, 1994	212
Table 10.8	Annual Risk of Dying by Selected Age, Sex, and Major Cause of Death, 1994	213
Table 10.9	Annual Mortality Risks From Several Sources	216
Table 10.10	Summary of Uncertainty	219

Abbreviations

ABS	Antilock Braking System
AIDS	Acquired Immune Deficiency Syndrome
AMI	Acute Myocardial Infarction
BMI	Body Mass Index
CDC	Centers for Disease Control and Prevention
CEPA	Canadian Environmental Protection Act
CHD	Cardiovascular Heart Disease
CI	Confidence Interval
CPR	Cardiopulmonary Resuscitation
DALYs	Disability-Adjusted Life Years
DNA	Deoxyribonucleic Acid
EPI	Exposure/Potency Index
HDL	High-Density Lipoprotein
HERP	Human Exposure dose/Rodent Potency dose
HIV	Human Immunodeficiency Virus
IARC	International Agency for Research on Cancer
ICD	International Classification of Diseases
IHD	Ischaemic Heart Disease
ILSI	International Life Science Institute
IRIS	Integrated Risk Information System
LD_{50}	Median Lethal Dose
LDL	Low-Density Lipoprotein
LLE	Loss of Life Expectancy
MTD	Maximum Tolerated Dose
NOAEL	No Observed Adverse Effect Level
PAR	Population Attributable Risk
PYLL	Potential Years of Life Lost
RfD	Reference Dose
RR	Relative Risk, Risk Ratio, or Rate Ratio
SAM	Smoking-Attributable Mortality
SMR	Standardized Mortality Ratio
TD_{05}	Tumorigenic Dose (5%)
TD_{50}	Median Tumorigenic Dose
TDI	Tolerable Daily Intake
US EPA	United States Environmental Protection Agency
US NRC	United States National Research Council
UCD	Underlying Cause of Death
UV	Ultraviolet
UVR	Ultraviolet Radiation
WHMIS	Workplace Hazardous Materials Information System
WHO	World Health Organization

"Life Expectancy" by Sidney Harris, reproduced by permission of the artist.

Preface

Risk is a pervasive concern in our society. Over the past century, as the Canadian standard of living has risen, we have seen a substantial change in the nature of the challenges to our individual health and well-being. Our ancestors faced enormous obstacles to survive the rigors of our climate and wilderness and the scourges of infectious disease. Recently, we have experienced a well-documented transition from acute diseases as major causes of death to the dominance of chronic diseases such as cancer and cardiovascular disease. This transition to chronic diseases parallels the increasing age of our population.

As we learn more about disease prevention and cure, we naturally focus increasingly on those diseases most responsible for mortality and morbidity in our society. At the same time, we have experienced an explosion of technological interventions in every aspect of our lives. We are exposed to new drugs, pesticides, food additives, and industrial and consumer products at an accelerating rate. Some of these exposures can cause serious disease, most notably in workplace exposures (e.g., asbestos and mesothelioma, vinyl chloride and angiosarcoma). For many other types of cancer, the evidence is much weaker or unclear. In addition, an understanding of the role of ionizing radiation in causing cancer has increased our knowledge about health risks that range from the blatantly obvious to the remarkably subtle.

Our progress in improving overall health in our society has allowed us to explore and attempt to manage smaller or more subtle risks. This progress has not been the same for all parts of our society. We see a great difference in the health of the rich and the poor, a gulf that some argue is increasing despite overall improvements in health across society. As risks and benefits are not uniformly distributed, many issues involving risk have become contentious. Different parties in any risk debate will commonly see the risks and any risk-benefit trade-offs very differently. The intensity of these risk controversies has led to great interest in the communication of risk, mostly among those who are looking for approval of a new activity or those who grant such approvals. When health risks are debated, risk comparisons are often used to provide some perspective on the proposed risk.

Risk comparisons are invariably oversimplified and are thus not very useful in individual decision-making. Yet risk comparisons remain popular and may often be quoted in the media. The motivation for this book is the prevalence of comparative risk estimates that do not clarify how they arrived at individual risk estimates. We clearly know different things about health risks with different degrees of certainty. Health risk comparisons are not useful if they fail to acknowledge the important differences in how each risk estimate is generated.

This project began as a citizen's guide to health risk in Canada: a comprehensive overview of what we knew about health risks and how we knew what we claimed to know. Based on the qualitative research conducted by Christina Lindsay for her MA in anthropology (Lindsay 1996) and our experience in gathering the information for this book, we decided that we needed to compile information that might be too comprehensive and detailed for many lay readers. We also recognized that keeping the scope of this activity manageable required limiting our scope to fatality risk, rather than a comprehensive evaluation of health risk (Thomas 1996).

Our target audience for this book includes students in the health sciences and professions, practising health professionals, and anyone else who may be interested in an overview of what is currently known about the risk of death in Canada. In our experience with environmental health issues, we have found that other texts may cover parts of the spectrum of information addressed in this book, but no single text covers the entire spectrum in the same way.

This book has two goals:

1. To provide a summary of accessible health risk information, and

2. To provide an explanation of the underlying source (evidence and inferential basis) and the certainty of the health risk information.

Even a summary of accessible health risk information could easily be many volumes long, making the summary itself unmanageable. Consequently, we limited the total amount of information covered to:

- direct human health risks, not risks to other animals or the environment, except environmental risks that pose a direct risk to human health,

- primarily mortality information,

- primarily accessible Canadian information.

Providing information that allows people to inform themselves about health risks is different from telling people what to do about the health risks. No data summary, including this book, can claim to present strictly impartial information. As far as possible, we have tried to provide data from a range of perspectives, so that your conclusions will be based on a critical and accurate understanding. We do not try to tell you what to do about any health risk and did not intentionally select or avoid any information with that purpose in mind.

The second goal of this book is to provide an explanation of the source and certainty of the information presented. The ideas of source of evidence and uncertainty in knowledge are closely linked. Currently, most published health risk information does not include an estimate or explanation of the uncertainty inherent in numerical estimates or causal inferences. As quantitative estimates of uncertainty are not readily available for most risk data, we used a more general approach to characterize the uncertainty.

Uncertainty arises from how the evidence was measured and interpreted. Basic information that can be measured accurately, is comprehensive in its coverage (e.g., death registration in Canada), and does not require substantial judgement or inference to link measurement with interpretation will have relatively low uncertainty. Basic information that cannot be measured directly, depends on population samples, and requires substantial inference to link measurements with their meaning will have relatively higher uncertainty. Following these premises, we used the primary source of any information on a health risk as the basis for explaining the uncertainty. By focusing on the information source, we could make a more detailed analysis of how the information was measured. Using this general approach, the range of the uncertainty can be estimated for health risk information from any given source, even if the source does not explicitly address uncertainty.

We seek to inform anyone who wishes to understand our state of knowledge about risks of death in Canada. In so doing, we believe that we can encourage informed discussions about important issues in our society. However, this book should not be used as a weapon to win battles in risk debates. The most contentious issues in risk debates are usually social issues of equity and fairness, issues which cannot be resolved by recourse to the data and inferential logic that we present.

Dedication

To Karina and everyone who believes that to risk is to live.

Simon P. Thomas

To Liz, who has always been able to remind me what is important in Life.

Steve E. Hrudey

Acknowledgements

This work was supported by funding for the Eco-Research Chair in Environmental Risk Management provided by the Tri-Council Secretariat representing the Medical Research, the Natural Sciences and Engineering Research and the Social Sciences and Humanities Research Councils of Canada; the Alberta Heritage Foundation for Medical Research; Alberta Environmental Protection; Alberta Health; The City of Edmonton; Syncrude Canada Ltd., Alberta Energy and Utilities Board; Acres International Ltd.; AGRA Earth and Environmental Ltd., Anderson Exploration Ltd.; Bovar Inc.; CanTox Inc.; EBA Engineering Consultants Ltd.; Golder Associates Ltd.; Gulf Canada Resources Ltd.; Milner Fenerty; O'Connor Associates Environmental Inc.; Reid Crowther and Partners Ltd.; The Wyatt Company; and UMA Engineering Ltd.

Statistics Canada information is used with the permission of the Minister of Industry, as Minister responsible for Statistics Canada. Information on the availability of the wide range of data from Statistics Canada can be obtained from Statistics Canada's Regional Offices, its World Wide Web site at http://www.statcan.ca, and its toll-free access number 1-800-263-1136.

We gratefully acknowledge the technical assistance received from Nola Low and Weiping Chen, the feedback from Christina Lindsay's M.A. research and the helpful comments from Kathryn Wilkins, Statistics Canada, Dr. Barry Thomas, Dr. Louis Francescutti, Dr. Warren Kindzierski, Dr. Steve Stanley, Dr. Wei-Ching Chang and the external reviewers consulted by the University of Alberta Press.

Introduction

Most of us recognize that good health is our most important asset. Consequently, we are concerned about things that may negatively affect our health, so-called "health risks." As our society is preoccupied with many health risks, we are inundated with information about what is healthy and what is not. Most of us find this flood of often contradictory information confusing and unhelpful. So what can we do about this lack of good information? We have a matter of intense personal interest, but encounter a fog of confusing and conflicting information when we seek answers.

A detailed analysis of most competing claims about health risks is simply not practical. We also cannot provide every individual with guidance about which health risks are personally most important. However, it is possible to understand fairly confidently what we know about health risks and how we come to know anything about health risk. This book very generally classifies knowledge of the risk of death, first by presenting and explaining the most recent and available mortality statistics for Canada. Then we progress from the most consistent and complete data source, the death registration information recorded for every individual fatality in Canada, to epidemiological studies done on selected samples of human populations, and, ultimately, to risk assessment predictions based primarily on toxicology experiments with animals.

Clearly humans cannot eliminate health risks altogether because everyone who is born is certain to die of some cause. But we can try to understand what is known about risks of death and what is inferred about the causes of death. This knowledge may not answer all or even most of the questions each of us has about health risk. However, our understanding of fatality risk does provide a frame of reference for understanding any health risk.

Understanding health risks requires more than just a probability estimate of the risk, it also requires an explanation of the evidence and inferential basis used to develop the estimates, and the degree of the certainty of the information.

The remainder of this introduction has three sections. The first (Categories of Health Risk Information) describes in more detail the three categories of information that are based on the source of the information. These categories, Direct Evidence, Indirect Evidence and Inference, and Predictive Inference, are the titles of the first, second, and third parts of this book. The second section in this introduction (Health Risk Evidence and Inference) evaluates the components of health risk information. These components include explanations of health and risk, as well as a brief overview of risk perception. The third section in this introduction (Numerical Data Information) discusses several topics relating to number interpretation.

Categories of Health Risk Information

We used three categories of mortality-based health risk information: direct evidence from death certificates, indirect evidence and inference from epidemiology and predictive inference from toxicological risk assessment. These categories were selected after reviewing readily available health risk information in Canada. These categories are introduced here to explain the similarities and differences between them. The last part of this book, Discussion and Summary Observations, provides a more detailed comparison of the three categories.

Direct evidence is collected and summarized from the death certificates that are completed for everyone who dies in Canada. This evidence is from across Canada and is published annually by Statistics Canada, along with other vital statistics. Key components of direct evidence are the age and gender of the individual and the apparent cause of death reported on the death certificate.

Indirect evidence and inference is based on epidemiological studies designed to determine risk factors relating to health risks. Unlike direct evidence from death certificates, where all evidence is related to mortality, epidemiological studies can address non-lethal (morbidity) health conditions as well. For most risk factors, the indirect evidence and inference was not limited to Canada in this text because there are not enough epidemiological studies performed on Canadians to address the main recognized risk factors. For these risk factors, evidence and inference from similar, industrially developed countries was used.

Predictive inference is based on a toxicological risk assessment of specific chemical substances. Predictive estimates of risk are usually based on evidence from animal studies that must be interpreted for human health risk. Toxicological risk assessment protocols have different approaches for carcinogens and non-carcinogens. For non-carcinogens, risk estimates mainly provide estimated exposure levels below which adverse health effects are not expected to occur. This approach only predicts health consequences for people exposed at levels well above tolerable levels (which include uncertainty factors in an attempt to ensure the relative safety of the specified tolerable level). There is generally no quantitative estimate of the number of individuals likely to be affected at these higher exposure levels. Carcinogens, in contrast, have usually been treated as a matter of public health policy, as if cancer might be caused at any level of exposure. This approach has allowed calculation of a hypothetical number of predicted cancer cases for any specified exposure level.

Table 1.1 identifies several items that help to distinguish the three categories of health risk evidence and inference. The knowledge in the three categories is based on evidence,

Table 1.1 ◆ Three Categories of Health Risk Evidence and Inference

Factor	Direct	Indirect	Predictive
Knowledge Source	Evidence	Evidence and inference	Inference
Information Source	Death certificates	Epidemiological studies	Toxicological risk assessment
Coverage	Everyone	Population sample	Experimental laboratory animals
Information Type	Age, gender, and cause of death	Association between exposure and effect for exposure to a risk factor	Estimate of risk associated with specific exposure

inference, or a combination of both. Evidence is information measured directly for individuals. Inference is information extrapolated to the general population from information that has been measured collectively. Coverage describes how much of the affected population is measured in the health risk information. For direct evidence from death certificates, all published values are based on individual measurement of each person involved and include everyone who dies (with a very few, relatively insignificant number of exceptions). Indirect evidence and inference from epidemiological studies are based on a selected sample of the population. How well the sample represents the relevant population characteristics will determine the applicability of the findings to people outside the sample. Predictive inference from toxicological studies is usually based on experiments with animals combined with estimates of exposure in humans. Although animal models clearly cannot be as representative as human population samples, laboratory experiments with animal models can be more closely controlled for extraneous factors than observations of human populations. Likewise, estimated human exposures must represent actual exposures to lead to valid predictions.

There are several other sources of useful direct evidence that are similar to the direct evidence on death certificates, but which are generated in other ways. Some more widely distributed examples include hospital discharge records, the Canadian Cancer Registry, Transport Canada's tracking of all motor vehicle accidents, and Workers' Compensation's tracking injuries and fatalities on the job. All these sources are based on a one person/one record, direct approach. As some other sources involve a more careful corroboration of the cause of death, sources such as cancer registries or specific outcome verification in major epidemiological studies are substantially more reliable than the basic death certificate evidence.

There is a fundamental difference between direct and indirect evidence and predictive inference. Both direct and indirect evidence require the existence of the effect (death) and each seeks to determine the cause (e.g., what caused the death?, does diet affect heart disease?). Some types of epidemiological studies (cohort) that gather potential causal evidence by tracking a cohort for the appearance of effects begin with the knowledge that some relevant effects will appear in a large enough population sample. In contrast, predictive toxicology begins with a cause (exposure to some hazard) and seeks to determine what effect will arise.

Health Risk Evidence and Inference

Defining Health

Health is a complex concept that has a different meaning for different people. The World Health Organization (WHO) comprehensively defined health in its founding charter almost fifty years ago: "health is a state of complete physical, mental and social well-being and not merely the absence of disease or infirmity" (Beaglehole et al. 1993, 13). Many other definitions and concepts have been proposed since, but the WHO definition is adequate for our purposes.

Although the focus of this book is on the risk of mortality, we do not consider only physical aspects. Although direct evidence, based on death certificates, uses only physical evidence, risk factors associated with mortality include mental and social factors as well.

There is no simple distinction between a healthy and unhealthy status. Health is a continuum from an ideal state of health to severe impairment and, ultimately, death. Figure 1.1 shows health as a function of impairment and disability. The vertical, disability axis goes from health to death, and the horizontal, impairment axis goes from normal to failure. The box in the lower left corner is homeostasis, where the body is in good health. Throughout life, people move back and forth along the line. Depending on the cause of death, people may gradually move to the right of this line over the course of months or years, or they may move along the line in a matter of seconds (e.g., fatal injuries).

Two important points about health are demonstrated in Figure 1.1. The first is that health is a continuum, not a dichotomy of healthy and unhealthy. The second is that health is dynamic, i.e., the health status of an individual can move back and forth along the line during a lifetime. Both of these points highlight the great difficulty in attempting to summarize health status for a population.

Given these complications, general indicators such as those related to mortality (e.g., life expectancy, age-standardized death rates) are often used. Other indicators include hospital admission rates and national surveys of common risk factors (e.g., smoking, alcohol consumption, economic status). Another measure gaining popularity is the use of disability-adjusted life years (DALYs) that adjust life expectancy to allow for long-term disability.

Figure 1.1 ◆ Disability versus Impairment

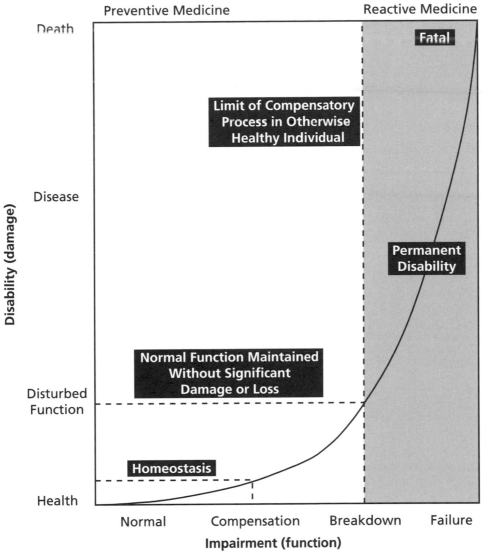

Adapted from Hatch, 1962, Figure 2

Mortality Data

The information presented in this book is based on mortality data. As William Rowe put it:

The only certainty in life is death; uncertainty lies in when and how death occurs, and whether it is final. Man strives to delay its onset and extend the quality of life in the interim. Threats to these objectives involve risks, some natural, some man-made, some beyond our control, and some controllable (Rowe 1977, 1).

As explaining the uncertainty associated with health risk evidence and inference is a major goal of this book, it is logical that we begin with the only certain piece of health risk information—death. People concerned about health risks already know that they will die, but, as Rowe puts it, many want to know "when" and "how." Many people want to know how they may productively delay the inevitable as long as possible.

A complicated series of "causes" can explain how someone died. Causes of death can be identified in several ways. Stating the cause of death involves selecting one of these ways. Ultimately, everyone dies of the same final cause-the heart stops beating, and oxygen is no longer supplied to the brain and throughout the body. In this book, the cause of death is what was reported on the death certificate, generally the most "direct" and widely available link to the actual death. Even on the death certificate, however, a selection is being made because multiple medical factors often contribute to a death. Considerable judgement must often be used to select a stated cause of death.

Epidemiological evidence and inference are sometimes used to estimate the cause of death from particular risks for groups of individuals in a population, and toxicological risk assessment may estimate the maximum number of cancer cases caused from a particular chemical exposure. Often summaries of fatality risks will mix estimates taken from an analysis of direct causal statistics, like motor vehicle fatalities, with epidemiological or toxicological risk estimates, which are much less direct and much more uncertain.

This book focuses on mortality mostly in Part One, Direct Evidence. So much direct evidence health data was available that we needed to limit consideration to mortality. In epidemiological studies, cancer incidence or some other measure of morbidity is sometimes used instead of mortality. For predictive inference, all the risk estimates are for cancer incidence, not mortality. Fortunately, there is a fairly well established relationship between cancer incidence and mortality, which is presented in Part One along with cancer mortality.

Focusing on mortality does not provide a comprehensive measure of health. Although mortality is a useful indicator for many of the most important health risks, such as cardiovascular disease, cancer, respiratory disease, and fatal injuries, it is much less useful for several others. These health risks include many common conditions that have a low mortality, such as colds, asthma, arthritis, mental conditions, non-fatal injuries, physical disabilities, malnutrition, and dental health. You can see the enormous difference between the scope and volume of mortality and non-mortality information in the fact that on any given day, for every person who dies, approximately twenty are admitted to hospital and 800 consult a health professional (Shah 1994, 103).

The subject of death is a very personal and often painful experience. This book does not attempt to personalize the facts and figures of death. However, we note that the social aspects of death and dying are receiving increasing research attention: a trend likely to continue with the increasing average age of our population. Kubler-Ross has been an active promoter of this subject for several decades and her work has led to university courses on death and dying accompanied by comprehensive textbooks (e.g., DeSpelder and Strickland

1992). In a best-selling book How We Die, the physician Robert Nuland provides a compassionate and personal outlook on dying: "Every life is different from any that has gone before it, and so is every death. The uniqueness of each of us extends even to the way we die. Though most people know that various diseases carry us to our final hours by various paths, only very few comprehend the fullness of that endless multitude of ways by which the final forces of the human spirit can separate themselves from the body. Every one of death's diverse appearances is as distinctive as that singular face we each show the world during the days of life. Every man will yield up the ghost in a manner that the heavens have never known before: every woman will go her final way in her own way" (Nuland 1993, 3).

Defining Risk

Risk and health risk management have been fundamental to human evolution. People who learned from danger survived to reproduce themselves, while those who did not perished from avoidable dangers. The formal concepts of risk and quantifying risk can be traced back to the seventeenth century, when it was discovered that mathematics, and specifically probability theory, could be used to estimate the odds (the probability component of risk) in games of chance or gambling (Trefil 1984). This ability evolved to the point where a whole industry, insurance, now depends on its ability to predict and quantify risks.

Defining risk is a study of its own. However, we can develop a general notion of risk that combines and expands on earlier studies of risk (Kaplan and Garrick 1981; Renn 1992). Risk may be viewed as a prediction or expectation made up of:

- a hazard (the source of danger);

- an uncertainty of occurrence and outcomes (expressed by probability distributions);

- adverse consequences (the possible adverse health outcomes);

- a time frame for evaluation;

- the importance of the risk for people affected by it.

This general concept of risk is focused for the purposes of this book in several ways. The hazards are the various causes of health risks. Where possible, these will use Canadian data. The uncertainty of occurrence and outcomes is limited by the available information to point estimates of probability rather than distributions. The adverse consequences focus on but are not limited to mortality outcomes. The time frame for evaluation varies with the source of the data and use both annual and lifetime risk. The perspectives of those affected by risk is largely beyond the scope of this book because the perspectives depend on individual values. However, the issue of risk perception is briefly introduced.

Mortality risk is defined in this book as the probability of death from a specified cause, for a specified time period, together with the uncertainty in the probability estimate. Probability of death includes two parts in addition to the numerical estimate. The first is the specific cause and/or factors that are involved and the second is the time frame being used (e.g., annual or lifetime).

The following sections describe probability and uncertainty in more detail. One difficulty in dealing with probability and uncertainty is that the different categories of health risk evidence and inference use different terms to describe uncertainty. In the direct evidence of death certificate data, terms like errors and accuracy are often used. In the indirect evidence and inference of epidemiological studies, terms like bias and confounding are used. To date, most attempts to define probability and uncertainty in health risks have come from research on the predictive inference of toxicological risk assessment.

Three Types of Probability

Similar to the concepts of health and risk, probability has different meanings in different contexts. People who misunderstand mortality risk may also misunderstand probability (particularly people who have a limited knowledge of probability and statistics). Kleindorfer et al. (1993) described three schools of probability: classical, frequency, and subjective. Most introductory courses emphasize classical probability and work with frequency statistics. Few introductory courses pay substantial attention to subjective probability or adequately distinguish classical probability from frequency statistics.

The classical school defines probability as the number of specified outcomes divided by the total number of possible outcomes. This definition requires that specified and possible outcomes be known completely. This definition of probability is commonly applied to games of chance such as coin flipping, dice rolling, card selection, and lottery playing. The probability of an event (e.g., coin: 1/2 probability of heads; dice: 1/6 probability of a one; cards: 1/13 chance of selecting an ace from a full deck) can be predicted strictly from an analysis of a set of circumstances. More complicated outcomes can then be calculated without actually performing the action, using the mathematical laws of permutations and combinations. The conditions necessary to classical analysis are generally too simple and hypothetical to be applied to health risk estimation. A hypothetical example would be that the chances of drawing the bullet in Russian roulette with a fair-six chamber revolver would be one chance in six.

The frequency school establishes probability by observing repeated events or trials. This type of probability is used in actuarial work (e.g., insurance is based on prior outcomes). The difficulty with the frequency school is that it only applies well to stable and repetitive processes. The advantage of this approach is that it can be applied to any situation that can be observed through many repetitions, including cases that can use classical analysis. Unfortunately, many events cannot be measured this way simply because they are rare or cannot be repeated often enough to extract relative frequency. Probability estimates can be derived from frequency data where enough relevant observations are available. One can estimate the future probability of motor vehicle fatalities in a given jurisdiction using historical data for that jurisdiction as long as future causative conditions remain unchanged. Even then, natural variability will yield differing outcomes from year to year.

The subjective school holds that probability estimates for real events cannot be measured in a strictly objective sense. Rather, probability estimates imply a degree of belief or confidence that a specified event will occur. The confidence of the estimator may come from classical analysis and/or substantial frequency evidence. However, the nature of the prediction demands some judgement and subjective belief from the estimator. As such, this type of probability is not strictly objective, even if the frequency evidence is substantial.

The subjective school involves uncertainty because knowledge based on experience is always limited. There is uncertainty at many levels. A probability value itself creates uncertainty for any future observations, because unless the probability is equal to one, you will not be certain which outcome will happen, only how likely a given outcome may be. But you are also subject to uncertainty in the probability estimate. You can be highly certain that the probability of rolling a six with a single die is one in six, if the die is fair, but you can be much less certain that your probability of getting bladder cancer from drinking chlorinated water is x, because the causal linkage itself is uncertain.

The advantages of the subjective school are that it is much more flexible than the frequency school, allows the probability estimate to be updated over time in response to new evidence, and also allows competing views of the probability.

The relationship between subjective and frequency probability may be illustrated with a hypothetical example. If you asked transportation experts to estimate the chance of a random driver suffering a fatal accident over the coming year in any Canadian province, they could check a well documented database of motor vehicle fatalities for several decades. The experts could make a prediction based on this evidence, taking into account any necessary adjustments. There is some subjectivity in this approach, but our confidence in the prediction will be based on the substantial relevant direct evidence (the frequency data of motor vehicle fatality statistics).

Suppose, for comparison, that the transportation experts could not look at any of the frequency data. Instead, they convened an expert panel made up of emergency room physicians, automotive engineers, traffic engineers, and various other experts. These experts were able to collect relevant data on the number of licensed vehicles, detailed road maps of the entire province, and basic science, engineering, or medical information. They could even conduct animal experiments with rodents and miniaturized vehicles. Obviously, the resulting estimate for motor vehicle fatalities would be much less certain and reliable than the estimates based on frequency statistics. Yet this latter process is much closer to what must be done in predictive risk assessment and even, to some degree, in the interpretation of epidemiological evidence.

Types of Uncertainty

Like probability, uncertainty has been defined in different ways in different contexts. In this book, uncertainty will consist of two parts: variability and inadequate knowledge. This distinction has received growing recognition among risk analysts (Hoffman and Hammonds 1994).

Before explaining these two types of uncertainty, it is useful to point out that some things do not have any uncertainty. These include statements made using the classical view of probability. For example, assuming fairness, there is a 0.25 probability that if you flip two coins, two tails will be face up. There is no uncertainty in the probability; the uncertainty is in the outcome of the actual coin tosses. Other numbers without uncertainty relate to things that can be counted thoroughly or discrete numbers. Examples include the number of brothers you have, your age in years, the date you received your first driver's licence, how much money you are now carrying. These statements are objective; they need not contain any uncertainty if the numbers are known accurately. Unfortunately, most health risk information contains uncertainty, due either to a lack of knowledge or inherent variability.

Inadequate knowledge is usually the largest cause of uncertainty. The inadequacy of the knowledge means that the full extent of the uncertainty is also unknown. Finkel (1990) in his focus on risk assessment issues identified three areas that could fall under lack of knowledge: parameter uncertainty (measurement errors, random errors, systematic errors); model uncertainty (errors arising from incorrect conceptions of reality); and decision-rule uncertainty (not knowing how to interpret predictions).

Uncertainty due to variability occurs when a single number is used to describe something that truly has multiple or variable values. Variability is often ignored by using values based on the mean of all the values occurring within a group. A common simplifying assumption for health risk predictions has been that everyone has the same susceptibility to a particular risk factor, when, in reality, large inter-individual variations exist. Similarly, mean values are often used to estimate exposure for a group, when large variations in individual exposure actually occur. A second type of variability is when a single value exists but changes constantly over time. The population of Canada is a single value at any instant, but it varies daily (most of the uncertainty in the population is due to lack of knowledge—the difficulty of accurately measuring the population on one day).

Figure 1.2 shows a causal chain model linking an agent or hazard to the effect or outcome. This model shows how an agent with hazardous properties may be exposed to a receptor via environmental media (air, water, soil, food). The causal process may act through a dose-response process to yield different effects or outcomes. Epidemiology was born by considering adverse outcomes and searching back up the causal chain to find the agent or hazard responsible. Toxicology, in contrast, has tended to begin with the agent and then to work through the causal chain to determine if any adverse outcome resulted from exposure and the dose-response relationship that governed that process.

Figure 1.2 ◆ Causal Chain Model for Environmental Health Risks

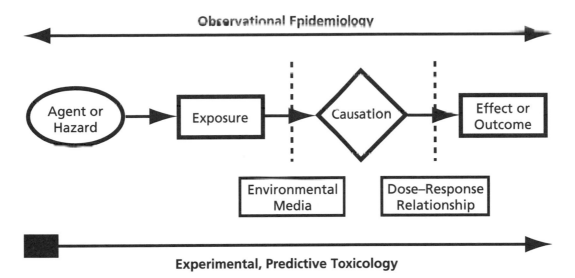

Adapted from Hrudey, 1997, Figure 1

Different types of uncertainty (variability and inadequate knowledge) occur at each stage in this model. This book only focuses on uncertainty in health risk estimates associated with effect or outcome in relation to cause. Levels of uncertainty would be characterized differently if all the other stages in the causal chain model were also analysed.

Figure 1.3 contrasts substantially certain health risk knowledge with the relative uncertainty of most health risk predictions. We can gain knowledge about any issue by collecting information. Relevant knowledge may be considered evidence on that issue. In most aspects of knowledge, logic and inference must also be used to interpret this evidence to establish knowledge. All knowledge involves varying degrees of evidence combined with inference. Figure 1.3's hierarchy of uncertainty shows the changing emphasis from evidence to inference for the different types of health risk information. At the base, direct evidence requires limited inference and the uncertainty is relatively low. Moving up from this base involves greater reliance on inference to compensate for the increasing shortage of direct evidence. In the middle, both evidence and inference are used to supply knowledge. Near the top, the uncertainty in the knowledge increases to the point where relevant certain knowledge may become only a tiny fraction in relation to a much larger degree of uncertainty. At the top, where we have no evidence, only inference, the uncertainty is enormous.

The foregoing description of knowledge about health risks has been generalized to address the enormous range of information used to form judgements about health risk. A sharp distinction between evidence and inference may be difficult to apply to many specific cases where observations alone will have little meaning without some level of interpretation. At all

Figure 1.3 ◆ Health Risk Evidence, Inference and the Uncertainty Hierarchy for Adverse Outcomes

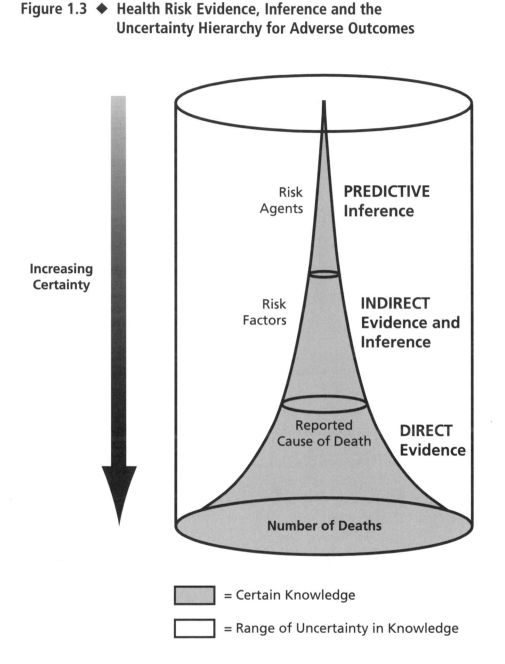

Increasing Certainty

Risk Agents — **PREDICTIVE Inference**

Risk Factors — **INDIRECT Evidence and Inference**

Reported Cause of Death — **DIRECT Evidence**

Number of Deaths

▨ = Certain Knowledge

▢ = Range of Uncertainty in Knowledge

stages of interpreting our knowledge about health risks, inference and evidence will be interactive Yet, in general, the more we must rely on interpreting observations, rather than letting observations speak for themselves, the greater our uncertainty about the accuracy of our conclusions.

Risk Perception

The expression "risk perception" almost inherently establishes a dichotomy between quantitative risk predictions and beliefs about risk. People think a risk probability is larger or smaller than a quantitative risk prediction because they perceive the risk differently from those who made the risk prediction. Much of the early work on risk perception originated with attempts to explain differences between the prevalent public opinion and various estimates of the technological risks of energy production and, in particular, nuclear power (e.g., Rasmussen 1981). Even though the numerical estimates of the annual risk from nuclear power are much smaller than most common health risks, many people regard nuclear power as an unacceptably high health risk. Experts who engage in risk predictions tend to see their estimates as correct or perhaps even "real." Although popular risk perceptions are sometimes inconsistent with risk predictions founded on substantial relevant risk evidence (e.g., tobacco companies and smokers denying the health risk of tobacco use), risk predictions are sometimes based on very little relevant evidence. In these latter cases, the risk estimates of non-experts may be as valid as the predictions of experts.

A problem will arise when anyone (expert or non-expert) presumes that a numerical probability estimate for a risk is a "real" risk. People who claim that a risk prediction is real inevitably characterize anyone who disagrees with that estimate as emotional or irrational. Seeing any risk estimate as a "real risk" ignores the subjectivity and multiple dimensions of risk. Multidimensional entities cannot be assigned a single numerical value without weighting the numerical values for each of the dimensions. Even a decision to weight each dimension equally for the purposes of aggregation requires a judgement that equal weighting is appropriate (Hrudey 1997).

Risk perception research has sought to explain some of the reasons that non-expert and expert estimation of risk may differ. This book presents numerical information that could be used, unwisely, to dismiss some concerns about specific health risks. The numerical values in this book summarize the most reliable information about health risk probabilities, but these frequency numbers cannot be interpreted as the "real" risk to any individual. Although high frequencies of death for particular risk categories suggest higher risks for an individual exposed to those risk categories, many individual factors determine the risk level that applies to any individual risk. All of these modifying factors and their quantitative effect on individual risk cannot normally be known for any individual. Many valid non-numerical or qualitative factors affect how important any particular health risk will be to any individual. For example, a prolonged painful death is clearly not the same as a sudden, painless death, yet death statistics make no distinctions between the two.

However, an individual may benefit from understanding the available frequency values and how this information was generated. This information may help them to understand the underlying uncertainties in the risks that apply to them or people they are concerned about. Some of the factors that influence individual perceptions of risk include the framing, choice, timing, and characteristics of the risk. These issues are discussed briefly and generally here. Every risk issue will be influenced by a complex array of factors that may differ markedly from one individual to another.

Framing is often used to explain why individuals, including experts, underestimate large risk probabilities and overestimate smaller ones. Slovic et al. (1979) have surveyed this phenomenon. The framing explanation for this is that people grow accustomed to the more common causes of death. The media plays a large role in this process. Except in the obituary pages in the newspaper, the number of people dying from cardiovascular disease, cancer, or other chronic diseases is not routinely reported. Even car accidents, which are often reported, receive limited media attention unless there are special circumstances surrounding the event (e.g., multiple deaths or a famous person involved). However, whenever there is a plane crash or an increase in a rare disease (e.g., the hanta virus scare in 1995), extensive media coverage is devoted to these low frequency events. Framing has been demonstrated in experiments that compare individual preferences for alternative courses of action. For example, people had a much higher preference for a medical intervention when it was described as offering a high chance of success (say, 90%), but a much lower preference when it was presented as offering a correspondingly small chance of failure (10%). This preference effect was as strong with physicians as with the lay public (McNeil et al. 1982).

Choice is commonly described in terms of voluntary vs involuntary risks. Studies and experience have consistently shown that individuals are less concerned about risks that they choose than about risks that are imposed on them without choice, or, worse, against their will. The preference may be attributable to the benefit individuals derive from an activity. A person gains substantial personal benefit from operating a motor vehicle, but may see little or no direct benefit from a new factory being sited in their community. In addition to this risk-benefit trade-off, an imposed risk is logically seen to be greater than one that is voluntary, perhaps because the imposed risk is seen as unfair and unjustified. Reacting negatively to unjustified compulsion is entirely logical within a democratic society.

Another aspect of choice is whether or not a risk is controllable and the potential degree of harm associated with the risk. An example here is the nuclear industry, where the annual risk of harm to the public is predicted to be very low by most risk analysts, but the threat of harm perceived by most members of the public is large. In this case, the analysts have knowledge, experience, and confidence that the technology will control the extremely hazardous materials and processes involved in the nuclear industry. The lay public has much lower confidence, partly because they have no direct ability to manage the activities of this industry.

Timing of a risk is an issue because many individuals are less concerned about harm in the distant future than immediate danger or benefit. Most deaths are not immediate (i.e., a few minutes or hours), but involve a slow degenerative process. There are two important exceptions to this, heart attacks and fatal injuries. Over 10% of deaths in Canada are from acute heart attacks (acute myocardial infarction). Fatal injuries (external causes of death) accounted for 7% of deaths in Canada and include suicides, motor vehicle accidents, falls, and poisonings.

Characteristics and context are important determinants of how individuals will judge a risk. A sudden accidental death may be dreaded much less than a slow, debilitating fatal disease. For some, the severe disability may be feared more than death itself. Such distinctions will depend on individual circumstances. There are no objective methods to quantify the effect of these determinants on how an individual judges the importance of a risk. Thus, no numerical rating of risks can be strictly objective, because individual ratings are influenced by inherently subjective values. These limitations are as true for experts as for non-experts. The differences are only in the nature of the individual values that influence judgements. Although the fatality frequency data summarized in this book can help an individual form an opinion about the importance of a risk, no numerical data can ever capture the relevant characteristics and context involved in a personal judgement about the importance of a risk.

In part because of these variables, issues involving risk often become contentious. Experts often believe the public is irrational in not accepting the expert estimates of risk. There is now substantial research evidence to demonstrate that the public is not irrational about risk (Slovic 1997). Although lay individuals may not have access to the same type or quantity of evidence as experts, both are influenced by emotion, beliefs, and generally their views of the world. This book is designed to provide broader access to and understanding of the types of relevant evidence that may used by risk analysts.

Numerical Data Information

Log vs Normal Scale

People usually work with numbers that range within two factors of ten. For example, we are conditioned by our education to deal with being graded in percentages ranging from 1 to 100%. However, when dealing with health risks, the differences can easily range over more than eight factors of ten (i.e., 1 to 100,000,000). For this reason, log scales must often be used in presenting health risk data. Figures 1.4 (log scale) and 1.5 (normal scale) highlight the importance of using log scales to depict such a wide range of numbers and also show some of the potential difficulties in interpretation. The same eight values are shown in both Figures (0.5; 1; 50; 100; 5,000; 10,000; 500,000; and 1,000,000). Both Figures have a similar range on the vertical axis, except that 0.1 was used as the base value for the log scale because there is no zero on a log scale.

The need to use log scales to show all the numbers is clearly demonstrated with these Figures. All eight values are clearly shown on the log scale, while only four are shown (and two just barely) on the conventional scale.

Figure 1.4 ◆ Log Scale Example

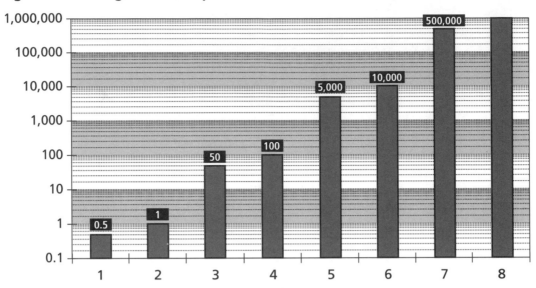

Figure 1.5 ◆ Normal Scale Example

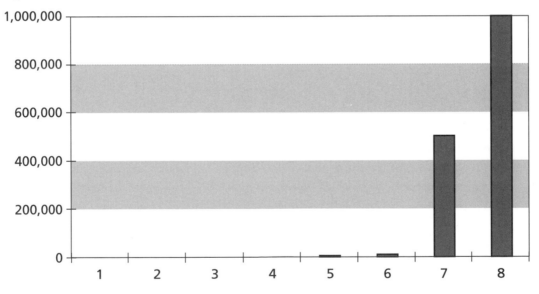

As log scales are used extensively in Part One, Direct Evidence, a few points need to be mentioned for those unfamiliar with interpreting them.

- All values are shown in a constant proportion (ratio) to each other. For example, Figure 1.4 shows the same vertical distance between successive pairs of plotted points nos. 1 and 2, nos. 3 and 4, nos. 5 and 6, and nos. 7 and 8. Each of these pairs are related by a ratio of two. Likewise pairs of points nos. 1 and 3, nos. 2 and 4, nos. 5 and 7, and nos. 6 and 8 show the same vertical distance because each pair is related by a ratio of 100.

- Reading values off the log figures must be done with caution if they are not located on a labelled grid line, because the corresponding changes in absolute values are not depicted in an intuitive way. For example, in Figure 1.4, point no. 1, with a value of 0.5, could easily be estimated as being very close to 1 on the log scale.

- Log scales appear to overemphasize low values. For example, in Figure 1.4, it is not possible to recognize that point no. 2 is 1 million times smaller than point 8 without considering the labels on the vertical scale.

- Log scales appear to minimize absolute differences. For example, point 7 on the normal scale is clearly one-half of point 8, while on the log scale they appear to be similar.

In addition to the proportionate increase in the axis number (e.g., 0.1, 10, 100), all log scale Figures in this book include horizontal grid lines.

Annual vs Lifetime Risks

A time frame must be included with a risk estimate for the numbers to be meaningful. For health risks, annual or lifetime risks are commonly used. Direct evidence is usually expressed annually because the information is collected and summarized annually. However, predictive information is commonly expressed as a lifetime probability, e.g., for expressing cancer risk. Knowing the time frame is important because a lifetime risk of one in a million could correspond to an annual risk of one in 70 million (or 0.014 chances in a million), based upon the standard seventy-year lifetime conventionally used in cancer risk assessment.

Manipulating Categories

A potential problem with any numbers is that they are easily manipulated to emphasize various perspectives. For example, categories can be chosen to emphasize or de-emphasize a particular health risk. Ways in which this may be done include the following.

- Categorization. To make one category seem larger than others you can subdivide all the other categories into smaller ones, making the undivided category appear larger.

For example, to emphasize cardiovascular disease more than cancer, you could divide cardiovascular disease into two categories (heart disease and stroke), and divide cancer into several specific types of cancer (e.g., lung, colo-rectal, breast, prostate, bladder).

- Age range. As health risks vary tremendously with age, selecting a specific age range can highlight a particular factor. A leading cause of death in a specific age range (e.g., early in life) may account for less than 1% of deaths overall.

As there is no single "correct" way to present frequency data, various methods are valid, provided the presentation shows what has been done. However, this presentation can create confusion because, using the example above, there may appear to be several different "leading" causes of death.

Health Risk as Relative Changes or Total Increases

To emphasize a health risk, the frequency data can be selectively shown as a relative change or as a total increase. Consider the following two scenarios.

- Small total increase, large relative change. For example, if the annual number of deaths from a cause increased from two to twenty (an increase of eighteen deaths), you could state that the number of deaths from the cause increased by a factor of ten or add more emphasis by expressing the increase as 900%.

- Large total increase, small relative change. For instance, if the annual number of deaths from a cause increased from 50,000 to 51,000 (a 2% increase), you could state that there were 1,000 more deaths from the cause.

A more informative compromise in these cases is to include the numbers (e.g. two to twenty; 50,000 to 51,000), together with any statement about relative increase.

Rare Events

Rare events happen all the time. However, there is a big difference between predicting an individual rare event (e.g., the chance of a *specific* ticket winning the lottery) and looking at all occurrences and identifying a rare event (the chance of *any* ticket winning the lottery). Another illustration of the difficulty is trying to predict the blade of grass a golf ball will rest on if it lands on the fairway. The probability that it will land on any specific blade of grass is incredibly small (one chance in many millions), while the probability that it will land on any blade of grass approaches one (one chance in one for the specified conditions). Similarly, it is impossible to predict who will die from a rare event, but with approximately 200,000 annual deaths in Canada, it is very likely there will be deaths arising from rare causes (e.g., deaths caused by lighting strikes were approximately five per year between 1991 and 1994).

Population vs Individual Risk

All of the quantitative data about human mortality discussed in this book has been obtained for populations, i.e., groups of individuals. The study of populations allows the calculation of frequency data for various outcomes in the group. These frequency data can be readily expressed as probability to provide estimates of risk. When risks are viewed in terms of the frequency of adverse effect in a population, they represent a tangible concept which may be observable as a number of cases, even if they are estimated for some future population.

In contrast, risk to an individual, expressed in terms of probability, is necessarily a less tangible concept because it cannot be verified by subsequent observations of a single individual. Suppose you contract a serious fatal disease and your physician advises you, from experience, that you have a 90% probability of dying in the next year. In this individual case, you will either die or not die in the coming year. Neither outcome can confirm or refute the probability estimate, although death would be more consistent with the prediction. An attempt at experimental verification of the individual risk estimate might be attempted if you had 9 or more clones who also had the identical disease. The proportion of clones who succumbed within a year could be taken as stronger evidence about the relative accuracy of the probability estimate. Any such hypothetical experiment would amount to a specialized population experiment.

The foregoing example illustrates that individual risk is most like a subjective probability, because it estimates a degree of expectation of what will happen. However, it is not possible to develop frequency-based estimates on individual risks. Rather, we can only infer what we may expect for any individual from observing frequencies in a population.

Conclusion

In conclusion, health risk information must be interpreted with caution. The media, catering to public interest, often shows the greatest interest in the most novel and rare events. Every day, new risks are identified, often in activities once believed to be relatively safe. Often reports contradict one another, leaving people confused about the risks' importance. Some of these contradictions arise because of how the numbers are expressed, others because of tangible differences in the information. All of this information seems to lead to an undeniable fact, "everything involves some risk." Even not doing something involves a risk associated with the alternative. Lying in bed involves some risk, eating, breathing, walking, driving—all involve varying levels of risk. However, the most important questions to ask ourselves when judging evidence about a risk is not whether there is a risk, but how large is the probability estimate of the risk and how confident can we be about the risk estimate?

Part

Direct Evidence

one

2 Background Mortality Information

Thishis chapter provides background information on the numerous tables and Figures that are presented in Chapters 3 to 5. Chapter 2 is divided into three sections. Evidence Source (below) describes the types of information collected and where this information came from. Population Evidence (p. 25) presents evidence on Canada's population. Rates (p. 31) describes mortality rates and explains why they are needed to make useful comparisons.

Evidence Source

Most of the information in this section is generated from vital statistics published annually by Statistics Canada and its predecessor the Dominion Bureau of Statistics. Most evidence in Chapters 2 to 5 has been divided into two parts: 1994 evidence, and trend evidence for the years 1930 to 1990. The year 1994 was chosen because it was the latest available year for detailed evidence on mortality. Although some types of evidence, like population estimates, are more current, they are of little use when evidence on mortality is not available.

One of the main advantages of direct evidence is its comparability over time (and place), which helps to highlight cumulative changes. Mortality evidence between 1930 and 1990 is summarized in five-year increments rather than annually. Since 1930, some significant changes in mortality patterns in Canada have occurred. However, changes in most aspects of mortality from year to year have been relatively small, which is why five-year increments can be used. We chose 1930 as the starting year even though different provinces began compiling vital statistics in 1921. This was done because Quebec, accounting for a significant portion of Canada's population, was not included until 1926. Even though Newfoundland and the Territories were added after 1930, their small populations had less effect on Canadian mortality statistics.

Table 2.1 summarizes evidence for 1994, and Table 2.2 summarizes evidence for 1930 to 1990. As it was the most current in late 1996, 1994 evidence has been summarized in more detail. However, all years have information separated by sex, age, and cause of death.

Evidence by sex is presented for males and females separately in most cases since important differences in mortality between sexes often exist. When the sexes are combined the data are labelled "both."

Table 2.1 ◆ 1994 Evidence

Category	Divisions	Division Names
Year	1	1994
Sex	2	Male, Female
Age	20	<1, 1–4, 5–9, 10–14, 15–19, 20–24, 25–29, 30–34, 35–39, 40–44, 45–49, 50–54, 55–59, 60–64, 65–69, 70–74, 75–79, 80–84, 85–89, 90+
Marital Status	3	Single, Married, Divorced/Widowed (1990 used)
Usual Residence	12	Nfld, PEI, NS, NB, Que., Ont., Man., Sask., Alta., BC, Yukon, NWT.
Cause of Death	6	Infectious, Cancer, Cardiovascular, Respiratory, External, Other
	17 Detailed	17 Major Categories (see Table 4.2) see Appendixes 1 and 2

Source: Statistics Canada 1996A

Table 2.2 ◆ 1930–1990 Trend Evidence

Category	Divisions	Division Names
Year	13	1930, 1935, 1940, 1945, 1950, 1955, 1960, 1965, 1970, 1975, 1980, 1985, 1990
Sex	2	Male, Female
Age	19	<1, 1–4, 5–9, 10–14, 15–19, 20–24, 25–29, 30–34, 35–39, 40–44, 45–49, 50–54, 55–59, 60–64, 65–69, 70–74, 75–79, 80–84, 85+
Cause of Death	6	Infectious, Cancer, Cardiovascular, Respiratory, External, Other

Source: Dominion Bureau of Statistics 1933, 1937, 1942, 1948, 1953, 1956, 1962, 1967, 1968; Statistics Canada 1970, 1972, 1975, 1978, 1980, 1983, 1985, 1987, 1990, 1994B

Age evidence is divided into five-year increments, except for the first two and last age categories. Recognizing the large difference in mortality between the first year of life and those immediately following, the first five-year increment is divided into 0–1 year and 1–4 year age categories. The upper age limit was determined by the available information. For 1994, this was 90+. Although much of the trend evidence included age categories until 100+, some contained only 85+, which became the limiting upper age category. Changing the last age category for 1994 from 90+ to 85+ would have allowed for better comparison with trend evidence. However, a much larger number of people currently live beyond 85, so that providing the extra age category in 1994 provides useful additional evidence.

For marital status, 1994 evidence was not readily available and 1990 evidence was used instead. For usual residence evidence, 1994 evidence was divided by province.

Detailed cause of death evidence is presented for 1994. This includes detailed breakdowns of all causes of death by major category (seventeen categories) and by age categories. For trend evidence, five major causes of death were selected for presentation (plus an "other" category). Currently, four of these five are the leading causes of death (based on the percentage of total deaths), while the fifth, infectious diseases, was a leading cause of death earlier in the century. The most detailed evidence for 1994 is presented in Appendixes 1 and 2. Annual evidence from 1991–1994 is presented in Appendix 3.

Population Evidence

The number of deaths is tied to the size of the population. A greater population will lead to a greater number of deaths. As many Tables and Figures use the population in their calculations, a summary of Canada's population since 1930 is presented in this section. Population evidence is presented in two ways: the total annual population and the annual population divided into age categories.

As the number of people dying in a year is related to the number of people living, the annual population must be used to calculate rates (number of deaths per unit population) to allow for comparison between years. Rates are discussed beginning on page 31.

1994 Evidence

The population estimate for Canada in 1994 was 29,251,285, which included 14,494,078 males and 14,757,207 females (Statistics Canada 1996A). The population passed the 30 million level in 1996. It should be noted that despite the apparent precision of the 1994 estimates (to the nearest person), these numbers are always uncertain because the true population is changing daily and is never known exactly. Clearly, it would be impossible to conduct an accurate count of every Canadian on any given day because of daily changes in births, deaths, immigration, and emigration. The section Uncertainty (p. 30) discusses some of the uncertainty associated with population estimates.

Table 2.3 shows the 1994 Canadian population broken down by age categories. Notice how the relative number of males and females changes with age. There are more males than females until the 55–59 age category. By the oldest age categories, there are over twice as many females as males.

Table 2.3 ◆ Population by Age Categories, 1994

Age Categories	Males	Females	Both
<1	198,055	186,949	385,004
1–4	830,231	790,295	1,620,526
5–9	1,008,998	967,065	1,976,063
10–14	1,015,782	969,683	1,985,465
15–19	1,005,139	957,239	1,962,378
20–24	1,043,671	1,015,008	2,058,679
25–29	1,163,762	1,137,939	2,301,701
30–34	1,359,190	1,322,565	2,681,755
35–39	1,280,910	1,266,974	2,547,884
40–44	1,128,735	1,127,675	2,256,410
45–49	1,002,308	989,987	1,992,295
50–54	765,479	761,143	1,526,622
55–59	631,052	638,052	1,269,104
60–64	597,308	618,551	1,215,859
65–69	519,102	589,405	1,108,507
70–74	416,873	534,165	951,038
75–79	265,163	382,778	647,941
80–84	162,937	273,445	436,382
85–89	69,957	148,195	218,152
90+	29,426	80,094	109,520
Total	14,494,078	14,757,207	29,251,285

Source: Statistics Canada 1996A, Appendix 2

Trend Evidence

Figure 2.1 shows the Canadian population between 1930 and 1990 for males, females, and both combined. The population has increased 2.6 times between 1930 (10.2 million) and 1990 (26.6 million). There was a greater number of males in 1930 (8% greater), a difference which disappeared by the 1970s, and a greater number of females by 1990 (3% greater). From 1970 to 1990, the total population increased by approximately 1 million every four years.

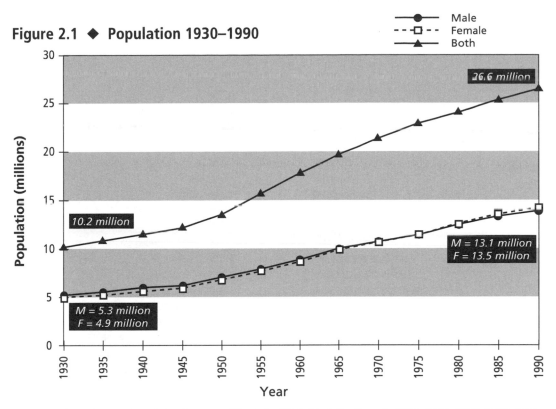

Figure 2.1 ◆ Population 1930–1990

Legend: Male, Female, Both

Data Source: Dominion Bureau of Statistics 1968; Statistics Canada 1970, 1975, 1980, 1985, 1990

When analysing mortality by age category, the matching population estimates are required as well. Information similar to Table 2.3 was collected for the years 1930–1990, although the 90+ age category was not used. In addition to the total number of people in each category, the relative number of people between categories is important as well. To show this number of people on a relative basis, population pyramids or population age distributions are used.

Figure 2.2 shows the male and female age distributions for the years 1930, 1950, 1970, and 1990. The lines represent the percentage of the total male and female populations found in each five-year age category (and one 85+ category). These numbers illustrate what has been called the baby boom. In 1950, the baby boom is in the 0–4 and 5–9 categories; by 1970, it was in the 0–4 to 25–29 categories; and by 1990, it is in the 25–29 to 40–44 categories. In addition, there has been an increase in the relative number of older people, especially females, indicative of an aging population. To highlight the aging population, Table 2.4 shows the percentage of the population younger than ten and older than sixty-five in 1930, 1950, 1970, and 1990. The greatest changes have taken place since 1970.

The differences in the age distribution between years and sexes can influence the results of some mortality calculations. The reasons for this and a method to compensate called age-standardization are discussed in Rates (p. 31).

Figure 2.2 ◆ Population Age Distributions, 1930–1990

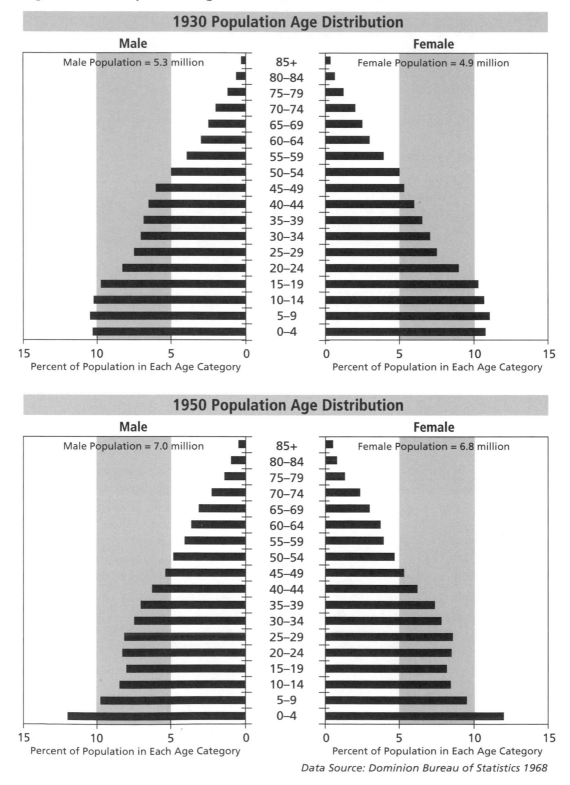

1930 Population Age Distribution

Male

Male Population = 5.3 million

Female

Female Population = 4.9 million

85+
80–84
75–79
70–74
65–69
60–64
55–59
50–54
45–49
40–44
35–39
30–34
25–29
20–24
15–19
10–14
5–9
0–4

15   10   5   0
Percent of Population in Each Age Category

0   5   10   15
Percent of Population in Each Age Category

1950 Population Age Distribution

Male

Male Population = 7.0 million

Female

Female Population = 6.8 million

85+
80–84
75–79
70–74
65–69
60–64
55–59
50–54
45–49
40–44
35–39
30–34
25–29
20–24
15–19
10–14
5–9
0–4

15   10   5   0
Percent of Population in Each Age Category

0   5   10   15
Percent of Population in Each Age Category

Data Source: Dominion Bureau of Statistics 1968

Figure 2.2 ◆ Population Age Distributions, 1930–1990 (Continued)

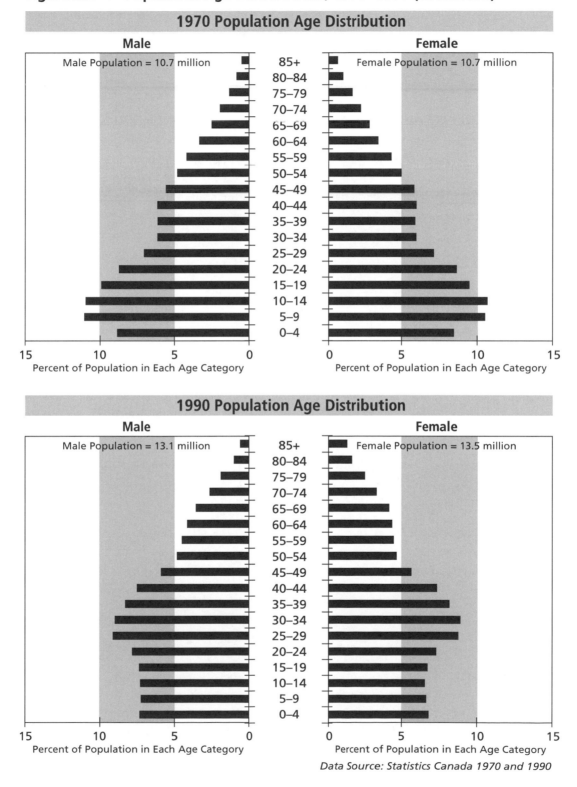

1970 Population Age Distribution

Male

Male Population = 10.7 million

Percent of Population in Each Age Category

Female

Female Population = 10.7 million

Percent of Population in Each Age Category

1990 Population Age Distribution

Male

Male Population = 13.1 million

Percent of Population in Each Age Category

Female

Female Population = 13.5 million

Percent of Population in Each Age Category

Data Source: Statistics Canada 1970 and 1990

Uncertainty

The population is a dynamic value that changes throughout the year, with people immigrating or emigrating, being born, or dying. Some other factors that can contribute to population uncertainty include changes in the method used to estimate population, adding the Territories and Newfoundland to Canadian totals, the availability of information, and use of non-census years.

In 1994, Statistics Canada changed the method they used to estimate the population. There were three changes: non-permanent residents were included; net census undercoverage was accounted for; and the reference date for the annual estimates was changed from June 1 to July 1. These changes applied retroactively to 1991 resulted in an estimated population increase of approximately 1 million people (or 3.6% of the total). These changes affected males more than females. The changes were also age dependent, with the largest changes in the 20–34 age categories. The largest change was ~9% in the 20–24 age category (Bender 1995).

Statistics Canada revised the population estimates back to 1971 using this new method. As the trend evidence summarized in this book starts in 1930, it was not worth making the changes. However, as the 1994 information uses the new populations method, comparison between 1990 and 1994 information in this book might appear several percentage greater than in reality. For example, the population for 1990 using revised numbers is 27.8 million instead of the 26.6 million used throughout this book. Although a difference of a few percent may seem small, it is a useful reminder that the population is only an estimate that can be altered because of changes in the method used to count the population.

The Yukon and Northwest Territories were not included in the five-year tabulations of mortality between 1930 and 1955, but were included in the population estimates. The population of the two Territories was always less than 0.2% of the total Canadian population during this time and only had a small effect on mortality rates.

As Newfoundland only joined Confederation in 1949, it was not included in the five-year population estimates between 1930 and 1945 and also not included in the mortality tabulations. Newfoundland represented approximately 2.5% of the population in 1950, and mortality rates in Newfoundland were not very different from the rest of Canada.

Population numbers used between 1930 and 1975 did not have separate age categories for the years 0–1 and 1–4. To promote comparisons with later years, it was assumed the listed 0–5 population estimate had a uniform distribution and was multiplied by 0.2 for the 0–1 age category and 0.8 for the 1–4 age category. Making this calculation for 1994 information would result in an overestimate of ~3% in the male and female 0–1 age categories. The difference in estimated population was less than 1% in the 1–4 age categories.

Table 2.4 ◆ Changes in Population Age Distribution, 1930–1990

Sex	Year	9 years and less	65 years and greater
Male	1930	21.1 %	5.4 %
	1950	21.6 %	7.7 %
	1970	20.0 %	7.1 %
	1990	14.6 %	8.7 %
Female	1930	22.0 %	5.5 %
	1950	21.4 %	7.6 %
	1970	19.1 %	8.6 %
	1990	13.5 %	13.2 %

Source: Dominion Bureau of Statistics 1968; Statistics Canada 1970 and 1990

The censuses took place one year following the five-year increments used in this book (i.e., 1931, 1936, 1941, etc.). However, because of the delay of approximately two years in publishing the vital statistics, the populations for the selected five-year intervals were extrapolated back one year, not ahead four years. Most information summarized by Statistics Canada is centred on the census years. The difference in values is likely less than those of other uncertainties in population estimates.

Considering all these factors together, the total population estimates would have an uncertainty of a few percent (less than 5%). Individual age categories usually have an uncertainty of less than 10%. The largest differences occur when comparing years that used the old population method with those that use the new.

Rates

Defining Rates and Participation

A rate is defined as the frequency with which an event occurs in a defined population. Rates enable comparison between populations at different times (e.g., between 1930 and 1990), different places (e.g., between different provinces), or different categories (e.g., sexes, age categories, different causes of death). A rate has a numerator, denominator, a specified time period, and usually a multiplier that converts the rate from an awkward fraction or decimal to a whole number (Last 1995):

$$\text{Rate} = \frac{\text{Number of events in specified period}}{\text{Average population during the period}} \times 10^n$$

In this book, the numerator is usually the number of deaths in a specific group (specific year, sex, age, and/or cause of death), the denominator is the population of the same group, the time period is usually one year, and the multipliers are usually 1,000 or 100,000.

Table 2.5 shows four population-based rate examples. A multiplier of 1,000 is used in the first two examples, while a multiplier of 100,000 is used in the last two examples. Larger multipliers are used when there is a small number of deaths in a large population group. Note that the denominator of the first, third, and fourth examples is deaths per population, while the second example is deaths per live births.

The latter limitation illustrates the importance of considering participation in stating the rate of an outcome. Infant deaths can occur only in infants, so expressing infant deaths as a rate per specified number of live births, rather than as a rate for the total population, is more informative about the risks of childbirth. Likewise, other risks may be relevant only to specific groups who possess a shared characteristic or participate in a risk-generating activity. Hence, the accidental-death rate from sky diving in the total population is less informative about risk to the individual than is the death rate among skydivers.

Other types of mortality rates used in this book include the following.

- **Maternal death rate:** annual deaths of mother resulting from pregnancy/annual live births (10,000).

- **Marital status death rate:** annual deaths in specific marital status category/total population in marital status category (100,000).

- **Provincial death rate:** annual deaths in specific province/total population of province (1,000).

For many examples in Chapters 3 and 4, two Figures divided into age categories are included. The first Figure shows the total number of deaths and the second the death rate. The total number of deaths must be interpreted carefully for two reasons. The first is that all age categories do not cover the same number of years. The first category is for only one year, the second includes four years (1–4), and then every category includes five years until the last category, which includes all people above a certain age (for 1994 information 90+; for 1930 to 1990 information, 85+). The second reason for caution is the large differences in population between different age categories and between sexes. As shown earlier in Table 2.3, differences in the population of age categories with the same five-year span can be twenty-fold. This is why the second Figure showing the death rate is included. Dividing the total number of deaths in the first Figure by the population accounts for the differences between age categories.

Population-based rates can also incorporate factors like occupational or transportation risks. However, using a base of those participating in any given risk is discussed in Part Two, Indirect Evidence and Inference, because these risks are based on a person's behaviour (risk factor).

Table 2.5 ◆ Rate Examples

A. Crude Death Rate Example, 1930 and 1990

Year	Sex	Deaths	Population	Crude Annual Death Rate (deaths per 1,000 population)
1930	Male	59,109	5,271,700	11.2
	Female	50,197	4,936,300	10.2
	Both	109,306	10,208,000	10.7
1990	Male	103,968	13,104,200	7.9
	Female	88,005	13,479,800	6.5
	Both	191,973	26,610,400	7.2

Note: Crude Annual Death Rate (annual number of deaths in specified sex group/total population in specified sex group) * (1,000).

B. Infant Mortality Rate Example, 1930 and 1990

Year	Deaths	Live Births	Infant Mortality Rate (deaths per 1,000 live births)
1930	22,677	~ 250,000	90.6
1990	2,766	~ 407,000	6.8

Note: Infant Mortality Rate (annual deaths less than one year of age/annual live births) * (1,000).

C. Cause-Specific Death Rate Example, 1994

Sex	Cause	Deaths	Population	Cause-Specific Death Rate (deaths per 100,000 population)
Male	Infectious	2,300	14,494,078	16
	Cancer	31,014	14,494,078	214
Female	Infectious	897	14,757,207	6
	Cancer	26,310	14,757,207	178

Note: Cause Specific Death Rate (annual number of deaths from specific cause in specified sex group/total population in specified sex group) * (100,000).

D. Age-Specific Death Rate Example, 1994

Age Categories	Deaths	Population	Age-Specific Death Rate (deaths per 100,000 population)
Less than 1	2,418	385,004	628
10–14	408	1,985,465	21
40–44	3,928	2,256,410	174
80–84	31,899	436,382	7,310

Note: Age-Specific Death Rate (annual number of deaths in specific age group/total population in specified age group) * (100,000).

Source: Dominion Bureau of Statistics 1933, 1968; Statistics Canada 1994B, 1996A

Age-Standardization

Age-standardization is used to compare two or more populations with different age distributions. Figure 2.2 highlights the differences in age distribution between sexes and different years. Provinces and other geographical areas also have differences in age distribution. Aside from standardization, the only way to accurately compare mortality rates is to include the individual age categories.

However, it is often not feasible to include all age categories, especially in a table or when comparing several years at the same time. For this reason, a process called age-standardization is done using the following equation:

$$\text{Age-standardized Death Rate} = \frac{\sum_{i=1}^{n} \left(\frac{d_i}{p_i}\right) P_i}{\sum_{i=1}^{n} P_i}$$

i = age category (1, 2, 3, ..., n)

n = 20 (for 1994 evidence), 19 (for trend evidence 1930–1990)

d_i = for age category i, the age and/or sex specific number of deaths for a specific cause and/or location

p_i = for age category i, the age and/or sex specific population for a specific cause and/or location

P_i = for age category i, the age specific population (1991 standard population, both sexes combined)

The death rate for an individual age category is represented by (d_i/p_i) (e.g., annual number of deaths in the 5–9 age category divided by the population in the 5–9 age category for a specified year). This rate is then standardized to P_i, the standard population. The standard population is the population distribution (with both sexes combined) to which the other distributions will be adjusted. The same standard population must be used in all calculations, so that results are comparable. The 1991 final post-censal population is currently used as the standard population. The number of people in the standard population is not important, but the distribution (percent in each age category) is important.

Table 2.6 presents crude and age-standardized death rates for 1930 and 1990. There are two big differences between the crude and age-standardized rates. The first is that the 1930 age-standardized rates are almost half as great again as the 1930 crude rates. The second is that the 1990 female age-standardized rate is lower than the 1990 female crude rate, while the

1990 male age-standardized rate is higher than the male 1990 crude rate. Why did these differences happen?

In the first case, Figure 2.2 shows that the population in 1930 was much younger than it was in 1991 (very similar to 1990). Age-standardization calculates how many more people would have died in 1930 if they had had fewer younger people and more older people as in 1991.

In the second case, Figure 2.2 shows that more males are alive at younger ages, but many more females are alive at older ages. Age-standardization calculates how many fewer females would have died in 1990 if there were more younger females and fewer older females. Likewise, age-standardization calculates how many more males would have died in 1990 if there were fewer younger males and more older males.

Age-standardization is the only way to use one number to properly compare groups that have different population distributions, aside from including numbers for each age-category. An example of the importance of using age-standardization is comparing the death rates between provinces (see Figures 3.18 and 3.19). Although crude rates show that the Territories have a lower death rate than the provinces, age-standardized rates show that the Territories actually have a greater death rate than the provinces. The Territories have a younger population than the provinces, which makes using crude rates misleading.

Table 2.6 ◆ Crude and Age-Standardized Death Rates, 1930 and 1990

Year	Gender	Crude Death Rate (deaths per 1,000 pop.)	Age-Standardized Death Rate (deaths per 1,000 pop.)
1930	Male	11.2	16.5
	Female	10.2	15.1
	Both	10.7	15.8
1990	Male	7.9	9.4
	Female	6.5	5.5
	Both	7.2	7.2

Source: Dominion Bureau of Statistics 1933, 1968; Statistics Canada 1994B

3

The Death Certificate

The death certificate (properly known as the death registration form) is one of several vital statistics that summarize information relating to human life. The primary vital statistics are births, deaths, marriages, and divorces. Stillbirths, abortions, and adoptions may also be included. Table 3.1 is a summary of vital statistics for 1994.

For the past several years, there have been approximately twice as many births as deaths in Canada. An interesting coincidence is that a similar ratio exists between marriages and divorces.

Table 3.1 ◆ Vital Statistics, 1994

Vital Statistic	Male	Female	Both
Live Births	198,173	186,939	385,112
Deaths	109,742	97,335	207,077
Marriages	–	–	159,316 (1993)
Divorces	–	–	78,226 (1993)

Source: Statistics Canada 1996; Colombo 1996

Historical recording of vital statistics began in Canada in the early 1600s when the church in Quebec began registering the information. However, it was not until 1921 that an annual publication combined vital statistics nationally for the other eight Canadian provinces. Quebec was added in 1926, Newfoundland joined in 1949 when it became part of Confederation, and information for the Territories was combined starting in 1956 (Statistics Canada 1996A).

Statistics Canada, the successor to the Dominion Bureau of Statistics, produces annual publications on vital statistics in addition to numerous other statistical data reports. These annual publications, and particularly those relating to mortality, have been used for most of the evidence presented in Part One, Direct Evidence. This evidence is the cumulative result of the experience of recording vital statistics that began hundreds of years ago.

A death certificate is filled in for every known death in Canada. Figure 3.1 is a copy of the standard death certificate designed and printed by Statistics Canada for use by provinces and Territories. A province may use its own form as long as it includes the same standard information. The death certificate supplies information that is the most "direct" link to mortality. For this reason, it is important to understand the process relating to and the contents of the death certificate.

Figure 3.1 ◆ Death Registration Form

Form reproduction:

```
                                    MODEL           (1971)
Province of                     Registration of              Registration No.(Department Use Only)
        (Canada)                    DEATH

(Do not write above this line)

NAME OF    1. Surname of deceased (print or type)                    Social Insurance Number
DECEASED
           All given names                                       2. Sex

PLACE OF   3. Name of hospital or institution (otherwise full  City, town or other place (by name)  Inside municipal limits?  County or district
DEATH         address where death occurred)                                                         (state Yes or No)

USUAL      4. Complete street address if rural give exact  City, town or other place (by name)  Inside municipal limits?  County or district
RESIDENCE     location (not PO or RR address)                                                   (state Yes or No)         Province (or country)

MARITAL    5. Single, married, widowed or divorced (specify)    MEDICAL CERTIFICATE OF DEATH            Approx
STATUS                                                       20. DATE OF DEATH: Month (by name), day, year  interva
                                                                                                        betwee
           6. If married, widowed or divorced, give full   21. CAUSE OF DEATH                           onset
              name of husband or maiden name of wife                     Part I                         and
                                                             Immediate cause       (a)                  death
OCCUPATION 7. Kind of work done during most of working life  of death          due to (or as a consequence of)

           8. Kind of business or industry in which worked  Antecedent causes,    (b)
                                                             if any, giving rise to  due to (or as a consequence of)
                                                             the immediate cause (a)
BIRTHDATE  9. Month (by name), day, year of birth           above, stating the
                                                             underlying cause last  (c)
AGE        10. Years If under(Months)(Days) If under(Hrs.)(Min.)       Part II
               1 year              1 day                    Other significant
                                                            conditions contribut-
           11. City or place, province (or country) of birth ing to death but not
BIRTHPLACE                                                  immediate cause (a) above

                                                            22. Autopsy Yes No  23. Does the cause of  Yes No  24. May further infor-  Yes
           This space reserved for optional item(s)            being              death stated above           mation relating to
                                                               held?              take account of               the cause of death
           12. Surname of father (print or type)                                  autopsy findings?             be available later?

           All given names                                  25. If accident, suicide,  26. Place of injury (e.g. home,  27. How did injury
FATHER                                                          homicide or undetermined   farm, highway, etc.)            occur? (descri
                                                               (specify)                                                  circumstances)
           13. City or place, province (or country) of
               birth - father                               28. I certify that the above named person  Signature:
                                                                died on the date and from the causes
           14. Maiden surname of mother (print or type)         stated herein:              X

           All given names                                  29. Desig-  Attending                Date certified: Month (by name)
MOTHER                                                          nation:  physician   Coroner   Other           day, year

           15. City or place, province (or country) of
               birth - mother                               30. Name of physician or coroner (print or type)  Address:

SIGNATURE  16. Signature of informant  17. Relationship to  DISPO-  31. Burial, cremation or other  32. Date of burial or disposition: Mont
OF             X                           deceased         SITION      disposition (specify)           (by name), day, year
INFORMANT  18. Date signed: Month(by   19. Address of              33. Name and address of cemetery, crematorium or place of disposition
               name), day, year            informant
                                                            FUNERAL  34. Name and address of funeral director (or person in charge of remain
                                                            DIRECTOR     (print or type)

For (Department Use Only)

CERTIFICATION  I certify this return  Signature of (Division) Registrar  Date: Month (by name), day, year  This space reserved for optional item(s)
OF (DIVISION)  was accepted by me
REGISTRAR      on this date:
               at
```

Source: Statistics Canada 1996A, Appendix 1

The process of registering a death is as follows:

The form for the registration of death consists of two parts, personal and medical. Personal data are supplied by an informant, usually a relative of the deceased. The informant signs this part of the certificate and is responsible for delivering the form to the undertaker. The part of the form comprising the medical certificate of death is completed by the medical practitioner last in attendance or by a coroner, if an inquest or enquiry was held. The undertaker, or person acting as the undertaker, enters details on burial or their disposition of the body on the death registration form. He is also responsible for filing the completed form with the local Registrar who then issues the burial permit (Statistics Canada 1996A, ix).

On the death certificate (Figure 3.1), the informant fills in sections 1–19, the medical practitioner or coroner fills in sections 20–30, and the undertaker fills in sections 31–34.

Although many parts of all death certificates are ultimately compiled by Statistics Canada, there are six aspects of the contents of particular relevance to direct evidence: registered deaths, sex, age, marital status, usual residence, and cause of death. These six aspects are listed in Table 3.2, with the related sections from the death certificate (Figure 3.1).

Other standard information collected and published by Statistics Canada includes the residence, birthplace, birthplace of parents, date of death, province of occurrence of death, place of accident, and autopsy (Statistics Canada 1996A).

Table 3.2 ◆ Death Certificate Sections Related to Direct Evidence

Name	Related Section on Death Certificate	Related Section in this Book
Registered Death	Form itself	Total Registered Death Evidence (p. 40)
Sex	2	Evidence of Sex Differences (p. 42)
Age	10	Evidence on Age (p. 44)
Marital Status	5	Evidence on Marital Status (p. 54)
Usual Residence	4	Evidence on Usual Residence (p. 56)
Cause of Death	21	Cause of Death Evidence (p. 59)

Total Registered Death Evidence

The annual number of deaths is the starting value from which all other annual mortality evidence derives. Subsequent divisions of this number provide more detailed, but often less precise, evidence. Divisions are made based on sex, age, marital status, residence, and cause of death, with varying degrees of increased uncertainty. Deaths of non-Canadian residents are not included in these totals. Deaths of Canadians in the United States are included in the Canadian totals under a mutual agreement. Otherwise, deaths of Canadians in foreign countries are normally not included.

1994 Evidence

In 1994, a total of 204,912 deaths were registered. This corresponds to a crude death rate of 7.0 deaths per 1,000 population (standardized rates are discussed under Evidence on Age, p. 44). This total annual number of deaths corresponds to:

- a one in 143 annual chance of dying over the entire population;

- 561 deaths per day;

- twenty-three deaths per hour;

- one death every 2.5 minutes.

Trend Evidence

The Yukon and Northwest Territories were not included in the annual totals for 1930 to 1955 because their information was not regarded as complete or significant for the totals of the rest of Canada. For the years collected, the combined deaths of the two Territories were less than 0.5% of the total number of deaths in the rest of Canada.

Figure 3.2 shows the relationship between population, deaths, and crude death rate from 1930 to 1990. The crude death rate was shown earlier in Table 2.5. For Figure 3.2 only, it is important to recognize that the vertical axis has two different meanings. For population and deaths, it is an annual number, but for the crude death rate, it is the annual deaths per 1,000 population.

Between 1930 and 1990, the population increased 2.6 times, while the number of deaths only increased 1.7 times. The greater increase in the population in comparison with total deaths explains why the crude death rate has been decreasing.

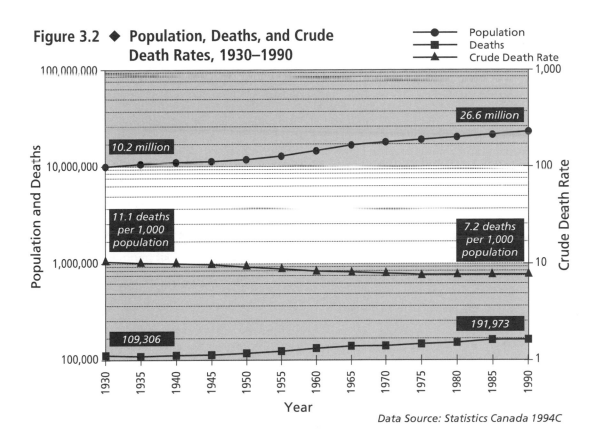

Figure 3.2 ◆ Population, Deaths, and Crude Death Rates, 1930–1990

Data Source: Statistics Canada 1994C

Method

In Figure 3.2, the population and the number of deaths for each fifth year between 1930 and 1990 were taken from Statistics Canada 1994C. The crude death rate was calculated by dividing the number of deaths by the population and multiplying by 1,000 for each year.

Uncertainty

The total annual number of deaths is the most accurate piece of mortality evidence available. Of those people registered, there is little doubt about whether or not they have died. However, there is uncertainty associated with whether all deaths are known and whether they have all been included in time for the annual publication of mortality statistics.

Knowing how many deaths are unknown and not registered is impossible. It is likely that more deaths were not registered earlier in this century than now, especially in the more remote areas of Canada.

Statistics Canada publishes their annual reports of vital statistics within time constraints. In 1990, there were eighty-four late registrations that were not included in the reports. However, this discrepancy was less than 0.05 % of the total registered deaths of 191,973 (Statistics Canada 1995A).

Evidence of Sex Differences

Males and females often have significant differences in their mortality patterns. For this reason, separate evidence is provided where possible. Wilkins, in the opening paragraph of a paper called "Causes of Death: How the Sexes Differ," writes: "Biological, social and behavioural factors have resulted in differences in the most common causes of death for males and females. In infancy, the causes are similar, but start to diverge sharply. However, as people advance into their senior years, differences in the leading causes of death for men and women tend to diminish" (Wilkins 1995, 33).

This quote highlights some general factors associated with differences in mortality between sexes, which will be discussed in more detail in Part Two, Indirect Evidence and Inference. As the differences are relatively large and consistent, where possible, all numbers will be presented separately for males and females.

1994 Evidence

In 1994, there were 109,407 registered male deaths and 95,505 registered female deaths. The crude death rates, in deaths per 1,000 population, were 7.5 for males and 6.5 for females. The larger number of male deaths (13% larger) and the smaller number of males in the population (2% smaller) meant that the crude death rate for males is 14% larger.

Trend Evidence

Figure 3.3 shows the deaths for males and females between 1930 and 1990. There have consistently been a greater number of deaths in males than females. This difference increased steadily from 1930, peaked in the 1960s and has since been decreasing. In 1960 and 1965, there were 29% more deaths of males than females, but, by 1990, this had decreased to 15%.

Figure 3.4 shows the crude death rate for males and females between 1930 and 1990. As the population has increased more rapidly than deaths, there has been a general lowering in the crude death rate. Caution needs to be used with Figure 3.4, since the crude rates are not age-standardized. Figure 3.9 compares the crude and age-standardized death rates, highlighting the importance of compensating for changing population age distributions.

Method

In Figure 3.3, the number of deaths for each sex for each fifth year between 1930 and 1990 was taken from Statistics Canada 1994C. In Figure 3.4, the crude death rate was calculated by dividing the number of deaths for each sex by the population for each sex (see Figure 2.1) and multiplying by 1,000 for each year.

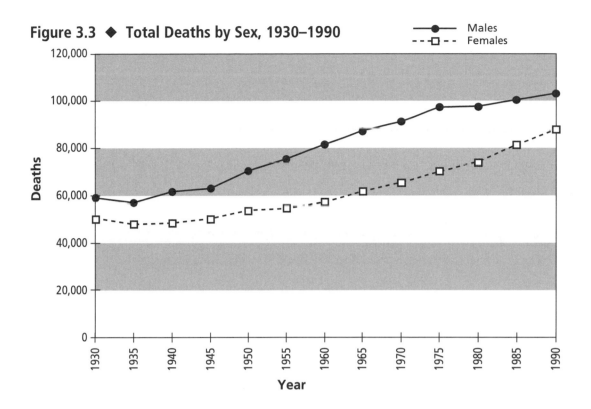

Figure 3.3 ◆ Total Deaths by Sex, 1930–1990

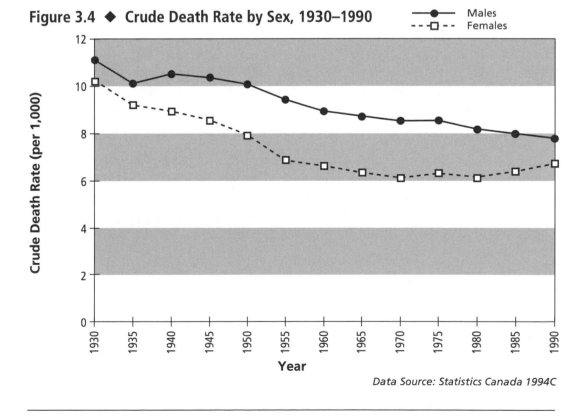

Figure 3.4 ◆ Crude Death Rate by Sex, 1930–1990

Data Source: Statistics Canada 1994C

Uncertainty

None of the cause of death summaries reported that the sex was not known or was uncertain. It is likely that any errors in recording the sex are very small. Overall, the uncertainty in the number of deaths by sex will be slightly greater than (or at a minimum equal to) the uncertainty in the number of total registered deaths (see p. 41). Overall, this uncertainty is likely less than 0.1%.

Evidence on Age

Age and mortality are strongly related. Age at Death (p. 44) summarizes the relationship between age and mortality. Infant Deaths (p. 48) deals specifically with deaths at less than one year of age and Life Expectancy (p. 50) discusses overall life expectancy.

On the death certificate, deaths of people aged one and older are completed in years, and deaths of those aged less than one are completed in months or days. Following the first few years of life, increasing age is strongly and exponentially associated with increasing mortality. In addition, the age at death provides valuable insights into different causes of death.

Age at Death

1994 Evidence

Figure 3.5 shows the total number of deaths for different age categories in 1994. This Figure can be used to identify how many males and females died in any age category. For example, in 1994, just over 2,000 females died at an age of between 50 and 54. Care must be taken in drawing conclusions from Figure 3.5 because it does not take into account the differences in population between age categories. Although there is a sharp drop in the number of male deaths past eighty-five years of age, there is an even sharper drop in the number of males alive. This is why Figure 3.6, death rate by age, is included.

Figure 3.6 shows the death rate for different age categories in 1994. Several conclusions can be drawn from Figure 3.6. Males are more likely to die than females in all age categories. The chances of dying in the first year of life are similar to the chances of dying in the mid to late fifties. After the first year of life, the risk of dying drops dramatically (approximately twenty times lower) until past middle age.

Trend Evidence

Figure 3.7 is similar to Figure 3.5 except that the sexes are combined and four different dates are compared. Care must be taken in interpreting Figure 3.7 because it does not take into account the differences in population between age categories and dates (the population increased 2.6 times between 1930 and 1990). In both 1930 and 1950, a significant number of people died in the first year of life.

Figure 3.5 ◆ Total Deaths by Age, 1994

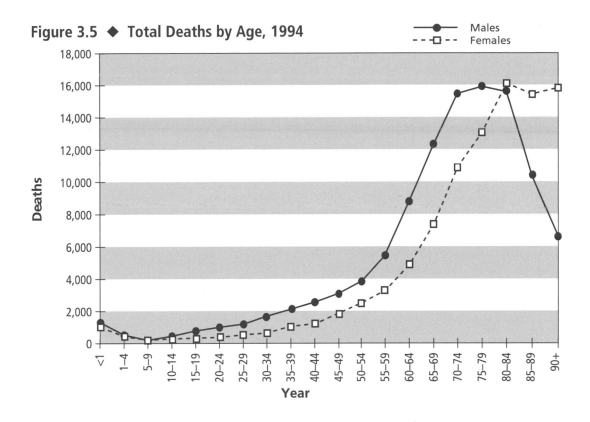

Figure 3.6 ◆ Death Rate by Age, 1994

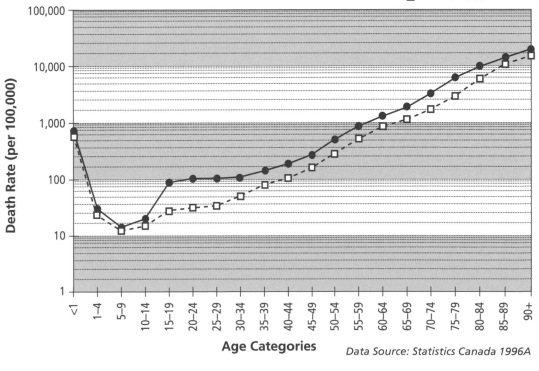

Data Source: Statistics Canada 1996A

Figure 3.8 is similar to Figure 3.6, except that four different years are compared instead of only one. The overall pattern of a high initial death rate followed by a rapid decrease and then an exponential increase with age is similar over the sixty years between 1930 and 1990. However, there is a significantly lower death rate in all age categories today than in 1930. The largest reduction in the death rate over this sixty-year period has occurred in the first fifteen years of life. Between 1930 and 1990, the chance of dying in the first year of life has decreased by a factor of thirteen. There is additional information on infant deaths beginning on p. 48.

Figure 3.9 shows the crude and age-standardized death rates for males and females between 1930 and 1990. Crude rates have shown a decreasing trend since 1930, with a slight increase for females between 1980 and 1990. However, age-standardized rates show a larger and consistent decrease for both males and females. The difference between the two rates is due to differences in the age distributions of each sex.

Figure 3.9 shows why using crude rates can be misleading. If the aging population since 1930 is not considered, the reduction in death rates appears much lower. The age-standardized rates not only highlight the larger decrease in death rates from 1930 to 1990 but also emphasize the difference between males and females, which is actually greater than indicated by the crude rates.

Method

In Figure 3.5, the number of deaths by age category for 1994 was taken from Statistics Canada 1996A. In Figure 3.6, the death rate was calculated by dividing the number of deaths by age category by the population in each category (see Table 2.3), and multiplying by 100,000 for each age category.

Figures 3.7 and 3.8 repeated the same method used for Figures 3.5 and 3.6 in 1994 for four years (1930, 1950, 1970, 1990), except that the sexes were combined and there was one less age category (90+).

In Figure 3.9, the crude death rates are repeated from Figure 3.4, and the age-standardized death rates were calculated using the formula shown on p. 34. The age-standardized rates were performed on a spreadsheet because of the large number of calculations required.

Figure 3.7 ◆ Total Deaths by Age, 1930–1990

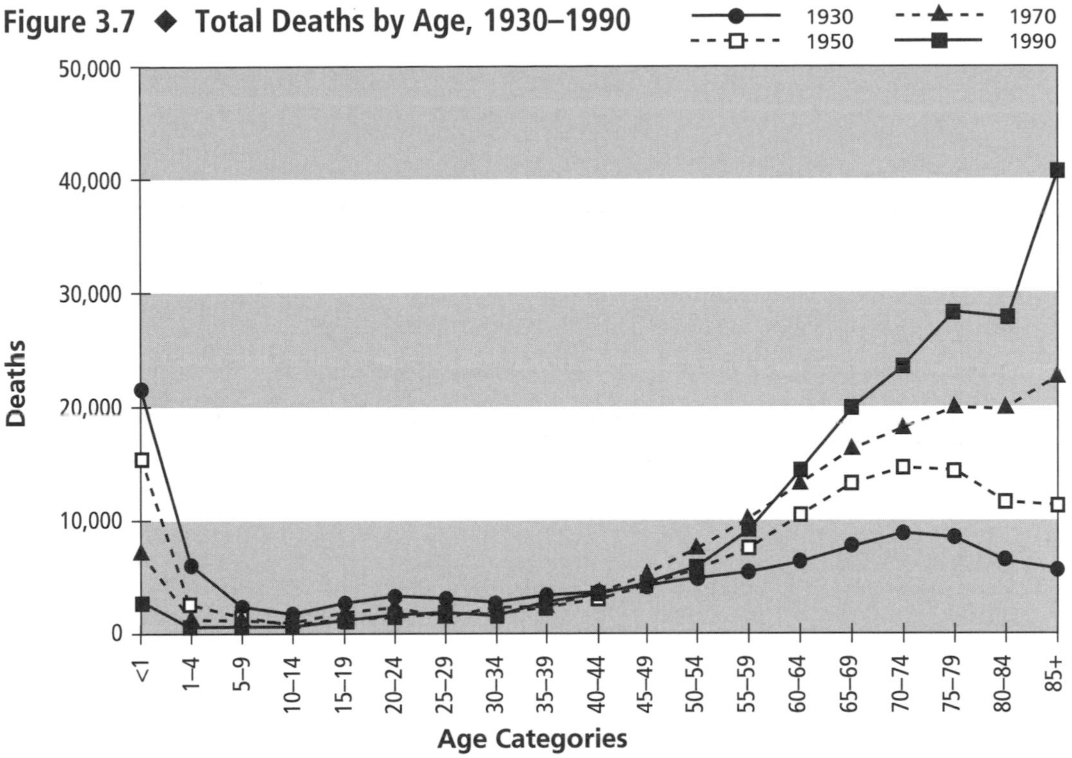

1930
1970
1950
1990
50,000
40,000
30,000
20,000
10,000
0
Deaths
<1
1–4
5–9
10–14
15–19
20–24
25–29
30–34
35–39
40–44
45–49
50–54
55–59
60–64
65–69
70–74
75–79
80–84
85+
Age Categories

Figure 3.8 ◆ Death Rate by Age, 1930–1990

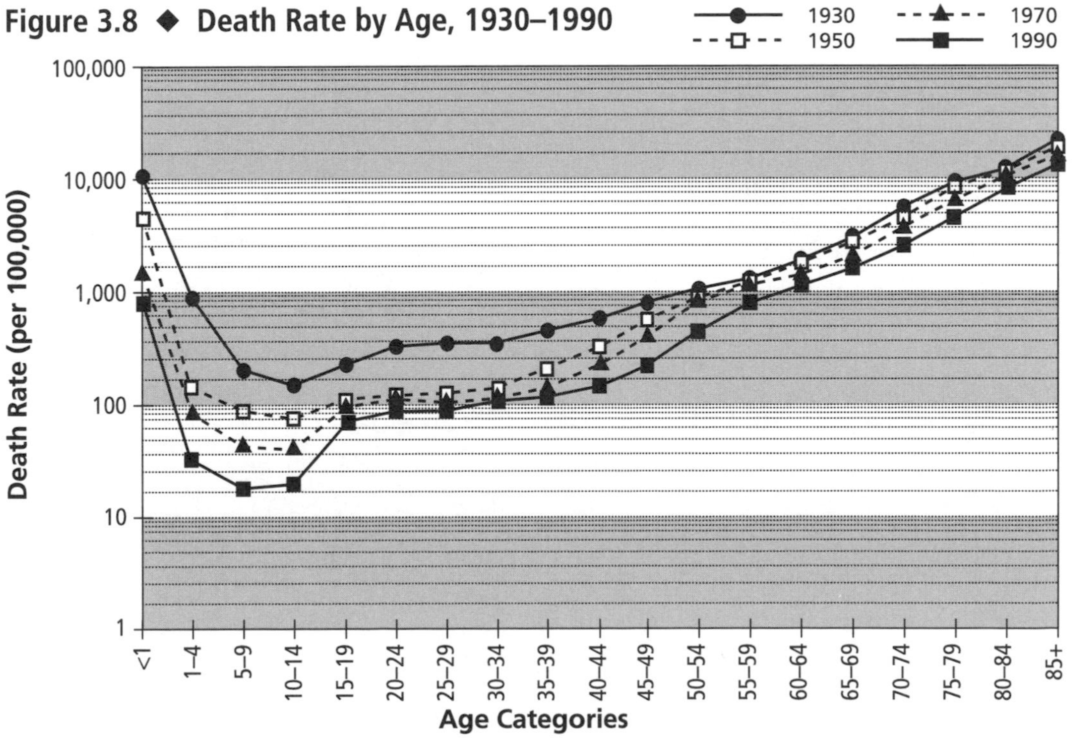

1930
1970
1950
1990
100,000
10,000
1,000
100
10
1
Death Rate (per 100,000)
<1
1–4
5–9
10–14
15–19
20–24
25–29
30–34
35–39
40–44
45–49
50–54
55–59
60–64
65–69
70–74
75–79
80–84
85+
Age Categories

Data Source: Dominion Bureau of Statistics 1933, 1937, 1942, 1948, 1953, 1956, 1962, 1967, 1968; Statistics Canada 1970, 1972, 1975, 1978, 1980, 1983, 1985, 1987, 1990, 1994B

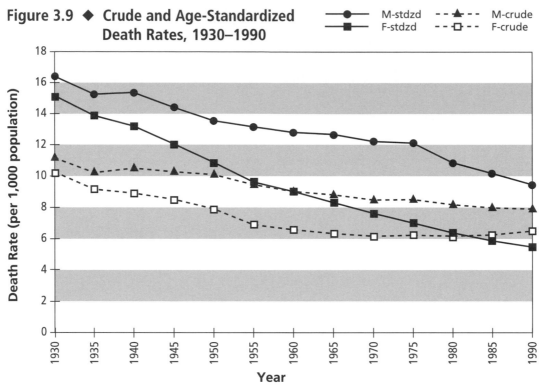

Figure 3.9 ◆ Crude and Age-Standardized Death Rates, 1930–1990

Legend: M-stdzd, F-stdzd, M-crude, F-crude

Data Source: Dominion Bureau of Statistics 1933, 1937, 1942, 1948, 1953, 1956, 1962, 1967, 1968; Statistics Canada 1970, 1972, 1975, 1978, 1980, 1983, 1985, 1987, 1990, 1994B

Infant Deaths

Infant deaths are those occurring at less than one year of age. Infant death rates, in addition to life expectancy, are often used as a measure of a country's prevailing health and indicate several factors, including the overall quality and accessibility of the health care system. As well as measuring the care of the newborn, the infant death rate also reflects the health of the community and may be assumed to reflect the health of parents (Alderson 1988).

If information is available, it is possible to standardize infant mortality rates using birth weights. This additional evidence was beyond the scope of this book, but a more in-depth analysis of infant deaths should include birth weight information.

1994 Evidence

In 1994, there was a total of 2,418 infant deaths (1,375 males and 1,043 females). As there were 385,112 live births in 1994, the corresponding infant mortality rate was 6.3 per 1,000 live births.

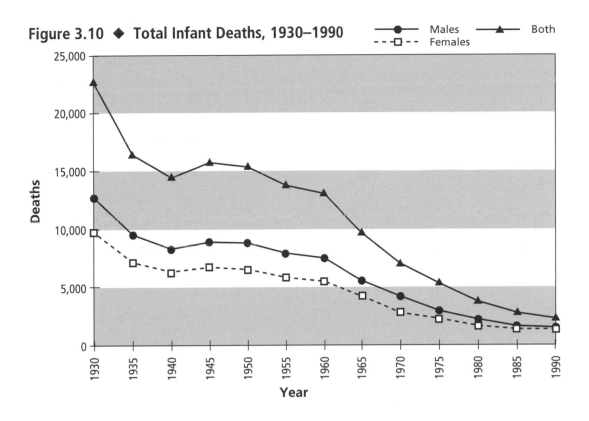

Figure 3.10 ◆ Total Infant Deaths, 1930–1990

Legend: Males ● Females □ Both ▲

Y-axis: Deaths (0 to 25,000)
X-axis: Year (1930 to 1990)

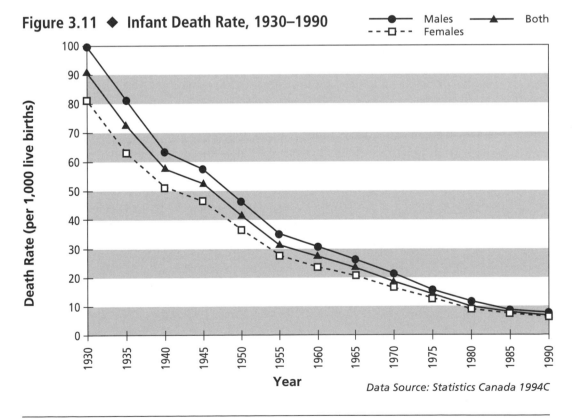

Figure 3.11 ◆ Infant Death Rate, 1930–1990

Legend: Males ● Females □ Both ▲

Y-axis: Death Rate (per 1,000 live births) (0 to 100)
X-axis: Year (1930 to 1990)

Data Source: Statistics Canada 1994C

Trend Evidence

Figure 3.10 shows the number of infant deaths between 1930 and 1990 for males, females, and both combined. Care must be taken in drawing conclusions from Figure 3.10 because it does not account for the number of births that actually took place each year. The total number of infant deaths decreased by a factor of eight from 22,677 in 1930 to 2,766 in 1990.

Unlike most other Figures that used five-year intervals because of relatively consistent annual changes over time, the number of infant deaths from year to year fluctuated more significantly. Not shown in Figure 3.10 is information for 1936 to 1938, when the infant deaths were 15,442, 17,762, and 15,233. This increase in 1937 was not due to increased births.

Figure 3.11 shows the infant death rate between 1930 and 1990 for males, females, and both combined. The infant death rate decreased by a factor of thirteen, from 90.6 per 1,000 live births in 1930 to 6.8 per 1,000 live births in 1990.

Method

In Figure 3.10, the number of infant deaths for each fifth year between 1930 and 1990 was taken from Statistics Canada 1994C. In Figure 3.11, the information was copied from the same reference, which calculated the infant death rate by dividing the number of infant deaths by the number of live births, and multiplying by 1,000 for each year.

Life Expectancy

Life expectancy is commonly used as a measure of the health of a country's population. Canada currently enjoys one of the highest life expectancies in the world. Life expectancy can also summarize trends in health over time. Canada's life expectancy has changed significantly over the past century.

Life expectancy (otherwise known as expectation of life) is the average number of years an individual of a given age is expected to live if current mortality rates continue to apply (Last 1995). Life expectancy does not necessarily mean the life expectancy at birth, although birth is most commonly used. Life expectancy is based on current mortality rates, which, as this book will show, can change significantly over the years. In the past, life expectancy predictions have underestimated the actual number of years people survived. Only when mortality rates remain relatively constant over a period of observation can life expectancy be accurate for predicting future rates.

A similar measure to life expectancy is the median age of death in a given year. For example, if 100,000 males died in 1994, the age of the 50,000th male (when they are ranked by age of death) is the median age of death.

Life expectancy can be used as a base for other health indicators. Disability-adjusted life years (DALYs) adjust the life expectancy using long-term disability estimated from official statistics. DALYs are a measure of the burden of disease and the effectiveness of interventions related to a defined population (Last 1995). However, DALYs require the use of additional, less certain information that is outside the scope of this book.

1994 Evidence

The life expectancy for Canadians in 1994 was 78.2 years: 75.1 years for males and 81.1 years for females (Statistics Canada 1996B).

Trend Evidence

Figure 3.12 shows the cumulative percentage of deaths by age for 1930, 1950, 1970, and 1990. Figure 3.12 is a good introduction to median age at death. The point at which the line for each year crosses the 50% approximates the median age at death for that year. The median age at death increased substantially between 1930 and 1950, and steadily at a lower rate over each of the next twenty years. Figure 3.12 highlights most of the gains in median age at death. In 1930, 20% of people did not survive past one year of age and the mortality increased more rapidly than in the later years. Between 1950 and 1970, most of the increase came from a reduction in infant mortality. Between 1970 and 1990, a continuing reduction in infant mortality helped, but starting around the age of forty, there was also a reduction in later mortality.

Figure 3.13 shows the median age of death for males and females between 1930 and 1990. As shown in Figure 3.12, a large gain occurred between 1930 and 1950, followed by more gradual increases. The median age at death for females increased at a greater rate than males. In 1930, males and females were similar, but by 1990, there was a six-year difference in median age at death.

Figures 3.14 and 3.15 show the remaining life expectancy at selected ages between 1930 and 1990 for males and females respectively. The actual years used for these Figures are averages of three years, centred around the census years. The top line, at birth, is similar to the life expectancy shown in Figure 3.13. The other lines represent the expected years of life remaining for an individual at different ages in the different years. For example, the median number of years of life remaining for a twenty-five-year-old male in 1930 to 1932 is forty-five, and in 1990 to 1992 is fifty-one. Therefore, a hypothetical twenty-five-year-old male in 1930 to 1932 could expect to live until seventy (twenty-five + forty-five), while a hypothetical twenty-five-year-old male in 1990 to 1992 could expect to live to seventy-six (twenty-five + fifty-one).

Figures 3.14 and 3.15 demonstrate that the gain in life expectancy over time has been primarily because of reduced mortality in the younger age groups. Though relatively fewer people reached eighty, in 1930, both males and females could expect six more years of life, while in 1990, a similar-aged male could expect seven more years and a female ten more years of life.

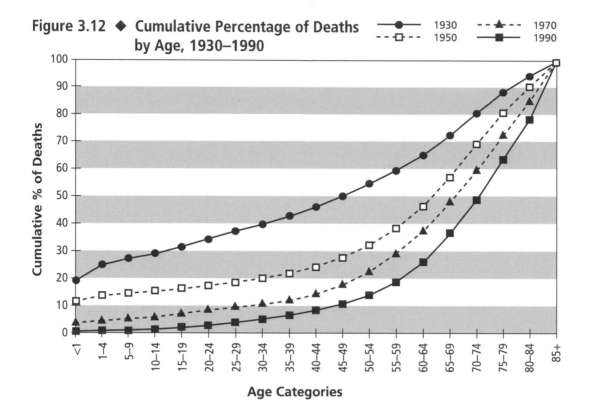

Figure 3.12 ◆ Cumulative Percentage of Deaths by Age, 1930–1990

Legend: ● 1930 ▲ 1970 □ 1950 ■ 1990

Y-axis: Cumulative % of Deaths

X-axis (Age Categories): <1, 1–4, 5–9, 10–14, 15–19, 20–24, 25–29, 30–34, 35–39, 40–44, 45–49, 50–54, 55–59, 60–64, 65–69, 70–74, 75–79, 80–84, 85+

Age Categories

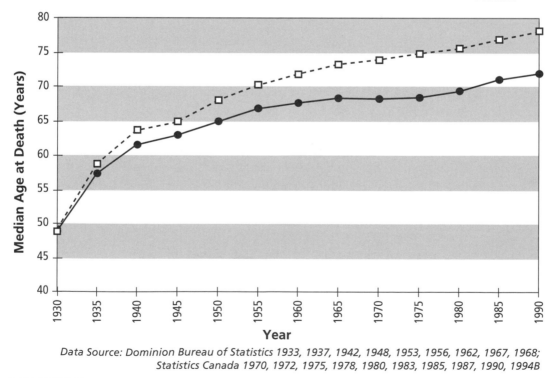

Figure 3.13 ◆ Median Age at Death, 1930–1990

Legend: ● Males □ Females

Y-axis: Median Age at Death (Years)

X-axis (Year): 1930, 1935, 1940, 1945, 1950, 1955, 1960, 1965, 1970, 1975, 1980, 1985, 1990

Year

Data Source: Dominion Bureau of Statistics 1933, 1937, 1942, 1948, 1953, 1956, 1962, 1967, 1968; Statistics Canada 1970, 1972, 1975, 1978, 1980, 1983, 1985, 1987, 1990, 1994B

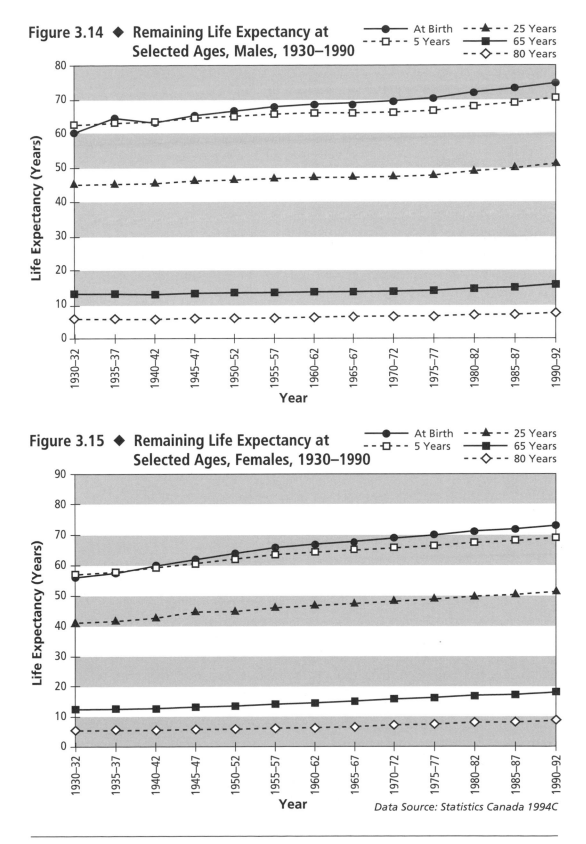

Figure 3.14 ◆ **Remaining Life Expectancy at Selected Ages, Males, 1930–1990**

Legend: ●—At Birth ▲--25 Years □--5 Years ■—65 Years ◇--80 Years

Figure 3.15 ◆ **Remaining Life Expectancy at Selected Ages, Females, 1930–1990**

Legend: ●—At Birth ▲--25 Years □--5 Years ■—65 Years ◇--80 Years

Data Source: Statistics Canada 1994C

Method

In Figure 3.12, the percentage of deaths in each age category was calculated, starting with the first age category, for four different years (1930, 1950, 1970, 1990). In Figure 3.13, the median age at death for each fifth year between 1930 and 1990 was taken from the references listed at the bottom of the Figure.

In Figures 3.14 and 3.15, the life expectancy at five different ages (at birth, five years, twenty-five years, sixty-five years, eighty years) for each fifth year between 1930 and 1992 was taken from Statistics Canada 1994C. The life expectancies were calculated using three years of information, centred around census years (1931, 1936, 1941, etc.).

Uncertainty

The annual mortality publications list the number of deaths where the age was unknown. The number of unknown ages used in this book ranged from eighty-five in 1930 to three in 1994. Similar to the total number of deaths and the sex of those who died, the age at death is an accurate statistic, with an uncertainty only slightly greater than the total number of deaths. Over the entire number of reported deaths, uncertainty about the age at death is likely less than 0.1%.

Evidence on Marital Status

The marital status of the deceased is shown as single, married, widowed, or divorced. Associations between marital status and mortality occur, but the reasons are uncertain. Although measurement of marital status evidence is direct, reasons for the observed differences in mortality are indirect (see Marital Status Risk Factors, p. 148).

Figure 3.16 shows the death rate for different age groups by marital status for males in 1990. Figure 3.16 reveals that the death rate for all three categories of marital status increases with age, as highlighted in Evidence on Age (p. 44). Married males had a consistently lower death rate than single and widowed or divorced males. For the first three age categories, the death rates were approximately three times lower for married people. For those aged 65+, the difference was approximately two times lower. Because these age categories are fairly large and were not age-standardized, some of the apparent differences may be over- or underestimated. For example, the average married person who dies may be much younger than the average widowed or divorced person in the same age category. Differences in age within each age category may account for some of the apparent gap in death rates.

Figure 3.17 represents the death rate for different age groups by marital status for females in 1990. Figure 3.17 also shows that the death rate for all three categories of marital status increases with age. Similarly, to married males, married females have a consistently lower death rate than single or widowed or divorced females. For the first three age categories, the death rates were two to four times lower for married females, clearly an interesting observation.

Figure 3.16 ◆ Death Rate by Marital Status, Males, 1990

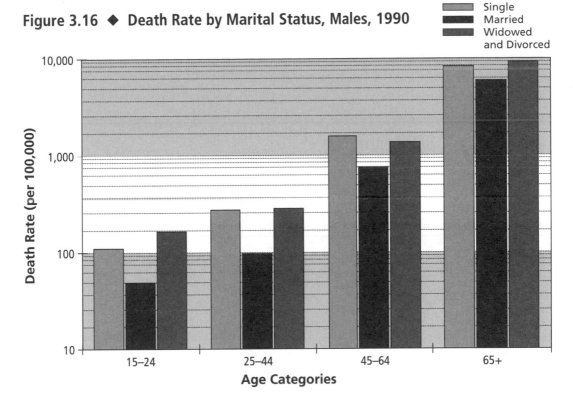

Figure 3.17 ◆ Death Rate by Marital Status, Females, 1990

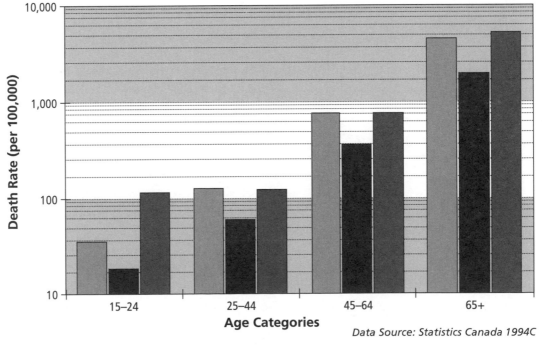

Data Source: Statistics Canada 1994C

Method

In Figures 3.16 and 3.17, the death rate by marital status for four age categories (different from any other categories in the book) was taken from Statistics Canada 1994C. The information was calculated by dividing the number of deaths by marital status for each age category by the total population in each age category. This process was done separately for males and females.

Uncertainty

There was no information included concerning the completeness of the marital status information. It is likely that incompleteness is a more important factor than errors in completing the form. However, with no additional information, it is assumed that the uncertainty is greater than in total registered deaths, sex, and age, but less, possibly by several times, than 1%.

Evidence on Usual Residence

The usual residence information includes province (or Territory), census division (or county), and locality (city, town, or village). Similarly to marital status, an association with geographical residence and mortality exists, but reasons for this are uncertain.

Place of residence is commonly used to compare mortality rates between provinces and Territories. On the death certificate, both the place of death and the usual residence are recorded (see Figure 3.1). Divisions can also be made by urban or rural residence, or for more detailed comparisons by counties. Often epidemiological studies will use place of residence and the cause of death to identify locations of disease clusters. More detailed studies then identify any possible associations with risk factors.

Figure 3.18 shows the total number of deaths by province for 1994. A significant proportion of all deaths takes place in Ontario and Quebec, with their large populations.

Figure 3.19 shows the age-standardized death rates by province for 1994. Figure 3.19 shows the large difference in death rates between males and females, which is not as apparent in Figure 3.18. Age-standardization emphasized that males die at a relatively younger age than females, even though the total number of deaths was only slightly greater. Age-standardized rates must be used when including the Territories because they have a significantly younger population than the provinces. Otherwise, comparisons would be meaningless. The crude death rates for the Territories are actually lower than those of the provinces.

Method

In Figure 3.18, the total number of deaths in each province was taken from Statistics Canada 1996B. In Figure 3.19, the information came from the same reference, which calculated the

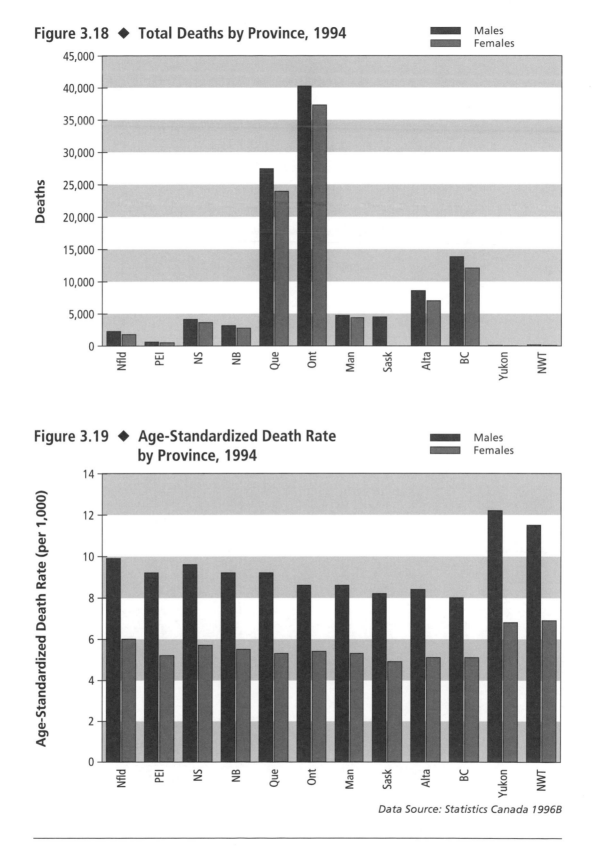

Figure 3.18 ◆ Total Deaths by Province, 1994

Males
Females

Figure 3.19 ◆ Age-Standardized Death Rate
by Province, 1994

Males
Females

Data Source: Statistics Canada 1996B

age-standardized rates using the equation from p. 34. Instead of using the age distribution for the entire country (like all other age-standardized calculations in this book), the age distribution for each province was used.

Uncertainty

No information was included about uncertainties in provincial mortality evidence. As each province collects information within its own boundaries before sending it to Ottawa for compilation, the provincial assignment should be accurate. The uncertainty is likely only slightly greater than that of total registered deaths or total deaths by age, or sex.

Uncertainty related to residential information would be significantly greater.

4 Cause of Death Evidence

Of all sections on the death certificate, the cause of death is the most useful for understanding health risk, but the most difficult to complete accurately. Unlike the other types of direct evidence provided by an informant (relative or acquaintance), the cause of death must be filled in by a medical practitioner or coroner. As it is so different from other types of direct evidence, Chapter 4 begins with the background behind the reported cause of death.

International Classification of Diseases (ICD)

History of the ICD

Classifying the cause of death has been a compromise for both medical and statistical reasons. Medically, the cause of death could be classified according to several factors, including biomedical cause (etiology), anatomical site, and circumstances of onset. Statistically, cause of death evidence can be used for several purposes, including vital statistics, hospitals records, and social and illness surveys.

Systematic classification of diseases, including the cause of death, began in the eighteenth century. Modern-day classification can be traced back to William Farr, who worked for the General Register Office of England and Wales starting in 1837. At the first International Statistical Congress in 1853, Farr and another person were asked to make a list that classified causes of death applicable to all countries. Farr's list, submitted at the next congress in 1855, was adopted in 1864 and underwent revisions over the next three decades. Farr's classification distinguished between particular diseases and those of a particular organ or anatomical site. Farr's 1855 classification was arranged into five groups: epidemic diseases, constitutional (general) diseases, local diseases arranged by anatomical site, developmental diseases and diseases directly resulting from violence. Although never universally accepted at that time, Farr's classification served as the basis for the modern International List of Causes of Death (Alderson 1988).

In 1891, the International Statistical Institute, successor to the International Statistical Congress, asked a committee chaired by Jacques Bertillion to prepare a classification of causes of death. At the meeting in 1893, Bertillion presented his report, which was based on the same principles as Farr.

In 1898, the American Public Health Association, which included participants from Canada, adopted the Bertillion Classification. The first International Conference for the review of the Bertillion Classification (or the International Classification of Causes of Death) took place in 1900, with delegates from twenty-six countries. In addition to this first review, it was proposed that the classification be reviewed every ten years. The second conference took place in 1909, the third in 1920, the fourth in 1929, and the fifth in 1938.

A major change took place in 1948 at the sixth conference, when the World Health Organization (WHO) took responsibility for organizing the classification scheme. Major changes at this conference included adopting a comprehensive list for mortality and morbidity and agreeing on rules for selecting the underlying cause of death. Subsequent conferences organized by the WHO took place in 1955 (seventh), 1965 (eighth), and 1975 (ninth) (WHO 1975).

Major changes are planned for the tenth revision, including using alphanumeric coding and having several health related classifications. For this reason, the usual ten-year revision cycle was increased to fourteen. However, further delays have occurred. The implementation date of the tenth code in Canada is anticipated for 1999.

The Underlying Cause of Death

The Medical Certificate of Death is Section 21 of the death certificate (see Figure 3.1). This section is divided into two parts:

- Part I is for the sequence of events leading to the death, proceeding backwards from the immediate cause;

- Part II is for other significant contributions to death.

For some causes of death only Part I needs to be filled in, for others all parts must be filled in. The last cause listed in Part I is termed the underlying cause of death (UCD). This term was established at the sixth conference on the ICD. For our purposes, the UCD is the most important cause as this is what is used in the published statistics. The underlying cause of death is defined as:

(a) the disease or injury which initiated the train of events leading directly to death, or

(b) the circumstances of the accident or violence which produced the fatal injury (WHO 1975, 763).

Table 4.1 shows three examples from a WHO booklet (1979) on filling out the Medical Certificate of Death. These examples show the difficulty and potential confusion involved in identifying the UCD.

One potential development is the use of multiple cause coding for the cause of death. Instead of recording only the UCD, all the causes may be recorded in the database (they are always

Table 4.1 ◆ Identifying the Underlying Cause of Death

Example 1	
	A man of forty-seven without a previous history of coronary disease suffered a myocardial infarction and died twenty-four hours later.
I	(a) Myocardial infarction
	In this case, the UCD is myocardial infarction, which is also the immediate cause of death.

Example 2	
	A woman of fifty-nine died of asphyxia following inhalation of vomitus some hours after suffering a cerebellar haemorrhage. Three years previously she had been diagnosed with adrenal adenoma with aldosteronism, which manifested itself as hypertension. Congestive heart failure was also present.
I	(a) Asphyxia by vomitus (b) Cerebellar haemorrhage (c) Hypertension (d) Aldosteronism (e) Adrenal adenoma
II	Congestive heart failure
	In this case, extra lines were needed and the UCD is a benign neoplasm of the adrenal gland.

Example 3	
	A man of forty-nine died of a fracture of the vault of the skull shortly after the car he was driving collided with a heavy truck on a narrow road.
I	(a) Fracture of vault of skull (b) Collision between car he was driving and heavy truck on road
	In this case the UCD is the collision between the deceased person's motor vehicle and another motor vehicle.

Adapted from WHO 1979

Table 4.2 ◆ Major Categories and Shortened Names of Causes of Death

No.	Code	Family Names	Shortened Names
I	001–139	Infectious and Parasitic Diseases	Infectious Diseases
II	140–239	Neoplasms	Cancer
III	240–279	Endocrine, Nutritional, and Metabolic Diseases and Immunity Disorders	Endocrine and Others
IV	280–289	Diseases of Blood and Blood-Forming Organs	Blood Diseases
V	290–319	Mental Disorders	Mental Disorders
VI	320–389	Diseases of the Nervous System and Sense Organs	Nervous System Diseases
VII	390–459	Diseases of the Circulatory System	Cardiovascular Diseases
VIII	460–519	Diseases of the Respiratory System	Respiratory Diseases
IX	520–579	Diseases of the Digestive System	Digestive Diseases
X	580–629	Diseases of the Genito-Urinary System	Genito-Urinary Diseases
XI	630–676	Complications of Pregnancy, Childbirth, and the Puerperium	Pregnancy-Related
XII	680–709	Diseases of the Skin and Subcutaneous Tissue	Skin Diseases
XIII	710–739	Diseases of the Musculo-Skeletal System and Connective Tissue	Musculo-Skeletal Diseases
XIV	740–759	Congenital Anomalies	Congenital Anomalies
XV	760–779	Certain Conditions originating in the Perinatal Period (excluding Stillbirths)	Perinatal Conditions
XVI	780–799	Symptoms, Signs, and Ill-Defined Conditions	Ill-Defined
E XVII	E800–E999	External Causes, Injury, and Poisoning	External Causes

Source: Statistics Canada 1996A

available on the original death certificates). This may provide useful additional information for subsequent studies. Some provinces have already begun to record multiple causes in their databases. Multiple cause coding is referred to by Alderson (1988) and Nam (1990).

Cause of Death Categories

Since the sixth revision of the ICD in 1948, the same seventeen categories (I–XVII) have been used as the first division of causes of death. Table 4.2 lists the seventeen major categories under both their full names and shortened names. The full name is used in the ICD and the summaries by Statistics Canada. The shortened names were selected for this book to simplify tables and discussion.

Each of the seventeen categories have been divided into subcategories (ranging from none to twenty-two). As an example, the first category, Infectious Diseases (ICD-9, 001–139), has sixteen subcategories (001–009, 010–018, 020–027 ... 137–139). Each three-digit number represents one cause of death. Sometimes an additional fourth digit, a decimal, is also added. There are spaces left intentionally in the numbering system, so that there are not 1,000 distinct three-digit codes (001–E999). These spaces allow new subcategories to be added, if needed, such as 042–044 (HIV Infection).

Canada is currently using the four-digit ICD code. In most cases, however, the fourth digit is not useful because it is not consistently recorded. There are usually a large number of "unspecified" fourth digits. Table 4.3 is an example of the different divisions within the ICD system. Table 4.3 starts with a four-digit code for a malignant neoplasm of the sigmoid colon (a specific section of the colon) and works backwards.

The ICD actually contains two levels of coding, both used by Statistics Canada in reporting mortality data. The first is the annual Causes of Death, which contains the detailed four-digit codes. This was our main source of information for 1994 mortality data. The second is a summary list of approximately 280 individual causes of death, with no extra levels of detail. This is published in an annual publication called Mortality—Summary List of Causes.

Table 4.3 ◆ Example of Four-Digit ICD-9 Coding

ICD-9 Code	Label
153.3	Sigmoid Colon
153	Malignant Neoplasm of the Colon
150–159	Malignant Neoplasm of the Digestive Organs and Peritoneum
140–239	Neoplasms
000–E999	All Causes of Death

Source: Statistics Canada 1996A

Detailed 1994 Evidence

Evidence from 1994 is presented in detail to provide an overview of mortality in Canada. By providing detailed evidence for only one year, the uncertainties of comparing years are not shown. The variability from year to year can be judged by the summary data for 1991–1994 provided in Appendix 3.

1994 Causes of Death

As mentioned, there are seventeen major categories in the ninth revision of the ICD. The mortality evidence for 1994 is shown in Table 4.4. There is a large difference, ranging from fourteen to 78,573, in the total number of deaths in the different major categories. Two categories, cardiovascular disease and cancer, accounted for two-thirds of all deaths in 1994.

Five of the seventeen categories are dealt with in more detail in the section Major Causes of Death (p. 67). In addition to extra information for 1994, trend information (1930–1990) is included in that section for these five categories. Appendix 1 also summarizes the 1994 causes of death in detail. Subcategories for all seventeen major categories are included. In addition some three-digit codes (and a few four-digit codes) were added because these additional entries were useful in some cases where the categories were very broad or were "other" categories.

1994 Causes of Death by Age

Unfortunately, many popular summaries of information relating to causes of death do not include information on age because of the increased detail needed. Where one number summarizes all ages, ten or more numbers are often required to include age categories. This book includes divisions by age wherever possible.

Appendix 2 contains the leading causes of death by age and sex categories for 1994. Appendix 2 separates the information for males and females into twenty age categories and lists the five leading causes of death.

Figures 4.1 and 4.2 show the cause of death by age for males and females in 1994. Eight of the seventeen major categories from the ICD code were selected to minimize the "other" category (the remaining nine major categories). The total number of people dying in each category varies tremendously, with most deaths occurring in the last three age categories (see Figure 3.7). Figures 4.1 and 4.2 highlight the importance of age when discussing mortality. External causes (fatal injuries) are the leading cause of death for males between one and forty-four, and between one and thirty-four for females. However, external causes are only ranked fourth in the total number of annual deaths.

Table 4.4 ◆ Mortality by Major Category, 1994

No.	Shortened Name	Males	Females	Both	% Total
I	Infectious Diseases	2,300	897	3,197	1.5
II	Cancer	31,496	26,815	58,311	28.2
III	Endocrine and Others	3,194	3,416	6,610	3.2
IV	Blood Diseases	336	377	713	0.3
V	Mental Disorders	1,963	2,710	4,673	2.3
VI	Nervous System Diseases	2,643	3,331	5,974	2.9
VII	Cardiovascular Diseases	39,885	38,688	78,573	37.9
VIII	Respiratory Diseases	10,087	8,255	18,342	8.9
IX	Digestive Diseases	3,912	3,767	7,679	3.7
X	Genito-Urinary Diseases	1,670	1,691	3,361	1.6
XI	Pregnancy Related	–	14	14	<0.1
XII	Skin Diseases	76	112	188	0.1
XIII	Musculo-Skeletal Diseases	259	664	923	0.4
XIV	Congenital Anomalies	630	527	1,157	0.6
XV	Perinatal Conditions	572	487	1,059	0.5
XVI	Ill-Defined	1,673	1,434	3,107	1.5
E XVII	External Causes	9,046	4,150	13,196	6.4
Total		**109,742**	**97,335**	**207,077**	**100.0**

Source: Statistics Canada 1996A

Figure 4.1 ◆ Cause of Death by Age, Males, 1994

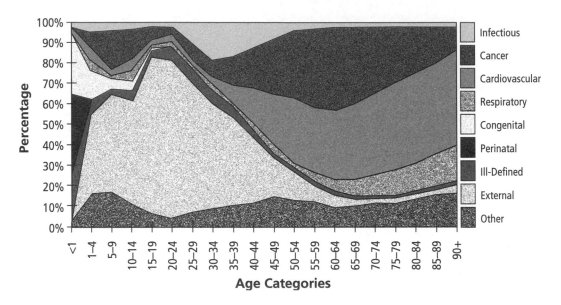

Figure 4.2 ◆ Cause of Death by Age, Females, 1994

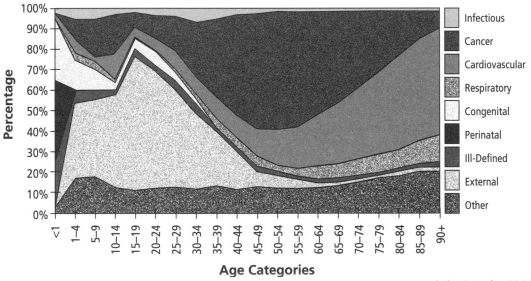

Data Source: Statistics Canada 1996A

Major Causes of Death

Five of the seventeen major categories have been selected for a more detailed discussion. Currently, four of the five are leading causes of death, the fifth, infectious disease, was a leading cause of death earlier in the century.

Evidence for All Major Causes of Death

Figures 4.3 and 4.4 show the major causes of death for males and females in 1994. These simple Figures highlight the importance of cardiovascular disease and cancer in total annual mortality for both males and females. Males have a significantly higher percentage of deaths from both external causes and infectious diseases compared with females.

Trend Evidence

Tracking and comparing mortality between years, especially many years, is difficult, but provides insight into changes in mortality. We know from life expectancy and age-standardized death rates that people are living longer. But how is increased life expectancy related to cause of death?

Figures 4.5 and 4.6 show age-standardized death rates for the major causes of death for males and females between 1930 and 1990. Changes in the significance of the major causes of death for sixty years are shown. These comparisons provide a useful summary of the trends in mortality over this period. For males, cardiovascular disease rose steadily until 1950 and remained level until approximately 1965, when a steady decrease began. For females, cardiovascular disease also rose steadily until 1950, but then soon started to decrease. Cancer mortality has gradually increased in males since 1930, but has remained constant in females. Infectious diseases dropped significantly for both males and females. Respiratory disease remained relatively constant, as did external causes, until a slight decrease started around 1980 for both sexes.

The large drop in the "other" category until approximately 1960 is partially linked to decreases in infant mortality. The unexpected jump in the "other" category in 1950 is puzzling. A consistent increase in all causes of death included in the "other" category in 1950 was followed by a huge drop five years later. This increase does not appear due to a change in classification since none of the five major causes of death mirror the jump.

The next five sections focus on each of the five major causes of death: infectious diseases, cancer, cardiovascular diseases, respiratory diseases, and external causes. Each section has two subsections, one showing 1994 evidence and the other trend evidence from 1930 to 1990.

Figure 4.3 ◆ Major Causes of Death, Males, 1994

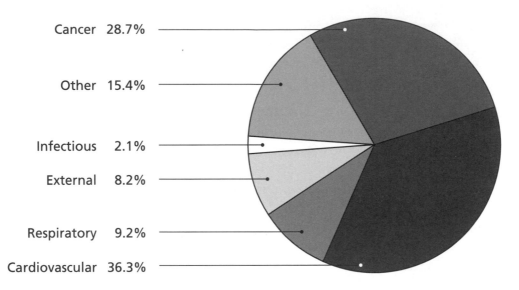

Cancer   28.7%

Other   15.4%

Infectious   2.1%

External   8.2%

Respiratory   9.2%

Cardiovascular   36.3%

Figure 4.4 ◆ Major Causes of Death, Females, 1994

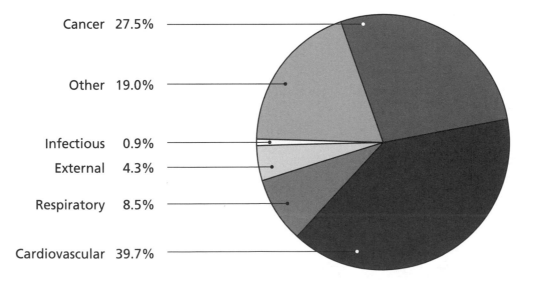

Cancer   27.5%

Other   19.0%

Infectious   0.9%

External   4.3%

Respiratory   8.5%

Cardiovascular   39.7%

Data Source: Statistics Canada, 1996A

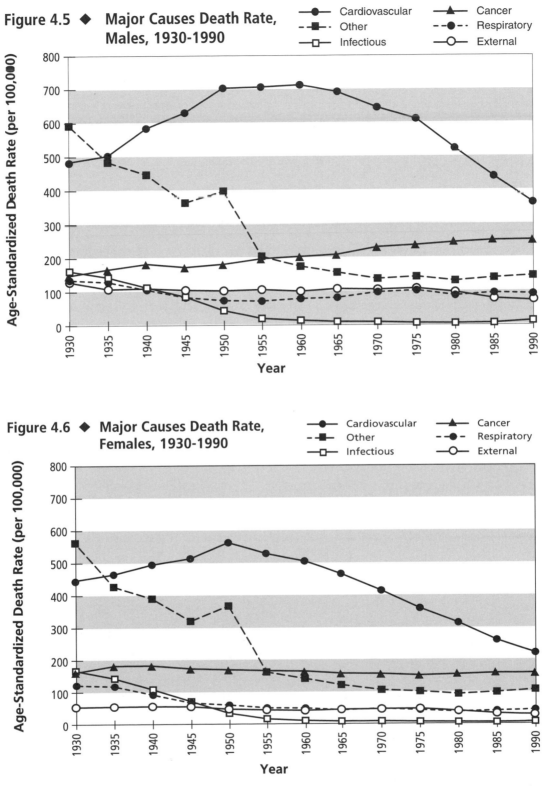

Figure 4.5 ◆ Major Causes Death Rate, Males, 1930-1990

Legend: Cardiovascular, Cancer, Other, Respiratory, Infectious, External

Figure 4.6 ◆ Major Causes Death Rate, Females, 1930-1990

Legend: Cardiovascular, Cancer, Other, Respiratory, Infectious, External

Data Source: Dominion Bureau of Statistics 1933, 1937, 1942, 1948, 1953, 1956, 1962, 1967, 1968; Statistics Canada 1970, 1972, 1975, 1978, 1980, 1983, 1985, 1987, 1990, 1994B

Method for Trend Evidence

This subsection will review how changes in the classification system made preparing Figures for trend evidence difficult. Table 4.5 summarizes how the classification system has changed between 1930 and 1990, including when provinces and Territories were included in the totals.

Canada has been using the ICD for causes of death since 1921, when it was based on the ICD-3 (Taylor 1992). However, the first mention of the ICD in the published reports used in this book was in 1945, when the ICD-5 was being used. Wilkins (1989) provided a useful table summarizing the changes in the classification system in Canada.

Alderson (1988) reviewed the major changes for the third to ninth ICD revisions. The only major change that affected this book related to cerebrovascular disease (stroke). Cerebrovascular disease was in the "Diseases of the Nervous System" major category until the ICD-8 in 1970, when it was moved into "circulatory diseases" (Cardiovascular Diseases). The cardiovascular disease category showed fewer deaths between 1930 and 1965. This difference was significant as cerebrovascular diseases accounted for more than one-quarter of deaths when added to the cardiovascular disease category. Therefore, cerebrovascular diseases were moved from the nervous system category to the cardiovascular disease category for 1930 to 1965.

A less significant difficulty occurred in 1930, when cancer was part of the major category "General Diseases Not Included in Class I." Cancer was list no. 43–49, which did not include "benign tumours and tumours not listed as malignant," list no. 50, and list no. 65, "leukaemia, lymphadenoma." These extra 560 deaths represented 6% of the reported 9,273 cancer deaths. This was a relatively small number and the extra deaths were not included under cancer. For 1935, 1940, and 1945, "leukaemia and aleukaemia" were not included with cancer. The total number of deaths for each year from this cause was 362, 484, and 415, respectively, approximately 3% of all cancer deaths each year. These extra deaths were also not included under cancer.

Table 4.5 ◆ Changes to the Classification System, 1930–1990

Year	ICD No.	No. Families	Comments
1930	3	XV	Newfoundland not included. Yukon and NWT in appendix. Neoplasms not its own family.
1935	4	XVIII	Newfoundland not included. Yukon and NWT in appendix.
1940	4	XVIII	Newfoundland not included. Yukon and NWT in appendix.
1945	5	XVIII	Newfoundland not included. Yukon and NWT in appendix.
1950	5	XVII	Yukon and NWT in appendix.
1955	6	XVII	Yukon and NWT in appendix.
1960	7	XVII	
1965	7	XVII	
1970	8	XVII	Cerebrovascular disease moved from nervous system to circulatory system.
1975	8	XVII	
1981	9	XVII	
1985	9	XVII	
1990	9	XVII	

Source: Dominion Bureau of Statistics 1933, 1937, 1942, 1953, 1956, 1962, 1967;
Statistics Canada 1972, 1978, 1983, 1987, 1994B

Note on Figures

For each 1994 subsection, four standard Figures have been prepared:

1. Death by Age, Males, 1994;

2. Death Rate by Age, Males, 1994;

3. Death by Age, Females, 1994;

4. Death Rate by Age, Females, 1994.

For each trend subsection, two standard Figures have been prepared:

1. Death Rate, 1930–1990;

2. Death Rate by Age, Both, 1930–1990.

The first and second Figures are meant to be used together. The first Figure shows the total number of deaths in 1994 for males from the three or four leading causes of death from within each of the five major causes of death. This evidence is shown for twenty age categories. The second Figure shows the death rate, which uses the evidence from the first Figure divided by the population in each age category. The three or four leading causes of death for each major cause of death were selected from the numbers in Appendix 1. The three-digit ICD-9 for each of the three or four leading causes of death is provided, so that it can be located in Appendix 1. The first Figure, showing the total number of deaths, is an arithmetic scale and has its vertical scale set by the data (varying from 80 to 3,000). The second Figure, showing the death rate, is a logarithmic scale and has its vertical scale fixed (from 0.1 to 100,000). The first and second Figures complement each other. The first Figure is easier to read because of its arithmetic scale, but there is a large difference in the population in each age category. The second Figure, though harder to interpret, more clearly displays differences in mortality between age categories.

The third and fourth Figures are similar to the first and second except that they are for females. The three or four leading causes of death are the same for both males and females, except for cancer, where a leading cause of cancer death for males, prostate cancer, is replaced with breast cancer for females.

For trends, the first and second Figures are not meant to be paired like the 1994 Figures. The first Figure simply combines Figures 4.5 and 4.6 (Major Causes Death Rate, Males and Females) into one Figure for a specific cause of death. This age-standardized death rate shows the change in the death rate over time and the difference between sexes.

The second Figure takes four years at twenty-years intervals (1930, 1950, 1970, and 1990) and compares the death rate by age. Age-standardization is not required because the age categories are used. The first and second Figures highlight the ages with the most significant changes in the death rate. Both sexes are combined because on a log scale the differences between the sexes are hard to distinguish. The first Figure shows the overall difference in the death rate between sexes.

Infectious Disease

In 1994, infectious disease was the cause of death for 2.1% of males and 0.9% of females. Although infectious diseases are currently no longer a leading annual cause of death, they were earlier in the century. The two infectious diseases of current concern in Canada are AIDS (HIV infection) and tuberculosis (on the rise). However, the Centers for Disease Control (CDC) have identified several emerging infectious disease threats in the US (CDC 1994):

- E. coli O157:H7 disease,

- cryptosporidiosis,

- coccidioidomycosis,

- multidrug-resistant pneumococcal disease,

- vancomycin-resistant enterococcal infections,

- influenza A/Beijing/32/92,

- hantavirus infections.

Another example of an infectious disease outbreak in Canada was meningococcal disease that killed several adolescents and young adults in 1991 and 1992 (Shah 1994).

1994 Evidence

The three sub-categories of infectious disease considered in more detail are:

- tuberculosis (ICD-9: 010–018, 137),

- septicaemia (ICD-9: 038),

- HIV infection (ICD-9: 042–044).

Figures 4.7 and 4.8 show the number of infectious disease deaths by age and the infectious disease death rate by age for males in 1994. Although tuberculosis kills a relatively small number of people annually, it is still a priority from a public health perspective. HIV infection has made a significant impact on male mortality. Considering that death can occur many years after the initial HIV infection, the youth of those dying stresses the impact of HIV infection on the young. HIV infection in males is the only cause of death of those summarized in this book where the death rate decreases with increasing age.

Figures 4.9 and 4.10 show the number of infectious disease deaths by age and the infectious disease death rate by age for females in 1994. When comparing the male infectious disease deaths by age (Figure 4.7) and the female infectious disease deaths by age (Figure 4.9), note that the numbers of deaths on the vertical axes are different. Unlike males, HIV infection has had only a small impact on female mortality to date. The death rates by age for septicaemia and tuberculosis are similar for males and females.

Trend Evidence

Figure 4.11 shows the infectious disease death rate for males and females between 1930 and 1990. An enormous decline in infectious disease deaths, which started before 1930, continued until approximately 1955, followed by a more gradual decline. The increase between 1985 and 1990 in males is due to HIV infection. After 1940, females had a lower mortality rate from infectious disease than males.

Figure 4.12 shows the infectious disease death rate by age for males and females combined between 1930 and 1990. Significant drops in the infectious disease death rate have occurred in most age categories. For example in the <1 age category, steady declines took place. The death rate per 100,000 fell from approximately 1,000 to five deaths between 1930 and 1990. The increase in the death rate between 1970 and 1990 between the ages of twenty to forty-nine is because of HIV infection.

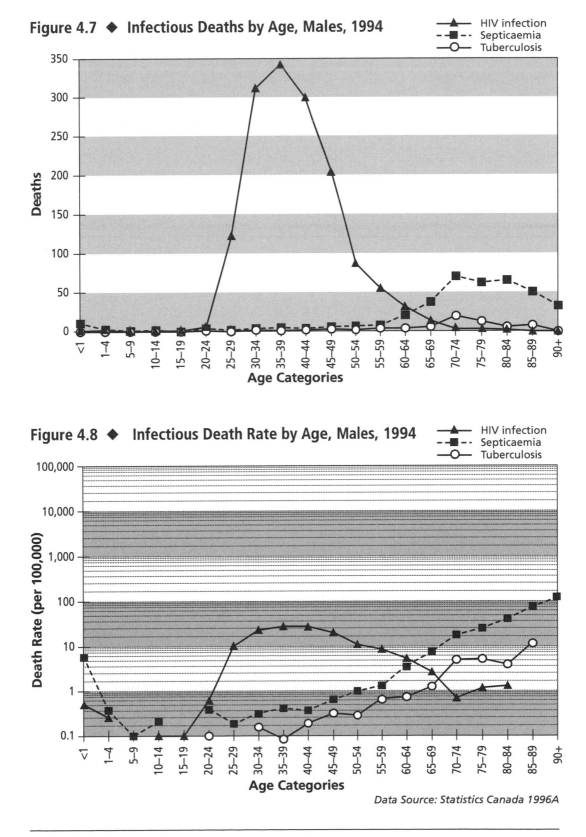

Figure 4.7 ◆ **Infectious Deaths by Age, Males, 1994**

HIV infection
Septicaemia
Tuberculosis

Deaths

Age Categories

Figure 4.8 ◆ **Infectious Death Rate by Age, Males, 1994**

HIV infection
Septicaemia
Tuberculosis

Death Rate (per 100,000)

Age Categories

Data Source: Statistics Canada 1996A

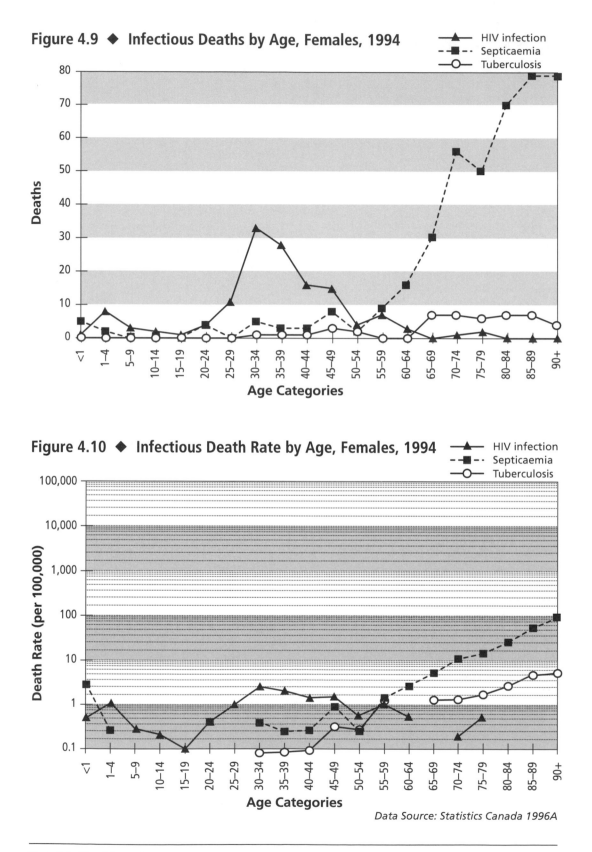

Figure 4.9 ◆ **Infectious Deaths by Age, Females, 1994**

Legend:
- HIV infection
- Septicaemia
- Tuberculosis

Y-axis: Deaths
X-axis: Age Categories (<1, 1–4, 5–9, 10–14, 15–19, 20–24, 25–29, 30–34, 35–39, 40–44, 45–49, 50–54, 55–59, 60–64, 65–69, 70–74, 75–79, 80–84, 85–89, 90+)

Figure 4.10 ◆ **Infectious Death Rate by Age, Females, 1994**

Legend:
- HIV infection
- Septicaemia
- Tuberculosis

Y-axis: Death Rate (per 100,000)
X-axis: Age Categories (<1, 1–4, 5–9, 10–14, 15–19, 20–24, 25–29, 30–34, 35–39, 40–44, 45–49, 50–54, 55–59, 60–64, 65–69, 70–74, 75–79, 80–84, 85–89, 90+)

Data Source: Statistics Canada 1996A

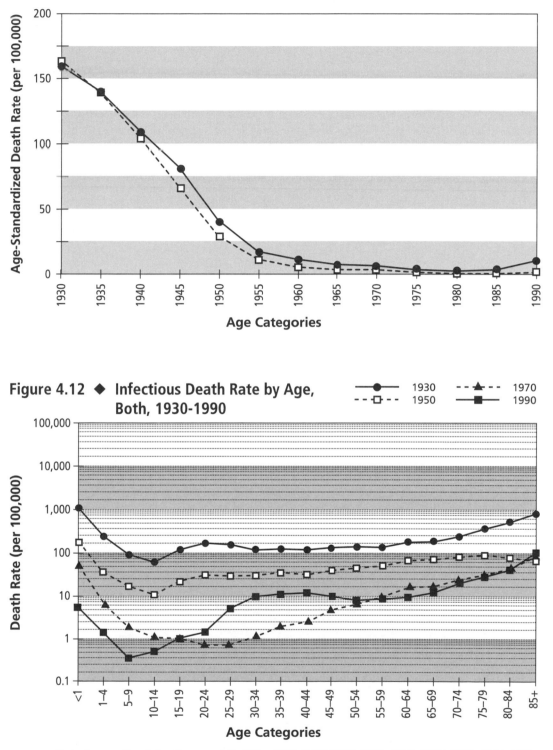

Figure 4.11 ◆ Infectious Death Rate, 1930–1990

Legend: Male (●), Female (□)

Figure 4.12 ◆ Infectious Death Rate by Age, Both, 1930-1990

Legend: 1930 (●), 1950 (□), 1970 (▲), 1990 (■)

Data Source: Dominion Bureau of Statistics 1933, 1937, 1942, 1948, 1953, 1956, 1962, 1967, 1968; Statistics Canada 1970, 1972, 1975, 1978, 1980, 1983, 1985, 1987, 1990, 1994B

Cancer

Cancer is a general term for neoplasms, which are abnormal tissue that grows by cellular proliferation more rapidly than normal and which continues to grow after its initial stimuli cease (Stedman's Medical Dictionary 1995). In 1994, cancer was the cause of death for 28.7% of males and 27.5% of females.

There are over 100 different types of cancer, which often have significantly different properties. One important measure for individual types of cancer is the relative survival rate. This rate can be determined by measuring the percentage of people surviving five years after diagnosis, or more indirectly by comparing the number of deaths with new cases in a year. The higher the ratio of deaths to new cases, the lower the relative survival. Some ratios for individual types of cancer include (National Cancer Institute of Canada 1996):

- pancreas, 1.02;

- lung, 0.85;

- stomach, 0.67;

- female breast, 0.28;

- prostate, 0.23;

- testis, 0.03.

As cancer incidence is so significant in relation to individual types of cancer, incidence data have been included in the Trend Evidence section. An extensive breakdown of cancer is beyond the scope of this book, but the annual publication Canadian Cancer Statistics (National Cancer Institute of Canada 1997) details the various types of cancer by site and also includes a section on childhood cancer.

1994 Evidence

The five subcategories of cancer considered in more detail are:

- colon (ICD-9: 153);

- pancreas (ICD-9: 157);

- lung (ICD-9: 162, includes trachea and bronchus);

- prostate (ICD-9: 185, males only);

- breast (ICD-9: 174, females only).

Figures 4.13 and 4.14 show the number of cancer deaths by age and the cancer death rate by age for males in 1994. Lung cancer is the most significant cancer in terms of total deaths and the age at which deaths start occurring. Prostate cancer, the second leading cause of cancer deaths in males, generally appears approximately fifteen years later than lung cancer. Virtually no cancer deaths occur in the young from these particular cancers; other types are more prevalent (e.g., leukaemia, brain, and spinal cancers).

Figures 4.15 and 4.16 show the number of cancer deaths by age and the cancer death rate by age for females in 1994. When you compare the male cancer deaths by age (Figure 4.13) and the female cancer deaths by age (Figure 4.15), you will see that the numbers of deaths on the vertical axes are different. Lung cancer for females, which surpassed breast cancer in annual deaths in 1991, has a nearly identical age distribution compared with males, but the numbers are approximately half. Breast cancer mortality in females occurs earlier in life than other types of cancer.

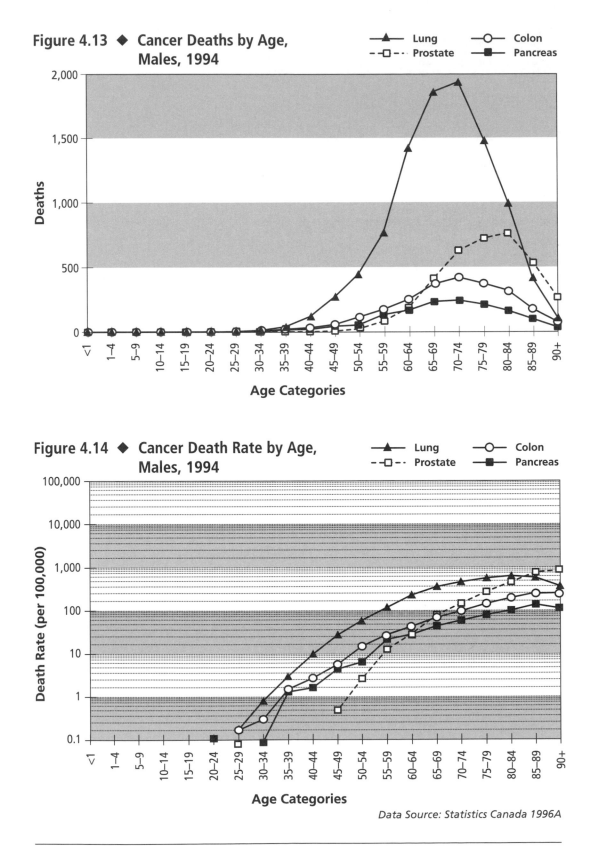

Figure 4.13 ◆ Cancer Deaths by Age, Males, 1994

Lung — Colon — Prostate — Pancreas

Deaths

Age Categories

Figure 4.14 ◆ Cancer Death Rate by Age, Males, 1994

Lung — Colon — Prostate — Pancreas

Death Rate (per 100,000)

Age Categories

Data Source: Statistics Canada 1996A

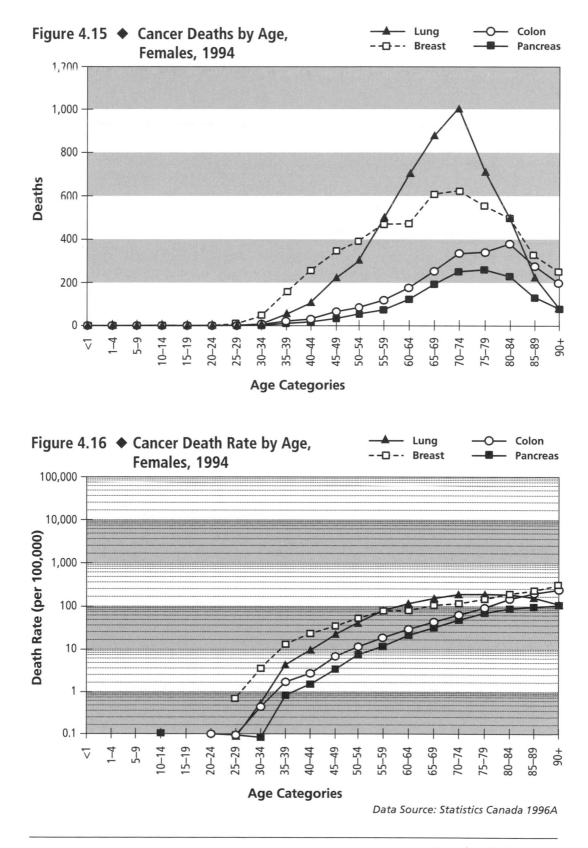

Figure 4.15 ◆ Cancer Deaths by Age, Females, 1994

Lung
Breast
Colon
Pancreas

Figure 4.16 ◆ Cancer Death Rate by Age, Females, 1994

Lung
Breast
Colon
Pancreas

Data Source: Statistics Canada 1996A

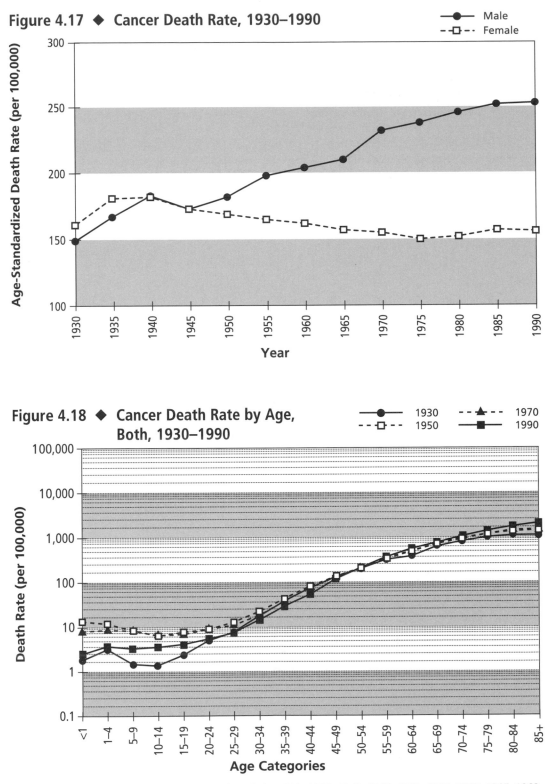

Figure 4.17 ◆ **Cancer Death Rate, 1930–1990**

Male
Female

Figure 4.18 ◆ **Cancer Death Rate by Age, Both, 1930–1990**

1930   1970
1950   1990

Data Source: Dominion Bureau of Statistics 1933, 1937, 1942, 1948, 1953, 1956, 1962, 1967, 1968; Statistics Canada 1970, 1972, 1975, 1978, 1980, 1983, 1985, 1987, 1990, 1994B

Trend Evidence

For this section, Figures for cancer incidence are also included.

Figure 4.17 shows the cancer death rate for males and females between 1930 and 1990. For males, the cancer death rate steadily increased until 1980, and has more gradually increased since 1980. The increase can be largely attributed to increases in lung cancer (National Cancer Institute 1997). For females, the cancer death rate has remained relatively constant.

Figure 4.18 shows the cancer death rate by age for males and females combined between 1930 and 1990. The apparently lower cancer rates in the young in 1930 are probably due to misclassification in diagnosis and the coding practices at the time. The lower rates in 1990, however, likely reflect decreases in mortality.

Figures 4.19 and 4.20 show the cancer incidence and mortality rates for males between 1969 and 1997. The incidence rates reveal the large differences in the ratio of deaths to new cases, which was discussed at the beginning of this section on cancer. Although prostate cancer is currently the most common form of cancer in males (Figure 4.19), lung cancer remains the leading cause of death from cancer (Figure 4.20). Some of the risk factors associated with specific types of cancer are discussed in Part Two, Indirect Evidence and Inference.

Figures 4.21 and 4.22 show the cancer incidence and mortality rates for females between 1969 and 1997. As with males, the incidence rates highlight the large differences in the ratio of deaths to new cases, which was discussed at the beginning of this section. Breast cancer is the most common form of cancer in females. One of the most alarming trends in females is the significant increase in the incidence of and mortality from lung cancer. Lung cancer recently passed breast cancer as the leading cancer cause of death in females. Some of the risk factors associated with specific types of cancer are discussed in Part Two, Indirect Evidence and Inference.

Figure 4.19 ◆ Age-Standardized Incidence Rates (ASIR) for Selected Cancer Sites, Males, Canada, 1969–1997

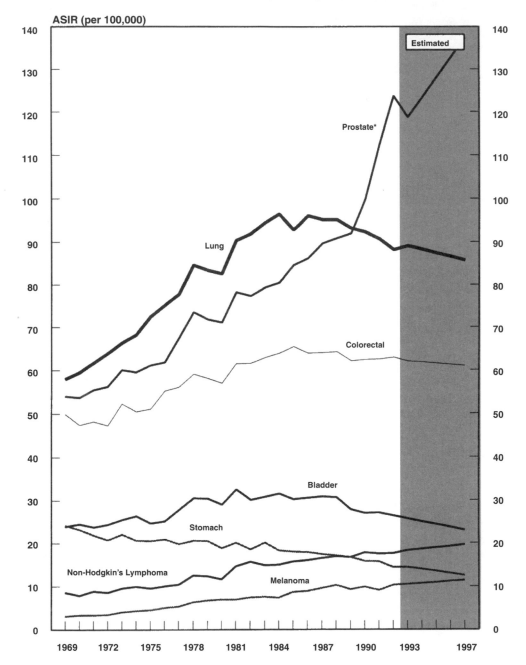

*Current rates for prostate cancer are possibly underestimated because they do not fully account for the impact of PSA testing in the 1990s.

Note: Rates are standardized to the age distribution of the 1991 Canadian population.

Source: Health Statistics Division, Statistics Canada.

Credit: *National Cancer Institute of Canada: **Canadian Cancer Statistics 1997** Toronto, Canada, 1997*

Figure 4.20 ◆ Age-Standardized Mortality Rates (ASMR) for Selected Cancer Sites, Males, Canada, 1969–1997

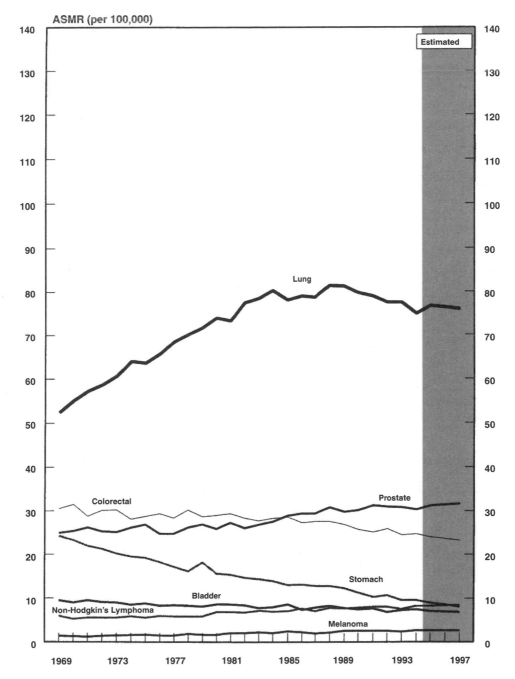

Note: Rates are standardized to the age distribution of the 1991 Canadian population.

Source: Health Statistics Division, Statistics Canada.

Credit: National Cancer Institute of Canada: **Canadian Cancer Statistics 1997** *Toronto, Canada, 1997*

Figure 4.21 ◆ Age-Standardized Incidence Rates (ASIR) for Selected Cancer Sites, Females, Canada, 1969–1997

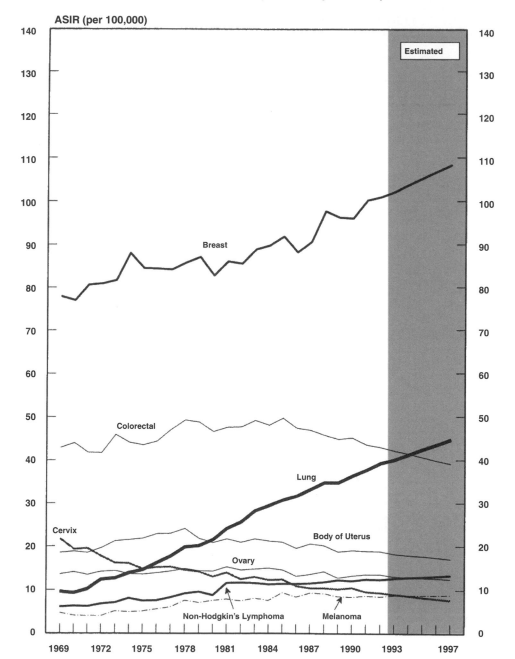

Note: Rates are standardized to the age distribution of the 1991 Canadian population.

Source: Health Statistics Division, Statistics Canada.

Credit: National Cancer Institute of Canada: **Canadian Cancer Statistics 1997** *Toronto, Canada, 1997*

Figure 4.22 ◆ Age-Standardized Mortality Rates (ASMR) for Selected Cancer Sites, Females, Canada, 1969–1997

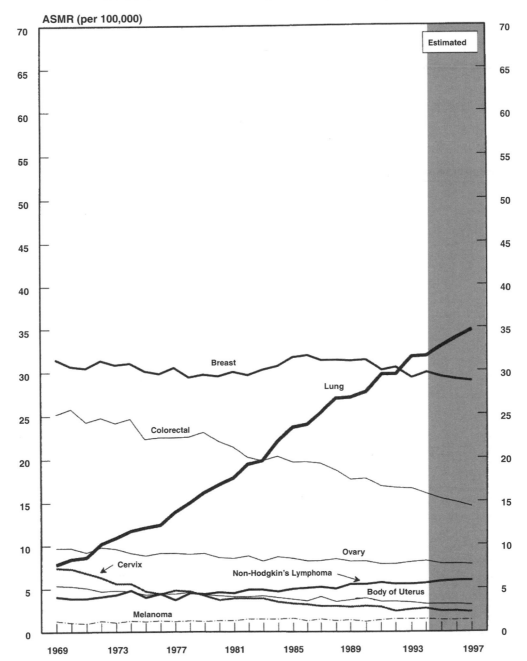

Note: Rates are standardized to the age distribution of the 1991 Canadian population.

Source: Health Statistics Division, Statistics Canada.

*Credit: National Cancer Institute of Canada: **Canadian Cancer Statistics 1997** Toronto, Canada, 1997*

Cardiovascular Disease

Cardiovascular disease includes heart disease and stroke (cerebrovascular disease). Cardiovascular disease is also known as circulatory disease. In 1994, cardiovascular disease was the cause of death for 36.3% of males and 39.7% of females. Most cardiovascular disease is a result of atherosclerosis, the build-up of lipid deposits in the arteries. Ischaemia refers to deficiencies in blood-flow due to constriction of blood vessels.

1994 Evidence

The four subcategories of cardiovascular disease considered in more detail are:

- AMI (ICD-9: 410, acute myocardial infarction—the medical term for a heart attack, which is ischaemia within the heart muscle);

- other IHD (ICD-9: 414, other forms of ischaemic heart disease);

- other heart (ICD-9: 420–429, other forms of heart disease);

- stroke (ICD-9: 430–438, cerebrovascular disease).

Figures 4.23 and 4.24 show the number of cardiovascular deaths by age and the cardiovascular death rate by age for males in 1994. Beginning around the age of forty, cardiovascular deaths increase significantly and exponentially with age. Deaths from heart attacks (acute myocardial infarctions) are the most significant because they are rapid and kill more people at earlier ages than other forms of heart disease. The sharp drop in the number of deaths for the last two age categories in Figure 4.23 occurs because the majority of males have already died.

Figures 4.25 and 4.26 show the number of cardiovascular deaths by age and the cardiovascular death rate by age for females in 1994. Overall, most deaths from cardiovascular disease in females occur approximately ten to twenty years later than in males.

Trend Evidence

Figure 4.27 shows the cardiovascular death rate for males and females between 1930 and 1990. Figure 4.27 shows the significant declines in mortality since 1965 in males and since 1955 in females. The gap in death rates from cardiovascular disease widened between sexes primarily between 1930 and 1965. Since 1975, the gap in death rates has been slowly closing.

Figure 4.28 shows the cardiovascular death rate by age for males and females combined between 1930 and 1990. Some significant declines in the death rate in children and young adults (ages five to twenty-four) have occurred. However, as relatively few people die from cardiovascular diseases at these young ages, the net reduction in mortality is small. A more significant reduction in mortality occurred in most other age categories between 1970 and 1990.

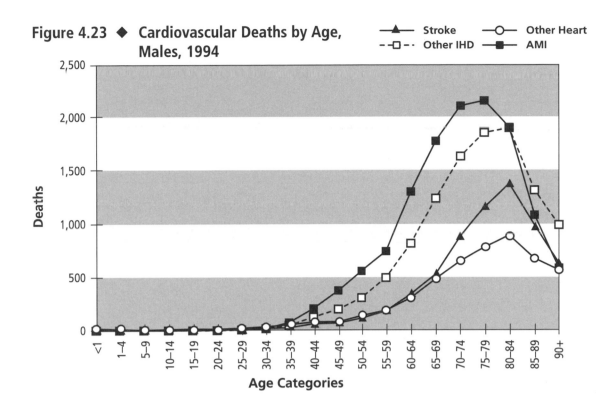

Figure 4.23 ◆ Cardiovascular Deaths by Age, Males, 1994

Legend: Stroke, Other Heart, Other IHD, AMI

Y-axis: Deaths
X-axis: Age Categories

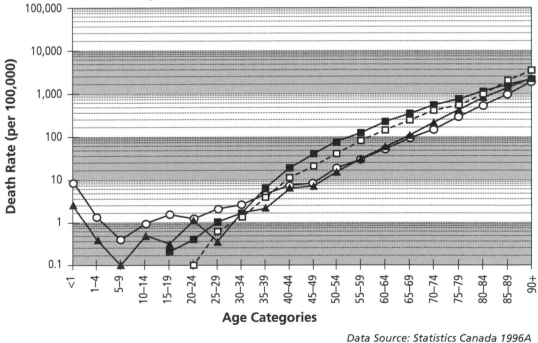

Figure 4.24 ◆ Cardiovascular Death Rate by Age, Males, 1994

Legend: Stroke, Other Heart, Other IHD, AMI

Y-axis: Death Rate (per 100,000)
X-axis: Age Categories

Data Source: Statistics Canada 1996A

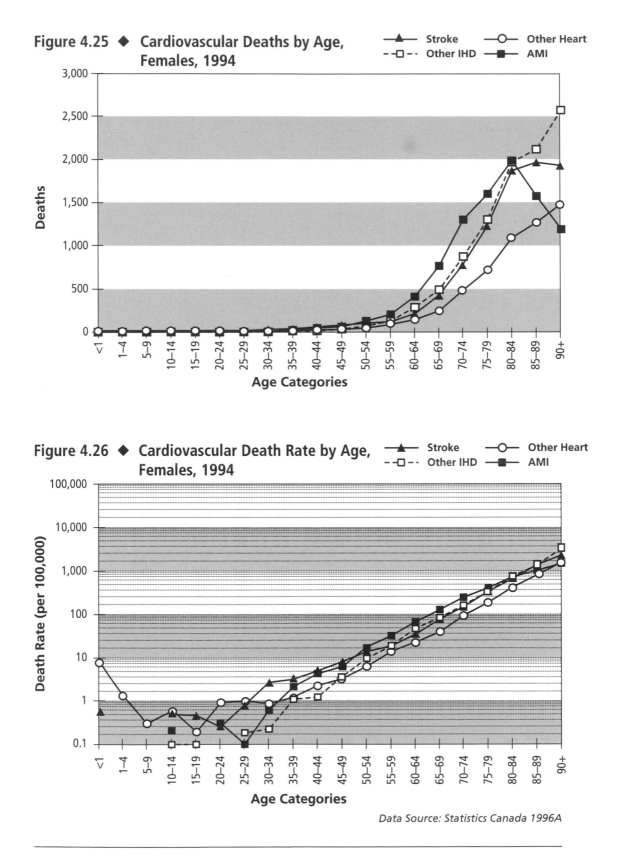

Figure 4.25 ◆ **Cardiovascular Deaths by Age, Females, 1994**

Legend: Stroke, Other IHD, Other Heart, AMI

Figure 4.26 ◆ **Cardiovascular Death Rate by Age, Females, 1994**

Legend: Stroke, Other IHD, Other Heart, AMI

Data Source: Statistics Canada 1996A

Figure 4.27 ◆ Cardiovascular Death Rate, 1930–1990

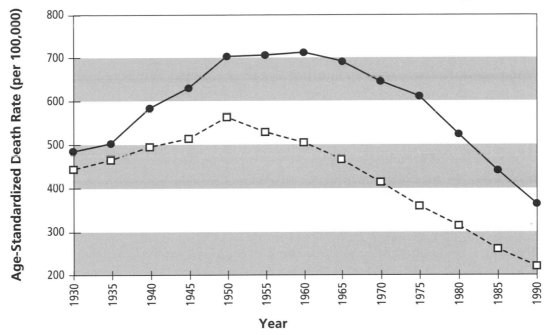

Figure 4.28 ◆ Cardiovascular Death Rate by Age, Both, 1930–1990

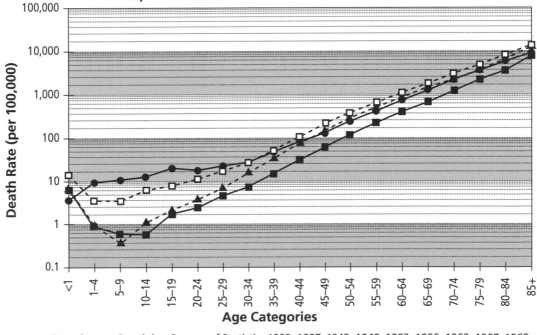

Data Source: Dominion Bureau of Statistics 1933, 1937, 1942, 1948, 1953, 1956, 1962, 1967, 1968; Statistics Canada 1970, 1972, 1975, 1978, 1980, 1983, 1985, 1987, 1990, 1994B

Respiratory Disease

Respiratory disease is associated with the lungs and airways. In this book (and in the ICD), respiratory disease does not include cancer. In 1994, respiratory disease was the cause of death for 9.2% of males and 8.5% of females.

1994 Evidence

The four subcategories of respiratory disease considered in more detail are:

- pneumonia (ICD-9: 480–486);

- emphysema (ICD-9: 492);

- asthma (ICD-9: 493);

- chronic obstruction (ICD-9: 496, chronic airways obstruction).

Figures 4.29 and 4.30 show respiratory deaths by age and the respiratory death rate by age for males in 1994. Unlike the other four major causes of death, respiratory deaths occur primarily in older age groups. Large numbers of deaths do not start occurring until the 60–64 age group.

Figures 4.31 and 4.32 show the number of respiratory deaths by age and the respiratory death rate by age for females in 1994. Female respiratory deaths also occur primarily in the older age groups. However, female deaths from chronic airway obstruction are not as significant as in males.

Trend Evidence

Figure 4.33 shows the respiratory death rate for males and females between 1930 and 1990. Respiratory deaths decreased sharply from 1930 to 1950. For males, respiratory deaths fluctuated, but, for females, these deaths continued to decrease. Changes in the classification system may have contributed to some of the fluctuations.

Figure 4.34 shows the respiratory death rate by age for males and females combined between 1930 and 1990. Most of the decrease in the death rates occurred for the younger age categories. For the <1 age category, there was an approximately 100-fold drop between 1930 and 1990.

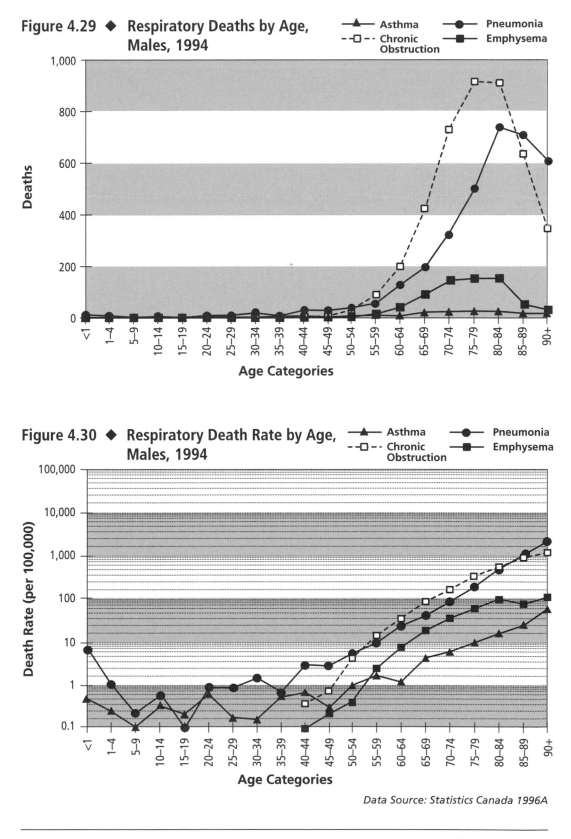

Figure 4.29 ◆ Respiratory Deaths by Age, Males, 1994

Asthma   Pneumonia   Chronic Obstruction   Emphysema

Figure 4.30 ◆ Respiratory Death Rate by Age, Males, 1994

Asthma   Pneumonia   Chronic Obstruction   Emphysema

Data Source: Statistics Canada 1996A

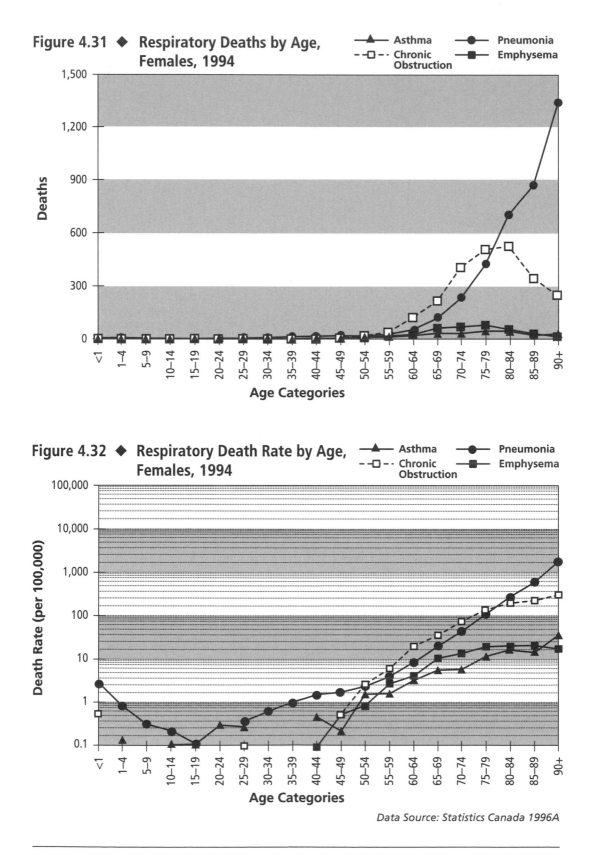

Figure 4.31 ◆ Respiratory Deaths by Age, Females, 1994

Figure 4.32 ◆ Respiratory Death Rate by Age, Females, 1994

Data Source: Statistics Canada 1996A

Figure 4.33 ◆ Respiratory Death Rate, 1930–1990

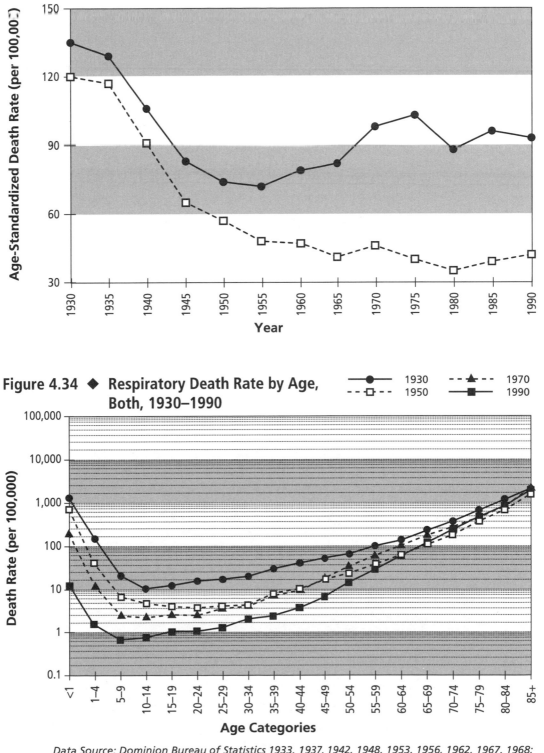

Figure 4.34 ◆ Respiratory Death Rate by Age, Both, 1930–1990

Data Source: Dominion Bureau of Statistics 1933, 1937, 1942, 1948, 1953, 1956, 1962, 1967, 1968; Statistics Canada 1970, 1972, 1975, 1978, 1980, 1983, 1985, 1987, 1990, 1994B

External Causes

External causes cover a variety of different causes of death. A more suitable label is accidents and adverse effects. Accidents (or, more appropriately, fatal injuries) include motor vehicle accidents, falls, drownings, etc. The other important cause of death included in this category is suicide. In 1994, external causes were the cause of death for 8.2% of males and 4.3% of females.

1994 Evidence

The four subcategories of external causes considered in more detail are:

- auto traffic (ICD-9: E810–E819, motor vehicle traffic accidents);

- falls (ICD-9: E880–E888, accidental falls);

- submersion/suffocation (ICD-9: E910–E915, accidents, submersion, suffocation, and foreign bodies);

- suicide (ICD-9: E950–E959).

Figures 4.35 and 4.36 show the number of external deaths by age and the external death rate by age for males in 1994. Due to the many subcategories in external causes, large differences in age distribution occur. Both motor vehicle accidents (auto traffic) and suicides are leading causes of death in male youth. Deaths from falls occur primarily in the elderly, with an exponential increase in death rates beginning in those aged 60 to 64. Submersion or suffocation deaths were low and remained relatively constant (within a range of ten) for all age categories.

Figures 4.37 and 4.38 show the number of external deaths by age and the external death rate by age for females in 1994. Figures for female motor vehicle accidents and suicides are significantly lower than males. The annual death rate from falls is less than one per 100,000 before the 50–54 age category, is 100 per 100,000 by the 80–84 category, and continues to rise exponentially after that age category.

Trend Evidence

Figure 4.39 shows the external death rate for males and females between 1930 and 1990. External death rates remained relatively constant until approximately 1975, when a decrease, more significant in males, began. Figure 4.39 shows the substantial differences in the external death rate between males and females. Females have consistently had a death rate from external causes two to three times lower than males.

Figure 4.40 shows the external death rate by age for males and females combined between 1930 and 1990. As mentioned for Figure 4.39, the death rate for external causes has remained relatively constant. The decrease in deaths between 1970 and 1990 has occurred at younger ages (<1 to 10–14) and middle ages (45–49 to 65–69).

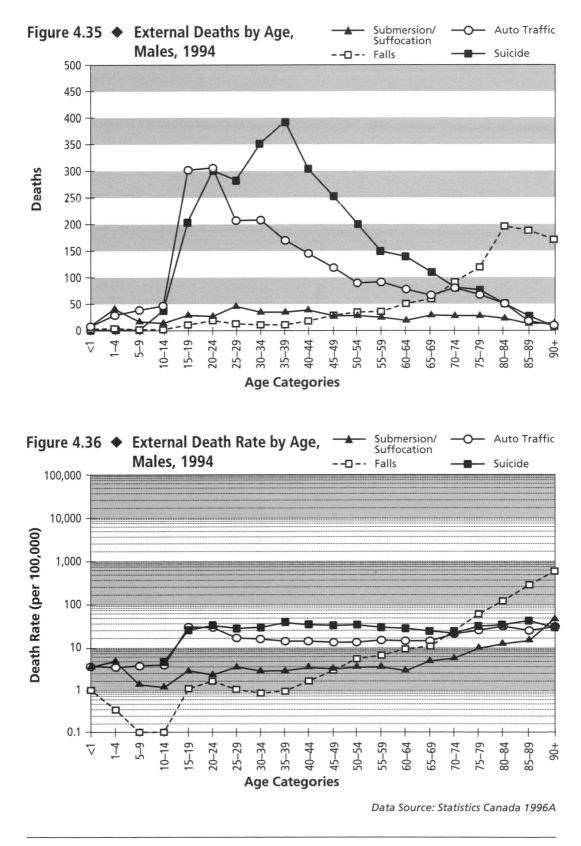

Figure 4.35 ◆ External Deaths by Age, Males, 1994

Legend: Submersion/Suffocation, Auto Traffic, Falls, Suicide

Figure 4.36 ◆ External Death Rate by Age, Males, 1994

Legend: Submersion/Suffocation, Auto Traffic, Falls, Suicide

Data Source: Statistics Canada 1996A

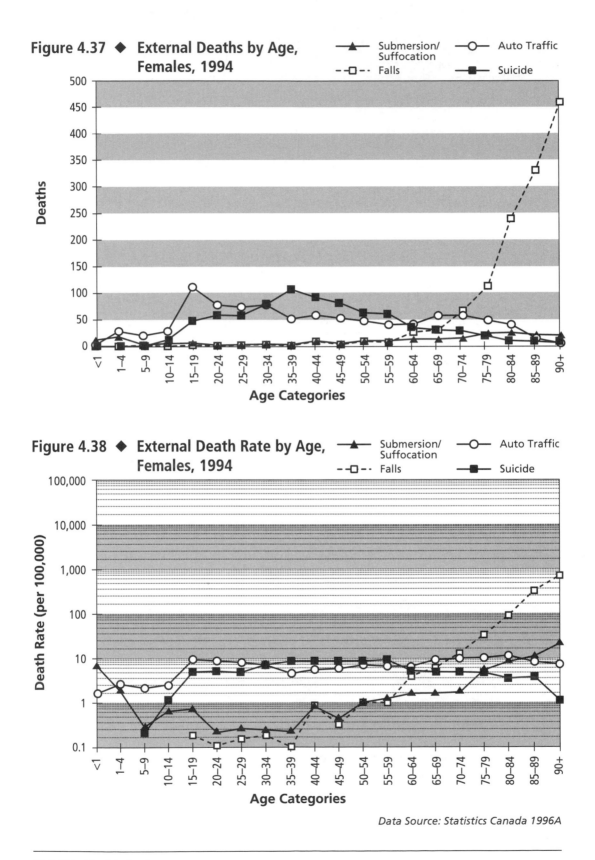

Figure 4.37 ◆ External Deaths by Age, Females, 1994

Legend: Submersion/Suffocation, Auto Traffic, Falls, Suicide

Figure 4.38 ◆ External Death Rate by Age, Females, 1994

Legend: Submersion/Suffocation, Auto Traffic, Falls, Suicide

Data Source: Statistics Canada 1996A

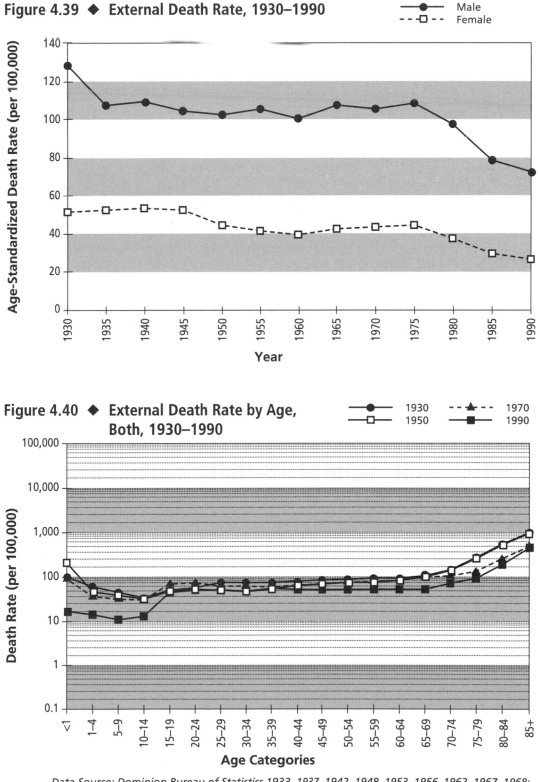

Figure 4.39 ◆ External Death Rate, 1930–1990

Male
Female

Figure 4.40 ◆ External Death Rate by Age, Both, 1930–1990

1930   1970
1950   1990

Data Source: Dominion Bureau of Statistics 1933, 1937, 1942, 1948, 1953, 1956, 1962, 1967, 1968; Statistics Canada 1970, 1972, 1975, 1978, 1980, 1983, 1985, 1987, 1990, 1994B

Maternal Deaths

A maternal death is defined as the death of a mother due to complications during pregnancy, childbirth, or the puerperium (Statistics Canada 1996A). Though maternal deaths are currently very low, they were a major cause of death earlier in this century. As maternal deaths are a specific cause of death listed in the ICD (as opposed to infant deaths, which are based on age), they were included in this chapter.

1994 Evidence

In 1994, there were fourteen maternal deaths. By comparison, there were over 385,000 live births.

Trend Evidence

Figures 4.41 and 4.42 show the maternal deaths and maternal death rate between 1930 and 1990. Of all changes in mortality between 1930 and 1990, maternal mortality has been one of the most significant: the number of maternal deaths dropped from over 1,400 in 1930 to less than twenty in 1990. When expressed as a rate, the drop has been even more significant, over 100-fold, as there are now more births than in the past. The drop in maternal deaths is similar to the decrease in infant deaths (see Figures 3.10 and 3.11).

Figure 4.41 ◆ Total Maternal Deaths, 1930–1990

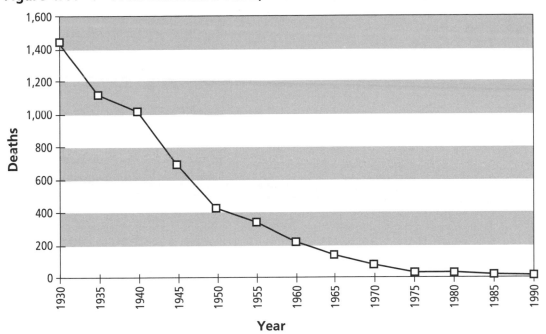

Figure 4.42 ◆ Maternal Death Rate, 1930–1990

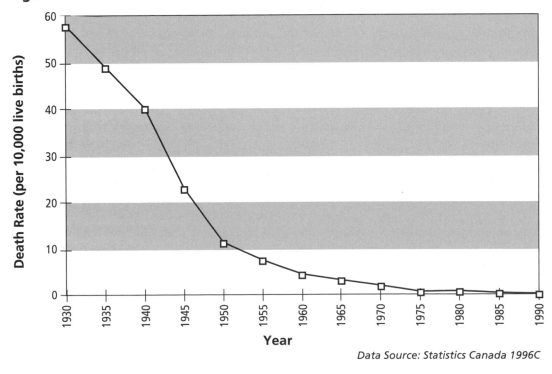

Data Source: Statistics Canada 1996C

Uncertainty in the Reported Cause of Death

Alderson (1988) has identified four areas where uncertainties or inaccuracies can arise in the reported cause of death:

1. incorrect diagnosis (last attending physician and/or autopsy);

2. incorrect completion of death certificate;

3. inaccurate processing and publication of the statistics;

4. invalid classification of diseases.

The diagnosis relies on the medical training of the individual, state of medical knowledge, and availability of diagnostic facilities. Different diseases or outcomes vary in the accuracy and consistency of diagnosis. Generally, diagnosis is less precise for older individuals, and acute and chronic outcomes can be more or less accurate depending on the disease. Determining the quantitative uncertainty in the diagnosis is very difficult. For mortality, comparisons between clinical and autopsy diagnoses have shown fairly large disagreements. In Ontario, autopsies are performed on approximately four out of every ten deaths: for all fatal injuries and other sudden or unexpected deaths (Young and Wagner 1994). Alderson (1988) summarized five studies that compared original and autopsy-verified causes of death. Alderson found only a 50% agreement at the three-digit level, and an 82% agreement at the chapter level. Lindahl et al. (1990) note that the concept of a principal cause of death is appropriate for well-defined diseases (cancer) and acute conditions (fatal injuries and infectious diseases). However, when the majority of deaths occur in old age and involve chronic diseases complicated by concurrent conditions, considerable difficulties occur in assigning a principal cause of death. Messite and Stellman (1996) tested several levels of New York physicians, based on training and experience, using a written test involving six different hospital deaths. The correct cause of death was identified only 56% of the time, with the accurate identification of each of the six deaths ranging from 15% to 99%. Messite and Stellman concluded that training on death certificate completion should be included in physician education and that substantial under-reporting may be occurring for specific causes of death.

Once a diagnosis is made, the classification form must be completed or encoded properly. There is little information on how many ways there are to complete a form for the same diagnosis. A survey sent to ninety-seven general practitioners with ten case histories resulted in seven to twenty-six different causes of death for the same hypothetical case history (Alderson 1988). Ease of use and training in using the classification system influence the reliability of the encoding. The classification system assumes that all information entered will be of equal quality, but this is not the case. Lilienfeld and Stolley (1994) showed that some significant differences do occur within a major category when the ICD is revised. However, the difference in the total number of deaths from cardiovascular disease using the ninth ICD rather than the eighth ICD for the same data was only 0.7%.

The final step in recording deaths is processing and publishing the statistics. Information must be collected in a timely manner for annual publications. For mortality, collection and publication take approximately two years after the end of a particular year. In Canada, a significant difference existed between the national publication compared with the provincial coroner database that provided the national data. The provincial coroner had 13% more accidental deaths, 51% more suicides and 58% more homicides because of the delayed transfer of autopsy results (Young and Wagner 1994). Wilkins (1994) observed that these differences in cause of death do not affect the total number of deaths.

For mortality, only the underlying cause of death is collected in the national database. Several provinces have started multiple cause coding, which uses information that is already present. This additional information could prove valuable for understanding health risks.

As mentioned previously, the ICD is a compromise between medical and statistical needs and perspectives, a fact that influences the validity of the classification system. The system must be detailed, easy to use, and flexible enough to allow for new developments.

Lilienfeld and Stolley (1994) summarized some of the uncertainties associated with mortality trends. These were divided into artifactual and real.

1. Artifactual:

   - changes in the recognition of disease;

   - changes in the rules and procedures for classification of causes of death;

   - changes in the classification code of causes of death;

   - changes in the accuracy of reporting age at death;

   - errors in the enumeration of the population.

2. Real:

   - changes in the age distribution of the population;

   - changes in survivorship;

   - changes in the incidence of disease resulting from genetic factors
     and environmental factors.

5 Other Ways of Accounting for Mortality

ge is an important factor to consider when discussing mortality. As shown in Chapter 4, a great deal of information must be presented to summarize the cause of death by age and sex. As a result of this difficulty, there are methods to reduce the information required to compare different causes of death. The two methods discussed in this chapter, potential years of life lost (PYLL) and loss of life expectancy (LLE), use techniques that combine the number of deaths in each category into one number.

Deaths of younger people are a concern because these deaths are often preventable. There is also a greater sense of loss when someone has not lived a full life. Both PYLL and LLE weight the deaths of younger people more than the deaths of older people. Because of the large amount of information required to generate this information, only calculations for 1994 have been included in this chapter.

Potential Years of Life Lost (PYLL)

As mentioned, PYLL is used to compare different causes of death and gives more weight to earlier deaths. As an example, you may decide only to be concerned with deaths before age seventy-five, what might reasonably be considered premature deaths. If a twelve-year-old dies, there are sixty-three years (seventy-five minus twelve) of life lost. The older the age at death, the fewer the years of loss, until at age seventy-five, there are no years of loss. Using this calculation for specific causes of death effectively weights deaths based on the age at death.

Normally, cause-specific information is divided into five-year age categories, so all methods use the midpoint of the age category as the age at death. For example, all deaths in the 10–14 age category are assumed to be deaths at age twelve.

One source of confusion with the PYLL is the variety of methods for doing the calculations. The first challenge in calculating the PYLL is to select the age that will be used as a reference. The choices include:

- selecting a single reference age for both males and females (e.g., seventy-eight years);

- selecting different reference ages for males and females, often the average life expectancy (e.g., males, seventy-five years/females, eighty-one years);

- selecting the expected years of life remaining for males and females in each age category with no age reference.

A second choice in using the PYLL is whether to use:

- the total number of deaths for each age category;

- the death rates for each age category.

In the past, people have also calculated the PYLL without including the deaths of those less than one year of age.

The Canadian Cancer Statistics (National Cancer Institute of Canada 1996) used the expected years of life remaining in each age category and the total number of deaths in each category. Other statistics have used a single age reference and age-standardized death rates that allow comparison of PYLL values from different years (Wilkins and Mark 1992).

This section does not attempt to judge the best method for calculating the PYLL. Each method weights the information differently and will yield slightly different results that are not directly comparable. However, all methods will emphasize causes of death in the young and will de-emphasize causes of death of older people.

This books uses the simplest method for calculating the PYLL: giving the same reference age for both males and females and using the total number of deaths for each age category.

1994 Evidence

To compare PYLL results with those from other types of direct evidence, we decided to compare the total number of deaths in 1994 with the PYLL. As the generated values are not comparable, the percentage of the total for each method in the seventeen major categories was calculated. In addition, three different age cut-offs were used to see what effect these have on the results. The results are shown in Table 5.1 (males) and Table 5.2 (females). The numbers of the five major causes of death are in boldface type.

As expected, the PYLL placed considerably more weight on causes of death in the young. For males, external causes, which only resulted in 8.2% of total deaths, had the highest percentage of PYLL at seventy-five years. Cancer remained in second place, while cardio-vascular disease dropped to third. There were over seventeen times as many deaths from respiratory diseases as from perinatal conditions, but the PYLL ranked perinatal conditions ahead because the respiratory deaths occurred primarily in the aged.

For females at seventy-five years, cancer was the number-one ranked PYLL, followed by cardiovascular diseases, and then external causes. For cancer, the PYLL shows how, overall, the effects of cancer influence mortality at younger ages in females than in males. The PYLL increased the percentage allotted to cancer in females, but decreased the percentage for males.

The information on the PYLL shown in Tables 5.1 and 5.2 can be manipulated by changing the age cut-off. People concerned with external causes can select a lower age cut-off to emphasize this category, while those interested in cancer or cardiovascular diseases can select a higher age cut-off to emphasize these categories.

One important point to remember is that when you calculate the PYLL using an age cut-off, you only use a percentage of all deaths in your calculations. The lower the age cut-off, the lower the percentage of all deaths being used in the calculations. Table 5.3 shows the percentage of all deaths included for three different age cut-offs. As males have a higher mortality at any given age than females, a greater percentage of males have died by each age cut-off. Using a seventy-five year age cut-off, 56% of the male population was included, vs 38% of the female population.

If you are only looking at one gender, percentages are much easier to use than PYLL values. However, PYLL values are useful when comparing genders because these values include the number of people dying. Table 5.4 shows the sum of PYLL values for all causes of death using three different cut-off years. Males have a substantially greater total number of PYLL than females. This total is related to the percentages in Table 5.3.

The PYLL stresses that causes of death have different impacts for different age categories. By placing more weight on younger deaths, the PYLL emphasizes causes of deaths that prevent individuals living into old age.

Table 5.1 ◆ Percentage of Total Deaths vs the PYLL, Males, 1994

No.	Shortened Name	% of Total Deaths	% of the PYLL		
			@65 yrs	@75 yrs	@85 yrs
I	**Infectious Diseases**	**2.1**	**7.0**	**5.6**	**4.4**
II	**Cancer**	**28.7**	**16.4**	**23.0**	**26.6**
III	Endocrine and Others	2.9	2.1	2.4	2.6
IV	Blood Diseases	0.3	0.3	0.3	0.3
V	Mental Disorders	1.8	1.1	1.2	1.3
VI	Nervous System Diseases	2.4	2.4	2.2	2.2
VII	**Cardiovascular Diseases**	**36.3**	**13.9**	**20.2**	**25.6**
VIII	**Respiratory Diseases**	**9.2**	**2.3**	**3.3**	**4.9**
IX	Digestive Diseases	3.6	2.8	3.3	3.4
X	Genito-Urinary Diseases	1.5	0.4	0.6	0.8
XI	Pregnancy Related	–	–	–	–
XII	Skin Diseases	0.1	<0.1	<0.1	<0.1
XIII	Musculo-Skeletal Diseases	0.2	0.1	0.2	0.2
XIV	Congenital Anomalies	0.6	5.5	3.6	2.5
XV	Perinatal Conditions	0.5	6.0	3.9	2.6
XVI	Ill-Defined	1.5	5.3	4.1	3.1
E XVII	**External Causes**	**8.2**	**34.3**	**26.2**	**19.7**

Note: The five major causes of death are **bolded**.

Data Source: Statistics Canada 1996A

Table 5.2 ◆ Percentage of Total Deaths vs the PYLL, Females, 1994

No.	Shortened Name	% of Total Deaths	% of the PYLL		
			@65 yrs	@75 yrs	@85 yrs
I	**Infectious Diseases**	**0.9**	**2.4**	**1.9**	**1.5**
II	**Cancer**	**27.5**	**31.8**	**38.0**	**38.2**
III	Endocrine and Others	3.5	2.5	2.8	3.1
IV	Blood Diseases	0.4	0.3	0.3	0.3
V	Mental Disorders	2.8	0.7	0.8	1.0
VI	Nervous System Diseases	3.4	3.4	3.1	3.1
VII	**Cardiovascular Diseases**	**39.7**	**10.4**	**15.6**	**22.5**
VIII	**Respiratory Diseases**	**8.5**	**2.5**	**3.5**	**5.0**
IX	Digestive Diseases	3.9	2.7	3.1	3.4
X	Genito-Urinary Diseases	1.7	0.6	0.8	1.1
XI	Pregnancy Related	<0.1	0.1	0.1	0.1
XII	Skin Diseases	0.1	<0.1	0.1	0.1
XIII	Musculo-Skeletal Diseases	0.7	0.5	0.6	0.6
XIV	Congenital Anomalies	0.5	7.9	5.1	3.2
XV	Perinatal Conditions	0.5	9.4	5.9	3.6
XVI	Ill-Defined	1.5	4.7	3.4	2.5
E XVII	**External Causes**	**4.3**	**20.0**	**14.9**	**10.6**

Note: The five major causes of death are **bolded**.

Data Source: Statistics Canada 1996A

Table 5.3 ◆ Percentage of All Deaths Considered by Three Age Cut-offs, 1994

Gender	PYLL @ 65 yrs	PYLL @ 75 yrs	PYLL @ 85 yrs
Male	30%	56%	84%
Female	19%	38%	68%

Data Source: Statistics Canada 1996A

Table 5.4 ◆ Comparison of Male and Female Total PYLL, 1994

Gender	PYLL @ 65 yrs	PYLL @ 75 yrs	PYLL @ 85 yrs
Male	618,229	1,093,764	1,877,116
Female	331,784	608,006	1,129,903

Data Source: Statistics Canada 1996A

Loss of Life Expectancy (LLE)

The loss of life expectancy (LLE) is another way to incorporate the age at death into calculations. An advantage of this method is that it results in a number that can be understood in personal terms.

The concept behind the LLE is fairly straightforward. The LLE is based on the death rates by age categories (see Figure 3.6). Other methods can be used to calculate the LLE if information by age category is not available (Cohen 1991). The death rate in the first year of life is high, but is followed by a sharp drop and then an exponentially rising rate starting in the teens. This same population has a fixed, calculated life expectancy for 1994. The LLE takes a cause of death, say cancer, which has a death rate of its own, and subtracts it from the total death rate for the year. The LLE calculation operates as if a cure were found and people only die from other causes, now at a lower rate. By reducing this death rate, life expectancy increases. The difference between the new life expectancy (without cancer mortality) and the actual life expectancy (with cancer mortality) is the LLE from cancer.

The greater the reduction in the death rate from a cause, the larger will be its impact. Age is an important factor, since reducing the death rate earlier in life causes a larger improvement in overall life expectancy.

Table 5.5 shows a life table used to calculate the LLE for males to help describe how the LLE is calculated (a similar table was used for females). There is no need to detail how the life table works. There are only two important areas. The first is the fifth column from the left, labelled q_x. This column is the annual mortality rate for that age category (and sex), based on data from Figure 3.6. The numbers in this column are used to calculate all the values in the rest of table. The second important number is the first one in the last column, e_x, which is the life expectancy. The difference between this number, 73.87, and the new number after the mortality rates change to reflect the absence of the disease is the LLE.

Several simplifications were made in calculating these values. The first is the life table itself. Ideally, you want to use a life table separated into individual years. Unfortunately, the only data on mortality were divided into the age categories used in previous sections. As the ages were limited by the 90+ cut-off and were in five-year age categories, the estimated life expectancy was several years lower than the actual life expectancy. The errors this will cause in the final results are unknown, but because the important value is the difference between life expectancies, the errors should be small.

Cohen and Lee (1979) prepared A Catalog of Risks using the LLE, which Cohen updated twelve years later (Cohen 1991). The Institute for Risk Research (Cherry et al. 1991) prepared a report for Health and Welfare Canada that provided a benchmark of risks for several different causes of death in Canada. This report used a method similar to the LLE called days of life lost (DLL).

Table 5.5 ◆ Life Table, Males, 1994

	l_x	d_x	p_x	q_x	L_x	T_x	e_x
<1	100,000	694	0.99306	0.00694	99,653	7,386,657	73.87
1–4	99,306	140	0.99859	0.00141	396,944	7,287,004	73.38
5–9	99,166	91	0.99908	0.00092	495,603	6,890,061	69.48
10–14	99,075	120	0.99879	0.00121	495,076	6,394,458	64.54
15–19	98,955	416	0.99580	0.00420	493,736	5,899,382	59.62
20–24	98,539	504	0.99489	0.00511	491,437	5,405,646	54.86
25–29	98,036	524	0.99466	0.00534	488,869	4,914,209	50.13
30–34	97,512	626	0.99358	0.00642	485,996	4,425,341	45.38
35–39	96,886	812	0.99162	0.00838	482,402	3,939,345	40.66
40–44	96,074	1,099	0.98856	0.01144	477,625	3,456,943	35.98
45–49	94,976	1,471	0.98452	0.01548	471,201	2,979,318	31.37
50–54	93,505	2,380	0.97455	0.02545	461,574	2,508,117	26.82
55–59	91,125	3,941	0.95675	0.04325	445,770	2,046,543	22.46
60–64	87,183	6,468	0.92581	0.07419	419,746	1,600,773	18.36
65–69	80,715	9,574	0.88139	0.11861	379,642	1,181,027	14.63
70–74	71,142	13,235	0.81396	0.18604	322,620	801,385	11.26
75–79	57,906	17,404	0.69945	0.30055	246,022	478,766	8.27
80–84	40,503	19,513	0.51822	0.48178	153,729	232,743	5.75
85–89	20,989	15,681	0.25290	0.74710	65,743	79,014	3.76
90+	5,308	5,308	0.00000	1.00000	13,270	13,270	2.50

Data Source: Statistics Canada 1996A

1994 Evidence

Tables 5.6 and 5.7 summarize LLE calculations for males and females in 1994. What is really useful about the LLE is that it provides a tangible quantitative measure. For example, if infectious disease were eliminated in males, the increase in life expectancy for the whole male population would be 116 days. We must be careful not to misinterpret this value. Although the increase in life expectancy for the entire male population is 116 days, the increase in life expectancy for those who actually die of an infectious disease would be much greater.

The difference between the percentage of total deaths and the percentage after LLE calculations is fairly small. In the most extreme case, perinatal conditions, the percentage is increased by a factor of approximately three. None of the three leading causes of death changed their rank after using the LLE. However, although the percentage assigned to cancer stayed the same for males, it increased almost 6% for females. Cancer has a greater impact at younger ages in females than in males compared with other causes of death.

What the LLE illustrates is that even if a major cause of death is substantially reduced, the overall increase in life expectancy for the population is moderate because people will continue dying at the same rate from all the other causes of death. Reducing the number of people dying of one cause of death increases the number dying of a different cause of death. The hope is that people will live longer (and be healthier) overall.

Table 5.6 ◆ Total Deaths and the LLE, Males, 1994

No.	Shortened Name	% Total Deaths	LLE % of total LLE	LLE Days
I	**Infectious Diseases**	**2.1**	**2.4**	**116**
II	**Cancer**	**28.7**	**28.7**	**1,357**
III	Endocrine and Others	2.9	2.5	120
IV	Blood Diseases	0.3	0.3	12
V	Mental Disorders	1.8	1.3	63
VI	Nervous System Diseases	2.4	2.1	101
VII	**Cardiovascular Diseases**	**36.3**	**34.5**	**1,633**
VIII	**Respiratory Diseases**	**9.2**	**6.9**	**325**
IX	Digestive Diseases	3.6	3.2	149
X	Genito-Urinary Diseases	1.5	1.1	51
XI	Pregnancy Related	–	–	–
XII	Skin Diseases	0.1	<0.1	2
XIII	Musculo-Skeletal Diseases	0.2	0.2	9
XIV	Congenital Anomalies	0.6	1.5	73
XV	Perinatal Conditions	0.5	1.6	78
XVI	Ill-Defined	1.5	2.0	97
E XVII	**External Causes**	**8.2**	**11.5**	**545**

Note: The five major causes of death are **bolded**.

Data Source: Statistics Canada 1996A

Table 5.7 ◆ Total Deaths and the LLE, Females, 1994

No.	Shortened Name	% Total Deaths	LLE % of total LLE	Days
I	**Infectious Diseases**	**0.9**	**1.1**	**40**
II	**Cancer**	**27.5**	**33.7**	**1,260**
III	Endocrine and Others	3.5	3.2	120
IV	Blood Diseases	0.4	0.3	12
V	Mental Disorders	2.8	1.6	60
VI	Nervous System Diseases	3.4	3.1	116
VII	**Cardiovascular Diseases**	**39.7**	**33.6**	**1,257**
VIII	**Respiratory Diseases**	**8.5**	**6.4**	**240**
IX	Digestive Diseases	3.9	3.4	128
X	Genito-Urinary Diseases	1.7	1.4	51
XI	Pregnancy Related	<0.1	<0.1	1.1
XII	Skin Diseases	0.1	0.1	3
XIII	Musculo-Skeletal Diseases	0.7	0.6	22
XIV	Congenital Anomalies	0.5	1.8	66
XV	Perinatal Conditions	0.5	2.0	76
XVI	Ill-Defined	1.5	1.7	62
E XVII	**External Causes**	**4.3**	**6.1**	**230**

Note: The five major causes of death are **bolded**.

Data Source: Statistics Canada 1996A

Part

Indirect Evidence
and Inference

two

Indirect evidence and inference are based on epidemiological studies. Chapter 6 looks at ways in which epidemiology evaluates risk factors influencing human health. Chapter 6 also discusses epidemiological risk factors. Chapter 7 focuses on major individual risk factors, while Chapter 8 deals with risk factors by major cause of death.

Epidemiology

Epidemiology can be defined as "The study of the distribution and determinants of health-related states or events in specified populations, and the application of this study to control of health problems" (Last 1995, 55). A more comprehensive definition that describes various aspects of epidemiological study is:

The study of the distribution and determinants of health-related states in human and other animal populations. Epidemiological studies involve surveillance, observation, hypothesis-testing, and experiment. Distribution is established by analyzing the time, place, and class of person affected by a disease. Determinants may include physical, biological, social, cultural, and behavioral factors. Epidemiological methods are most commonly applied to the study of disease; however, they also may be used to examine causes of death (e.g., homicides of various sorts) or behaviors (e.g., tobacco or alcohol use, practice of safe sex, use of health services). Epidemiology plays a key role in formulation and implementation of public health policy (Stedman's Medical Dictionary 1995, 582).

Analysing the distribution of disease has a long history and is the foundation of epidemiology. Identifying a cause of a disease and applying it to the control of health problems can be traced back to London, England, in the mid-nineteenth century. Dr. John Snow calculated the rates of cholera and found large differences in populations served by different water companies. Snow proposed that cholera was associated with the source of the water supply. Snow's analysis was the basis for many subsequent studies that have benefited human health. Most epidemiological studies of the mid to late nineteenth and early twentieth centuries have addressed communicable diseases. More recently, epidemiology has expanded its scope to include a wide variety of other health problems, including risk factors associated with chronic diseases and fatal injuries.

Measurement

Epidemiological studies try to develop evidence for an association between a determinant or cause and a health outcome. Studies do not provide "yes" or "no" answers. Rather, these studies provide evidence along a continuum, running from weak to strong, for an association between a determinant or cause and an effect or outcome. There are many types of measures of the strength of an epidemiological association. However, only two are described and used in this section: relative risk (RR) and population attributable risk (PAR).

Table 6.1 shows the four basic categories of exposure and disease in an epidemiological study. The horizontal rows indicate the exposure category. For example, the exposure could represent smokers vs non-smokers, high alcohol consumption vs low alcohol consumption, high vs low education level, or wearing vs not wearing a seatbelt. Some categories may be discrete (seat belt or no seat belt), while others may be continuous (non-smokers, non-smokers exposed to second-hand smoke, light smokers, heavy smokers). The vertical columns indicate the disease (or outcome) being studied, for example, the development of a specific cancer, mortality from cardiovascular disease, or all-cause mortality. Again, some categories may be discrete (death or no death), while others may involve a degree of impairment. We will simplify these complexities by dealing with these categories as if they are all discrete.

Table 6.1 ◆ Exposure vs Disease

	Disease	No Disease
Exposure	a	b
No Exposure	c	d

The relative risk (RR) is the ratio of the proportion of those with the disease (or outcome) who have been exposed, to the proportion of those with the disease who have not been exposed. Though still widely used, the term relative risk can be replaced with the less descriptive (though more accurate) term rate ratio. To add to the confusion, a third synonymous term, risk ratio, has also been used (Last 1995). Using the letters in Table 6.1, the RR is calculated with the following equation:

$$\frac{a/(a+b)}{c/(c+d)} = \frac{\text{disease (exposed)/total exposed}}{\text{disease (not exposed)/total not exposed}}$$

The RR indicates how an individual's risk of experiencing a disease might increase (as a multiplier) if he or she changed from unexposed to exposed, or, conversely, how much an individual could reduce risk (as a divisor) by eliminating exposure. The RR is usually accompanied by confidence intervals that indicate the statistical uncertainty of the RR estimate. The larger the confidence intervals (for the same specified confidence level), the less certain one can be about the true value of the RR. Commonly, 95% confidence intervals have been used in epidemiological studies. As there would be an RR of 1.0 if there was no association between the exposure and the disease, a study outcome is commonly regarded as statistically significant if the calculated confidence intervals do not include an RR of 1. However, these statistical confidence intervals do not account for many sources of uncertainty. These non-random uncertainties are discussed in more detail in Uncertainty (p. 127).

Many epidemiological studies only report the RR, which measures the strength of association between disease outcome and exposure to a suspected causal factor. Most diseases are the result of multiple causal factors which may interact in complex ways. The RR by itself does not provide a quantitative perspective on the proportion of a disease attributable to the suspected causal factor nor on the magnitude of the disease in the overall population. Although RR is of interest to individuals who may be exposed to any suspected causal factors, public health must be concerned with the overall impact of disease on society, in order to determine how to allocate resources for disease prevention. Consequently, additional quantitative measures for estimating the contribution from important causal factors are needed.

The population attributable risk percentage (PAR%) is one such measure. According to Northridge (1995), PAR%, which is also known as the etiologic fraction or excess fraction, can be defined as follows:

$$PAR\% = [(Rate_{TOTAL\ POPULATION} - Rate_{UNEXPOSED}) / (Rate_{TOTAL\ POPULATION})] \times 100\%$$

This measure, which expresses what fraction of the total occurrence of a disease may be attributed to a particular exposure factor, may also be expressed in terms of RR as follows:

$$PAR\% = \{P_{EXPOSED}\ (RR - 1) / [1 + P_{EXPOSED}\ (RR - 1)]\} \times 100\%$$

With the latter expression, PAR% can be calculated using only the RR and the fraction of the total population exposed ($P_{EXPOSED}$). Because PAR% depends on two independent parameters, Northridge found that four combinations may arise:

high RR with high $P_{EXPOSED}$,
high RR with low $P_{EXPOSED}$,
low RR with high $P_{EXPOSED}$,
low RR with low $P_{EXPOSED}$.

An example of the first case is lung cancer and smoking, where both the RR and proportion of the population exposed are high, resulting in a PAR% ranging over 90%. These estimates mean that the majority of lung cancers could be attributed to smoking. An example of the second case is the BRCA1 gene and breast cancer. In this case, the RR may be very high, depending on age, but the occurrence of this gene in the total population is very small. Taken together, the PAR% ranges from 8.2% for women under 40 to 1% for women over 50. An example of the third case is stratospheric ozone depletion and skin cancer incidence. In this case, the RR for increased UV-B exposure resulting from ozone depletion is small, but the exposed fraction approaches one, because virtually everyone has some exposure to sunlight. Assuming a 15% increase in UV-B exposure over the last 20 years, due to ozone depletion, results in a PAR% of 13% (Northridge 1995). Finally, any case with a low RR and a low proportion of the population exposed would be of limited interest to public health, because a low PAR% is assured.

The PAR% shows the importance of both the strength of association between cause and effect, as expressed by RR, and the proportion of the population exposed to the risk factor. The latter concept also applies to many specialized activities and direct risks. For example, the risk of death from rock climbing will appear small in the overall population, but the risk among the exposed population (those who engage in rock climbing) is much higher.

Even a large PAR% value may not rank as a major public health issue if the specific disease in question is rare. In such cases, a high proportion of the disease may be attributed to a particular cause, but the low prevalence of the disease results in a minor impact on the overall population.

Finally, if all possible risk factors for any given disease could be assigned a PAR%, they would not necessarily sum to 100%. The sum might fall short of 100% because important risk factors have not yet been identified. Likewise, the sum might exceed 100% because of the interactive and multi-causal nature of most diseases.

Types of Epidemiological Study

There are several ways to classify and name the different types of epidemiological studies. Table 6.2 summarizes several types of epidemiological studies using alternative names and units of study. The most basic division is between observational and experimental studies. Experimental studies require experimental intervention to control the exposures, as well as a variety of other elements that are more actively controlled.

The six types of epidemiological study identified in Table 6.2 are described in more detail below.

1. Observational studies include:

a. Descriptive studies are often the first step in any epidemiological investigation. Descriptive studies are often based on death certificates or other existing data sources. No analysis of exposure vs effect is done. An example of a descriptive study would be to compare age-standardized death rates for specific causes between regions or countries.

b. Ecological studies look at population rates, not individual responses. Therefore, no reliable associations with exposures can be made at this group level. The tendency of ecological studies to yield spurious correlation is termed the ecological fallacy. This kind of study is often used for studying rare diseases and for hypothesis generation. Examining the relationship between population rates of red wine consumption and population rates of heart disease would be an example of an ecological study.

Table 6.2 ◆ Types of Epidemiological Study

Type of Study	Alternative Name	Unit of Study
1. Observational studies		
a. Descriptive studies		
b. Ecological* studies	Correlational*	Populations
c. Cross-sectional studies	Prevalence	Individuals
d. Case-control studies	Case-reference	Individuals
e. Cohort studies	Follow-up	Individuals
2. Experimental studies	Clinical trials	Patients, healthy people or communities

Notes: *Although these names are widely used in epidemiological practice, neither is accurate in meaning for other scientific disciplines. Ecological studies have nothing to do with ecology and because all epidemiological studies are fundamentally assessing the correlation of exposure and outcome, so all studies are correlational.

Source: Adapted from Beaglehole et al. 1993, Table 3.1

c. Cross-sectional studies measure exposure and effect at the same time to estimate the prevalence of disease. However, this study design does not ensure that exposure preceded disease, as is necessary to support causal inference. Good questionnaires and appropriate study populations are needed to be sure that exposure represents earlier periods. An example of a cross-sectional study is a random telephone survey of health habits.

d. Case-control studies include people with a disease (or other outcome) and a control group that does not have the disease or outcome. Case-control studies are best for studying rare diseases, multiple exposures, and determinants with long latent periods. These studies select the cases and controls and then determine their status with regard to exposure. The studies of birth defects resulting from thalidomide exposure were examples of case-control studies.

e. Cohort studies begin with people free of disease who are followed over time, either by reviewing past records (retrospective cohort) or by tracking into the future (prospective cohort). A prospective cohort allows more accurate measurement of exposure without any potential bias in data quality between cases and controls. This study design provides much better information for inferring causation of disease and multiple outcomes. Major disadvantages of cohort studies include the long time required, high cost, and large size of cohort that must be followed for rarer types of diseases to yield enough cases for analysis. An example of a cohort study was the Framingham study of coronary heart disease (Kannel and Gordon 1976).

2. Experimental studies include several types such as randomized clinical trials, field trials, and community trials. Experimental studies can be used to assess new preventive or therapeutic methods. The high degree of intervention inherent in experimental designs limits their use in risk factor epidemiology for ethical and practical reasons. The ß-carotene cancer studies are an example of an experimental study.

Most epidemiological studies discussed in this book are either case-control or cohort. However, the largest number of environmental epidemiology studies found in the literature are ecological or cross-sectional studies because of their practicality and lower cost. The case-control or cohort study designs can both provide quantitative estimates of health risks and be used to study most risk factors.

Causal Inference

Types of epidemiological studies can be arranged similarly to the uncertainty hierarchy shown in Figure 1.3. At the top of this hierarchy are descriptive studies, the weakest type, followed by ecological, cross-sectional, case-control, cohort, and, at the bottom, experimental studies, the strongest type of epidemiological study. The stronger study designs are better at establishing associations or supporting causal inferences. On their own, epidemiological studies cannot prove causation, but better study designs can provide substantial evidence to support causal inferences.

Early epidemiological investigations focused on communicable diseases. Over 100 years ago, the Henle-Koch postulates for infectious diseases were proposed as follows (Evans 1976).

- The parasite occurs in every case of the disease in question and under circumstances that can account for the pathological changes and clinical course of the disease.

- The parasite occurs in no other disease as a fortuitous and nonpathogenic parasite.

- After being fully isolated from the body and repeatedly grown in pure culture, the parasite can induce the disease anew.

Robert Koch concluded that if all three conditions could be satisfied, the "occurrence of the parasite in the disease can no longer be accidental, but in this case no other relation between it and the disease except that the parasite is the cause of the disease can be considered." (Evans 1976, 175) Today, infectious diseases are only one part of epidemiologic study, and even many infectious diseases cannot meet the strict Henle-Koch postulates.

Newer guidelines have evolved to judge the causal inference of associations in epidemiological studies. As associations could result from biases, confounders, or random chance, additional evaluation is usually necessary to support causal inference. Hill prepared a famous set of nine guidelines to help determine the strength of the associations used to infer causation (Hill 1965). The WHO published a more recent list of eight guidelines for judging causation, several of which are the same as Hill's (Beaglehole et al. 1993).

1. **Temporal relation**. Does the proposed cause precede the effect? This is especially challenging to satisfy for cancer, because its effects may not be recognized until ten or more years after the initial exposure.

2. **Plausibility**. Is the association consistent with other knowledge of the biological mechanism of the disease?

3. **Consistency**. Do several studies, using a variety of designs in different settings, show similar results?

4. **Strength**. How large and statistically significant is the RR?

5. **Dose-response relationship**. Is there a consistent relationship between degrees of exposure to the cause (e.g., exposure to a chemical) and the proportion of individuals responding?

6. **Reversibility**. Does removal of a possible cause reduce the rate of response?

7. **Study design**. Do the study's results recognize the hierarchy of epidemiological studies and their different abilities to generate evidence in support of causal inferences (e.g., cohort studies can establish stronger causal inference than ecological studies)?

8. **Judging the evidence**. As there is always uncertainty and risk factors rarely meet all the criteria, judgements must be made when looking at the evidence.

These guidelines are ordered in a logical sequence for making judgements on causality. They are not weighted equally, and their relative contribution to a final judgement will vary from one situation to another.

Determining a temporal relationship is particularly important, because a cause must precede effects. Although eliminating ambiguity about the temporal relationship may be difficult in many cases, clear evidence that effects preceded a hypothetical cause fails to support causation. Despite the importance of temporal relationship for the interpretation of causation, evidence of a temporal relationship by itself is insufficient to conclude that the factor under study is causal.

Plausibility is a judgement about the existence of other knowledge which may support a mechanism by which the cause is able to act. This judgement is necessarily constrained by the existence of other knowledge. Knowledge of a plausible biological mechanism can support a judgement of causality. However, current lack of knowledge of a plausible mechanism usually cannot preclude the possibility of future discovery of a plausible mechanism of causation. Judgement on the issue of plausibility would be tempered by the amount of research that has been devoted to searching for evidence of a causal mechanism.

Consistency is a judgement about the pattern of results from several studies considering the same hypothetical cause. If many studies done in different situations, by different investigators, using different methods and study designs, find consistent results of an association between hypothetical cause and effect, this finding supports a judgement about causation. The logic of this criterion is that similar findings in many different studies should reduce concerns about potential bias undetected in individual studies. However, if many studies have been similarly performed, they may all suffer from a common bias. When several studies are being judged for consistency, it is necessary to evaluate the study designs and quality of study conduct carefully, to insure that apparent inconsistencies are not the result of comparing strong studies with weak studies. One or more good studies will be far more meaningful than several weak studies. As with plausibility, this test depends on the existence of other comparable studies. If few studies have been done on a possible cause, a meaningful judgement on consistency may not be possible.

Strength of association refers to the magnitude of the RR, with values greater than two being considered strong (Beaglehole et al. 1993). Generally, unrecognized bias can less likely explain a large RR than a small RR. Hence, finding a large RR tends to support a causal hypothesis. But finding a large RR does not in itself rule out a spurious result due to bias.

Evidence of a dose-response relationship, whereby a higher exposure corresponds to a higher response, provides strong support of a causal relationship. This logic follows from toxicological studies, which often focus on causal biological mechanisms after demonstrating a dose-response relationship. However, the absence of a clear dose-response relationship in epidemiological studies does not preclude causation, because the true dose-response relationship may not be linear or even consistently increasing with dose. Complex dose-response relationships may be demonstrated experimentally where doses can be selected and closely controlled. Epidemiological studies cannot discriminate doses as closely as experimental toxicology studies. Likewise, measures of actual individual exposures are often not available in epidemiological studies, so the ability to demonstrate clear dose-response relationships is limited by practical methodologies or available data.

Reversibility, whereby removal of a hypothetical cause leads to reduced chance of adverse effect, provides strong evidence in support of causation. Interventions to remove hypothetical causes can only rarely be prescribed, so evidence on reversibility normally depends on voluntary measures. This reality makes evaluating reversibility difficult for many hypothetical causes. Likewise, reversibility will only be meaningful as a measure of causality if the mechanism of causation is reversible. An exposure leading to infection with HIV, for example, would not exhibit reversibility if the exposure is withdrawn or avoided in the future.

The importance of study design was explained earlier. Because of the inherently different capabilities of various study designs, evidence for causation strongly depends on the quality of study design. Likewise, the quality of study conduct in dealing with issues of confounding and bias is critical to any meaningful interpretation of causation.

Other criteria, such as specificity and analogy, have been proposed (Hill 1965). Specificity proposes a single cause should be associated with a single effect. While this premise can work for acute infectious diseases, it is much less useful for chronic diseases, because of their multi-factorial nature. Consequently, specificity is often not regarded as a critical test for causality. Analogy suggests that the possibility of an association being causal is strengthened if other well-established causes are analogous to the one under study. This might be seen as a weaker version of plausibility. Analogy by itself does not provide strong evidence of causation.

Overall, there is no absolute test that can be applied to prove causation. Final conclusions rest on judging the available evidence in a comprehensive, critical fashion. Because judgements cannot be absolute, disagreement and controversy will often surround the discussion of whether a particular factor is truly known to cause any disease. Inevitably, this scope for disagreement creates substantial uncertainty about causal inference.

Uncertainty

The uncertainty in epidemiology is much greater than in direct evidence. As epidemiological studies rely on direct evidence that has its own uncertainties, any uncertainties in indirect evidence and inference are additional to the uncertainty of the original direct evidence.

However, major epidemiological studies often invest in collecting a more certain diagnosis of the cause of death than what is recorded on the death certificate. In such cases, epidemiological studies obtain and use more valid direct evidence than is commonly available from death statistics. The inferential process of assigning observed causes of death to any particular exposure or risk factor inevitably introduces additional sources of uncertainty.

Uncertainties in epidemiology can be separated into random and systematic errors. Random error is the difference between the measured (sample) and the true population value due to chance. Three major sources of random error are individual biological variation, sampling error, and measurement error. Random error can be reduced by increasing the size of the study (larger sample) and by using a more careful and specific measurement of exposure and outcome.

Systematic error (or bias) is related to the methods used to perform the study. Many possible sources of systematic error exist, but the principal types include selection bias, measurement bias, and confounding. Selection bias occurs when people in the study have a consistent difference from those not included in the study. A common example in occupational studies is that workers are healthier on average than the rest of the population (healthy worker effect). Measurement bias includes errors in key exposure or outcome measures such as biochemical or physiological measurements, and recall bias occurs when self-reporting of health conditions is involved. Confounding arises from a failure or inability to distinguish the effects of more than one process or factor upon the observed outcomes (Last 1995). Any factor that can cause or prevent the outcome of interest can confound the interpretation of other factors under study, unless it is possible to adjust the observations for the effects of confounding factors. For example, because smoking contributes to many different types of cancer, studies investigating other risk factors for these cancer types would need to account for the confounding effect of smoking behaviour on the observed cancer outcomes. Confounding can be a substantial source of error, and recognizing sources of confounding can be difficult. One of the WHO criteria for supporting causation was study design, because some designs deal with systematic errors better than others. Cohort and experimental studies can achieve lower systematic errors. Table 6.3 compares the bias and confounding factors of ecological, cross-sectional, case-control, and cohort studies, and the time and cost required for each type of study.

Table 6.3 Comparison of Observational Study Designs

	Ecological	Cross-Sectional	Case-Control	Cohort
Likelihood of:				
– Selection bias	NA	Medium	High	Low
– Recall bias	NA	High	High	Low
– Loss to follow-up	NA	NA	Low	High
– Confounding	High	Medium	Medium	Low
Time Required	Low	Medium	Medium	High
Cost	Low	Medium	Medium	High

Source: Beaglehole et al. 1993, Table 3.6

Often, greater weight is placed on confidence intervals and statistical significance than is warranted. Confidence intervals only account for the random error, not the systematic errors from bias and confounding. Media reporting of epidemiological studies often ignores this fact when discussing the significance of their outcomes (Taubes 1995). When a 95% confidence interval is used as the basis for statistical significance, it suggests less than 5% chance that the RR different from 1 could have been measured when the true RR=1. The more outcomes measured, the greater the likelihood of finding a statistically significant outcome. Specifying the hypothesis before performing a study is essential in this regard. Data dredging (i.e., looking for a significant association) after all the data are collected is very likely to find at least one statistically significant association.

This concept of prior hypothesis can be illustrated with a golf analogy. If you guess that your ball will land on a blade of grass, your probability of landing on any blade of grass is likely to be high (assuming there is no sand, water, etc.). But if you specify in advance that you will land on a specific blade of grass, the probability of you achieving this is infinitesimal. The same event, a ball landing on the grass, can be interpreted as very likely or very unlikely. This is most relevant for prospective cohort studies that commit to an hypothesis before they begin. The uncertainties of prior hypothesis are harder to argue for retrospective studies. People argue that the evidence already collected was not subject to a prior hypothesis, so that the hypothesis can be changed to fit the observations.

Shlyakhter et al. (1993) attempted to estimate systematic uncertainty using physical measurements from atomic and sub-atomic particle data. Original estimates of the physical measurements, including the confidence intervals, were compared with more recent, presumably more accurate, estimates. By comparing the original estimates with the recent estimates, they could verify whether the originally reported confidence intervals were sufficiently large to include the current estimates that approached the true value. They found that the original confidence intervals were far too narrow and the actual range of the 95% confidence intervals should have been almost twice as large for measures as experimentally verifiable as those encountered in particle physics: "By analogy with physical measurements, the results indicate that the usual 95% confidence intervals in epidemiology and environmental studies should be expanded to account for unsuspected systematic error" (Shlyakhter et al. 1993, 310). As epidemiological measures are harder to verify than those in particle physics, the case for larger confidence intervals is even more compelling in epidemiology.

The Measurement section (p. 119) explained how the population attributable risk (PAR) is a more important indicator of public health than relative risk (RR). However, if a PAR is low, but can be reduced fairly easily, then it may be worth taking action to avoid the risk (e.g., installing signals at crosswalks). Other factors include cost, potential future effects, and who is affected (voluntary vs involuntary risks).

For an association to be causal, it does not necessarily need to have a high RR. If exposures and effects can be measured accurately, then even risk factors with low RRs can have strong associations (e.g., the association between early maternal age of childbirth and reduced breast cancer risk) (Taubes 1995).

One important element in epidemiological studies is the accuracy of exposure estimates. Some, like age of first childbirth for females, are very accurate. Estimates of smoking are less accurate, but most people know approximately how many cigarettes or packs per day or week they smoke. Estimates for diet are usually very inaccurate. Can you remember what you ate last week? What was the fat content? What type of fat was it?

For environmental epidemiology, exposure estimates contribute a large part of the uncertainty. For carcinogens, estimates of exposure need to be made for ten, twenty, or more years earlier. Industrial processes change; different jobs or locations may have huge differences in concentrations. One of the basics of epidemiology and toxicology is the dose-response relationship-that higher exposures (e.g., more cigarettes smoked, more fat content in the diet, or higher and longer exposure to carcinogens) should result in higher risk. If the exposure cannot be measured or estimated accurately, then the uncertainty of the estimates is increased. In particular, not being able to distinguish exposed from unexposed populations or uncertainty about the degree of exposure are often critical limiting constraints in environmental epidemiology studies.

7 Major Individual Risk Factors

Epidemiology identifies risk factors to detect individuals and populations at elevated risk and to determine causes of death. Risk factors in this book are defined as anything apparently or potentially related to increases or decreases in mortality or other health effects. This intentionally broad definition allows for risk factors that may not be the primary, underlying causes of the health effect.

Beaglehole et al. (1993) summarized four factors that play a part in causing a disease:

1. **predisposing factors** may create a state of susceptibility to a disease agent (e.g., age, sex, previous illness);

2. **enabling factors** may favour development of disease (e.g., low income, poor nutrition, bad housing, inadequate medical care);

3. **precipitating factors** include exposure to a specific disease agent;

4. **reinforcing factors** involve repeated exposure to the disease agent.

There are two ways to summarize information on risk factors. The first is to look at individual risk factors and identify which causes of death they affect. The second is to start with a cause of death and identify the individual risk factors associated with it.

Ideally, working from individual risk factors towards the cause of death can be combined with reviewing the causes of death in relation to associated individual risk factors. Moore (1985) was able to combine these two methods into a large table with a list of risk factors along the top and causes of death along the sides. A shortened version of this summary table is included in Appendix 4. Moore (1985) divided his list of risk factors into four categories based on Lalonde (1974): human biology, environment, lifestyle, and health care. For this book, four similar categories were selected:

1. **biological factors** include predisposing factors;

2. **lifestyle / behavioural factors** include enabling, precipitating, and reinforcing factors;

3. **societal factors** include enabling factors;

4. **environmental factors** include precipitating and reinforcing factors.

We have broadened Lalonde's fourth category, health care, and labelled it societal. The usual type of risk factor (according to Beaglehole et al. 1993) is shown for each category as well.

Table 7.1 ◆ Individual Risk Factors Relating to Health

Biological	Lifestyle/Behavioural	Societal	Environmental
• Age	• Smoking	• Education Level	• Air Pollution
• Sex	• Alcohol	• Economic Status	• Water Pollution
• Genetics (Heredity)	• Drugs	• Employment Status	• Food Additives and
• Blood Pressure,	• Diet	• Marital Status	Contaminants
Cholesterol Levels,	• Exercise	• Occupation	• Chemicals
and Diabetes Risk	• Weight	• Geographic Area/	• Radiation Levels
Factors	• Sexual and	Region	• Natural Disasters
	Reproductive Factors	• Medical	
	• Risk-Avoidance	• Transportation	
	• Personality	• Recreational	
	• Stress	• Other	

A list of individual risk factors is shown in Table 7.1. Often, it is the combination of risk factors that greatly increases a person's risk, rather than a single risk (e.g., for cardiovascular disease, if the person is older, male, smokes, has high blood pressure, and is a diabetic). However, many people who develop disease or have accidents have none of the known risk factors.

Biological Risk Factors

Biological risk factors are summarized in four subsections: by age, sex, genetics and heredity, and health. The two basic biological risk factors are age and sex. Age, sex, and genetics and heredity are predisposing risk factors, i.e., ones that cannot be changed. The final risk factor in this section is a general one, overall health, which includes the health risks of blood pressure, cholesterol, and diabetes.

Age Risk Factors

Age is clearly one of the strongest health risk factors. Though a complete range of health status (healthy people through to those dying and deceased) occurs at all age levels, on average, there is a consistent and exponential increase in mortality and other health effects starting in the teens. This trend was shown in Part One, Direct Evidence (see Figure 3.6).

Age is such a strong risk because individual organs and systems accumulate damage over time, so that the body weakens and becomes more susceptible to injury and disease as it ages.

The overall mortality rate is not the only concern-the percentage of deaths from specific causes is important as well. Even though the mortality rate for accidents is higher at older ages (85+), accidents are not the leading cause of death in that age range. However, accidents are a leading cause of death in young adults. A similar relationship between age and different causes of death occurs for other individual risk factors.

Sex Risk Factors

Although the sex of an individual is not as strongly related to mortality as age, it is still an important and consistent risk factor. There are two basic differences in risk factors associated with sex: anatomical and non-anatomical risk factors.

Anatomical differences occur for causes of death related to the reproductive system. Men may die of prostate and testicular cancer, while women may die of breast and ovarian cancer. (Men also die of breast cancer, but at a rate over 100 times lower than women.) In addition, hormonal differences have been linked with mortality, because before menopause, female hormones help protect women against cardiovascular disease. In the case of breast cancer, hormonal differences may explain the large gap between men and women for cancer at an anatomical site common to both sexes.

Non-anatomical differences help to explain the increased mortality in men for most causes of death. Some of these differences are associated with lifestyle/behavioural and societal risk factors in addition to biology.

Genetic (Heredity) Risk Factors

We must distinguish between heredity and genetics. Heredity is the accurate transmission of characteristic traits and qualities from parents to their children in the form of genetic characteristics that are correctly transcribed in the offspring. Congenital defects, one of the leading causes of death in infants, are mostly genetic, but are not necessarily related to heredity because they can arise from errors in genetic transcription from the parent to the offspring. Genetic factors may be considered to be broader than hereditary risk factors.

Genetics are important in the development and contribute to the susceptibility or resistance to cardiovascular disease (WHO 1994): "the risk of heart disease in a given individual or community reflects the interplay between genetic susceptibility to disease and environmental factors such as diet, physical exercise, ambient temperature, and smoking habits" (Swales and de Bono 1993, 12).

Genetics plays a role in many forms of cancers. The US National Research Council (1994) identified several factors related to genetics that may affect cancer susceptibility: carcinogen metabolism, DNA-adduct formation, and DNA-repair rates. DNA adducts are sites on the genetic code that are damaged by the attachment of a reactive chemical compound. These adducts can give rise to subsequent errors in replicating DNA when cells divide or in reading the genetic code for guiding cellular metabolism. The National Research Council noted that:

- Variations of several thousand have been observed for some metabolic activities;

- Inter-individual and intertissue variation for forming DNA adducts ranges from a factor of ten to 150 among humans;

- five-fold variations have been observed in DNA repair rates.

A recent medical advance is to identify genes associated with increased risk for various diseases (notably cancer). People who have these gene sequences can have greater RRs than those without these sequences. Most of the discoveries to date have been for less common gene sequences. However, in the future, this research could help identify people more susceptible to common cancers, perhaps leading to more focussed prevention. This genetic research raises important ethical issues relating to genetic testing of fetuses, and identifying and notifying patients with incurable diseases.

Heredity depends on genetics, being the transmission of genetically determined characteristics from parents to children. Specific examples include physical characteristics such as eye colour and blood type.

Heredity appears to be a major factor in childhood and early adulthood cancers, but likely affects susceptibility to all cancers (Ames et al. 1995). A specific example of this is retinoblastoma, cancer of the eye, typically found in young children. Parents with susceptible genes have a 50% chance of passing it on to their offspring.

Blood Pressure, Cholesterol Levels, and Diabetes Risk Factors

This category highlights some of the risks associated with blood pressure, cholesterol levels, and diabetes. In addition to these, a general state of health is closely linked with other health effects. Poor health can increase the susceptibility of the body, which can allow other diseases or ill effects to occur. An extreme example of this is AIDS, which weakens the immune system, allowing otherwise innocuous diseases to ravage the body.

Blood pressure is a measure of hypertension, which was identified as a health risk by the US insurance industry in the late 1950s (Society of Actuaries 1980). High blood pressure can lead to heart attacks, stroke, blindness, kidney failure, and can double the risk of heart disease. High blood pressure can be present without symptoms and, unfortunately, researchers do not know the cause in the majority of cases. Overall, age-adjusted risk of stroke among hypertensives (with high blood pressure) compared with normotensives (with normal blood pressure) is 3.1 for men and 2.9 for women. There is good clinical evidence that treating isolated systolic hypertension in those over sixty years of age decreases the incidence of cardiovascular disease (Heart and Stroke Foundation of Canada 1995).

Cholesterol is mostly produced by our livers; only one-third comes from the food we eat. Diet, heredity, smoking, and weight influence our cholesterol level. The type of cholesterol and fat is important as well. Serum cholesterol levels increase with a higher intake of saturated fats, decrease with a higher intake of polyunsaturated fats, and are not changed by monounsaturated fats. Higher levels of low-density lipoprotein (LDL) have been associated with a higher cardiovascular disease risk, while higher levels of high-density lipoprotein (HDL) have been associated with a lower cardiovascular disease risk. Therefore, the amounts of LDL and HDL relative to total cholesterol are more important than the total cholesterol itself (Willett 1994). A 2% decrease in ischaemic heart disease has been associated with a 1% lowering of blood cholesterol in middle-aged men. Women who have low levels of HDL and high triglyceride levels have been associated with increased cardiovascular risk (Heart and Stroke Foundation of Canada 1995).

Some 4% of men and 5% of women report having diabetes (Heart and Stroke Foundation of Canada 1995). Diabetes (specifically diabetes mellitus) is a significant cause of death on its own (over 5,000 deaths in 1994), and is also a major risk factor for cardiovascular disease. Several risk factors are associated with diabetes, including blood glucose, lipids, blood pressure, and body weight.

Lifestyle/Behavioural Risk Factors

Lifestyle factors can be enabling, precipitating, and/or reinforcing. Most of the risk factors in this category are theoretically modifiable. However, the difficulty in actually changing these risk factors can be substantial (e.g., those with a genetic component).

Smoking Risk Factors

Smoking is the single largest, modifiable risk factor for mortality in Canada. Smoking is responsible for earlier mortality from cardiovascular disease, respiratory diseases, and many types of cancer, such as lung, mouth, pharynx, larynx, oesophagus, pancreas, bladder, kidney and, possibly, uterine cervix and colon (Ames et al. 1995; Illing and Kaiserman 1995; Miller 1995). Unlike several other risk factors, where moderate exposure does not increase health risks, even a moderate use of tobacco increases health risks. In addition, the addictive nature of tobacco prevents many people from limiting their smoking.

Among Canadians over the age of fifteen in 1990, an estimated 31% of males and 28% of females were current smokers. Back in 1965, the rates were approximately 60% for males and 38% for females. In 1990, Quebec had the highest level of current smokers (34%) and British Columbia the lowest (26%) (Health Canada 1993). There are fairly strong differences in smoking rates depending on education and income, which are discussed in Societal Risk Factors (p. 146).

Due to the tremendous influence of smoking on health, epidemiological studies of most risk factors must be adjusted for the effects of smoking, much as they standardize for age and sex. Sometimes, studies will look only at the effects on non-smokers to avoid confounding.

According to the Nurses Health Study and Framingham Study, one year after quitting smoking, people reduce their cardiovascular disease risk by 50%; after five years, they have the same risk as people who have never smoked (Heart and Stroke Foundation of Canada 1995). However, the same reduction does not occur for some cancers: ".. at least for lung cancer, and possibly other tobacco-associated lung cancers as well, the risk acquired by smoking remains at about the same level after cessation, and does not fall to normal. Thus even though many people have given up smoking, with benefits relating to no further increase in their risk, many cancers are now occurring in ex-smokers" (Miller 1995, 656).

Most estimates of health risks relating to risk factors are not available strictly for Canada. However, there have been several recent articles estimating the impact of smoking on health. Despite the large number of studies on smoking, there are currently no reliable estimates on the average number of years of life expectancy lost due to smoking.

Illing and Kaiserman (1995) used a variety of information to estimate smoking-attributable mortality (SAM) for Canadians in 1991 (Table 7.2). Illing and Kaiserman used direct evidence and RRs to estimate the number of deaths for twenty-two smoking-related diseases. They used additional evidence to estimate the number of deaths from fires and from passive smoking. Their figures report deaths down to an individual level, because the calculated estimates were not rounded off to reflect the level of confidence in the predictions. At most, estimated figures should not be quoted with more than two or three significant figures (e.g., reporting a total of 41,400, not 41,408), and for predictive risk estimates, only one significant figure is appropriate.

Illing and Kaiserman's report estimates that the SAM is approximately 26% of all deaths for males and 15% of all deaths for females. Separate estimates were included for the Atlantic Provinces, Quebec, Ontario, the Prairie Provinces, and British Columbia. For males, the SAM percentage for the regions ranged from 23% (Prairie Provinces) to 30% (Quebec), and for females, from 14% (Prairie Provinces) to 17% (British Columbia).

Comparing these SAM percentages with the percentage of smokers highlights the impact of smoking. If 60% of males smoked in the past, a SAM of 26% for all men implies that almost half of male smokers have their lives shortened by smoking. A similar conclusion could be made for female smokers.

Table 7.3 summarizes several studies that have estimated deaths attributed to smoking in Canada. Ellison et al. (1995) used the PAR from smoking and multiplied it by the total number of deaths from all causes. This method assumes that all the excess deaths of smokers were due only to smoking. This assumption overestimates the number of deaths attributable to smoking if smokers have a greater number of non-smoking related risk factors than non-

Table 7.2 ◆ Smoking-Attributable Mortality (SAM) by Disease Category, Canada, 1991

Disease Category	ICD-9	Males	Females	Both
Adult Diseases (35+ yrs of age)		**27,646**	**13,172**	**40,818**
Neoplasms		11,435	4,833	16,268
Lip, oral cavity, pharynx	140–149	673	174	847
Oesophagus	150	579	225	804
Pancreas	157	358	441	799
Larynx	161	355	90	445
Trachea, lung, bronchus	162	8,739	3,583	12,322
Cervix uteri	180	–	136	136
Urinary bladder	188	403	135	538
Kidney, other urinary	189	328	49	377
Cardiovascular Diseases		11,003	5,390	16,393
Rheumatic heart disease	390–398	41	56	97
Hypertension	401–405	123	134	257
Ischaemic heart disease	410–414			
– Ages 35–64		2,635	644	3,279
– Ages 65+		3,769	2,037	5,806
Pulmonary heart disease	415–417	99	76	175
Other heart disease	420–429	1,231	871	2,102
Cerebrovascular disease	430–438			
– Ages 35–64		401	351	752
– Ages 65+		1,178	319	1,497
Atherosclerosis	440	467	473	940
Aortic aneurysm	441	762	259	1,021
Other arterial disease	442–448	297	170	467
Respiratory Diseases		5,208	2,949	8,157
Respiratory tuberculosis	010–012	21	11	32
Pneumonia/influenza	480–487	912	966	1,878
Bronchitis/emphysema	491–492	962	376	1,338
Asthma	493	61	65	126
Chronic airways obstruction	496	3,252	1,531	4,783
Paediatric Diseases (<1 yr of age)		**101**	**70**	**171**
Low birth weight	765	19	17	36
Respiratory distress syndrome	769	23	14	37
Respiratory conditions—newborn	770	17	12	29
Sudden infant death syndrome	798.0	42	27	69
Fire Deaths (all ages)		**54**	**31**	**85**
Passive Smoking Deaths		**66**	**268**	**334**
TOTAL		**27,867**	**13,541**	**41,408***
SAM crude rate per 100,000		**210.2**	**99.2**	**153.9**
SAM as % of all deaths		**26.4%**	**15.0%**	**21.2%**

Note: *These estimates have not been rounded off in relation to the level of confidence in the predictions. At most, the figures should not be quoted with more than two or three significant figures and for passive smoking deaths only one significant figure is appropriate.

Source: Illing and Kaiserman 1995, Table 1

Table 7.3 ◆ Estimated Deaths Attributed to Smoking in Canada

Study	Year	Males	Females	Both
Illing and Kaiserman 1995	1991	27,867	13,541	41,408
Ellison et al. 1995	1991	31,698	13,367	45,065
	2000	30,359	16,551	46,910
Peto et al. 1992	1995	31,000	17,000	48,000
Single et al. 1996	1992	23,100	10,400	33,500

smokers (e.g., excessive alcohol consumption). Coincidentally, both Illing and Kaiserman and Ellison et al. used 1991 figures for their estimates; Ellison et al. (1995) estimated 12% more male deaths in 1991 than Illing and Kaiserman, but each had a similar number of female deaths.

Peto et al. (1992) used a cruder method to estimate smoking-related mortality in developed countries including Canada. Peto et al. used an indirect method, based on age- and sex-specific lung cancer rates, to estimate tobacco-related deaths from other diseases. This study estimated that smoking had killed 37% of Canadians aged thirty-five to sixty-nine and 26% of Canadians overall.

A recent report (Single et al. 1996) estimated that in 1992, 33,500 deaths were attributable to smoking. Single et al. stated that they estimated a lower number of deaths than Illing and Kaisermann (1995), partly because they used a lower RR for male lung cancer (thirteen versus twenty-two).

Based on the estimates in Table 7.3, the range of deaths attributed to smoking was at least +/- 15% (33,500 to 48,000) for similar years (1992 and 1995). This range indicates the degree of uncertainty associated with smoking risk: likely the most thoroughly studied and fully characterized risk factor.

Villeneuve and Mao (1994) focused on the probability of Canadians developing lung cancer based on their smoking status. They estimated that 17.2% of current male smokers will eventually develop lung cancer, as against 1.3% of non-smokers. For females, 11.6% will eventually develop lung cancer, as against 1.4% of non-smokers.

A survey by Stewart et al. (1995) of maternal smoking was conducted in 1983 and 1992 in the Ottawa-Carleton region. In 1983, 28.5% of women smoked after the first trimester, compared with 18.7% in 1992. Gradients were observed by age, education, marital status, and income. Pregnant women who smoke have higher rates of miscarriage, still-birth, premature birth, babies below average weight, and infant mortality soon after birth.

A high alcohol consumption combined with smoking is linked to cancers of the mouth, larynx, oesophagus, and upper respiratory tract. Alcohol and smoking apparently act synergistically and greatly increase the cancer risk at these sites compared with the risk from each factor alone (Doll and Peto 1981).

Smokeless tobacco, which has been gaining popularity in North America, increases the risk of mouth cancers and may increase the chance of heart attacks and strokes.

Second-hand Smoke

Second-hand smoke, also called passive smoke, affects non-smokers. Second hand smoke consists of inhaled smoke that has been exhaled by the smoker and sidestream smoke that comes directly from the smoker's cigarette. Although quantitative estimates of the health risks of smoking are well characterized, quantitative health risk estimates for second-hand smoke are very uncertain. It seems reasonable to assume that second-hand smoke could be a health risk to non-smokers, partly because the vast majority of people's time is spent indoors. Second-hand tobacco smoke contains the same noxious mix of chemicals as inhaled smoke and a substantial proportion of inhaled or sidestream smoke is released into the air for others to breathe. However, compared with the overwhelming evidence on smoking, the evidence for the health risks of second-hand smoke is relatively weak.

The mortality estimated for passive smoking is relatively low. The relationship between lung cancer, which poses the highest RR for smoking, and passive smoking has been more widely studied than any other aspect of passive smoking. Case-control studies of married couples, where one smokes and the other does not, have been commonly used to study this issue. The most widely quoted study associated with second-hand smoke estimated 3,000 non-smoker lung cancer deaths in the US (US EPA 1993). This study also estimated that 150,000 to 300,000 annual cases of lower respiratory tract infections related to passive smoking, and passive smoking worsened the conditions of 200,000 to 1,000,000 asthmatic children. Illing and Kaiserman (1995) estimated over 300 passive smoking deaths in Canada, mostly for females. The uncertainty in these estimates is substantially greater than the +/- 15% uncertainty range for total mortality estimates among smokers. Although the numerical estimates are uncertain, second-hand smoke is important because exposure to it dwarfs any other non-occupational source of indoor air pollution.

Alcohol Risk Factors

In a 1994 survey, 58% of adult Canadians reported that they were current drinkers (at least one drink per month), 21% drank on occasion, 12% were former drinkers, and 10% had never consumed alcohol (Statistics Canada 1995B).

The health effects of alcohol are complicated because there are both negative and positive associations with mortality. Alcohol is involved in many types of fatal accidents, most notably motor vehicle (see p. 165) and poisoning. In 1994, accidental alcohol poisoning was associated with the deaths of ninety-seven people (seventy-eight males, nineteen females) (Statistics Canada 1996A). Negative health effects include possible inflammation and cirrhosis of the liver and liver cancer (Ames et al. 1995). Alcohol is also a risk factor in suicide, as well as contributing to serious individual, domestic, and societal problems. The latter are outside the scope of this study, but must be recognized as substantial.

On the positive side, low to moderate alcohol consumption is related to lower mortality from heart disease. Since the late 1970s studies have found the consumption of alcohol associated with a decrease in mortality, specifically from heart disease. A famous study (St. Leger et al. 1979) that compared national rates in eighteen countries for ischaemic heart disease and wine consumption showed that countries with an increased wine consumption had lower heart disease rates. Although this was an ecological study, the weakest type of study and subject to ecological fallacy, hundreds of subsequent studies have generally found a lower rate of mortality from heart disease associated with moderate alcohol consumption. However, the beneficial effects apparently only apply to some people. The following quote from a recent study on women supports similar findings in men: "In conclusion, these findings indicate that for women as a group light-to-moderate alcohol consumption confers a significant overall survival advantage. Among younger women and those without risk factors for coronary heart disease, however, light-to-moderate alcohol consumption is not associated with a reduction in total mortality and heavier drinking is associated with a substantial increase in mortality. For older women and women with coronary risk factors, light-to-moderate alcohol consumption is associated with a reduction in total mortality, although with heavier intake mortality is increased" (Fuchs et al. 1995, 1250).

Health professionals generally advise that no alcohol should be consumed by pregnant women. Alcohol can readily cross the placental barrier and high levels of alcohol consumption during pregnancy can lead to fetal alcohol syndrome in the baby.

Drug Risk Factors

Mortality can result from drug overdosing (poisoning) and hormonally related drug use. Information on poisoning comes from direct evidence (death certificates), while information on hormonally related drug use is based on epidemiological study.

In 1994, 71% of males and 83% of females reported using at least one prescription or over-the-counter medication in the previous month. Pain relievers (62%), cough or cold remedies (15%), and allergy medications (10%) were the most common (Statistics Canada 1995B). Drug poisoning data is related to direct evidence that includes data for poisoning from drugs, medications, or biologicals. Poisoning was listed as the cause of death for 668 people in 1994; 245 of these deaths were caused by opiates and related narcotics. These figures do not include people who committed suicide using drugs.

An estimated 21% of women aged between fifteen and thirty-nine used birth control pills in 1994, and 15% of women aged forty-five and over used menopausal hormones (Statistics Canada 1995B). With a high hormonal dosage of oral contraceptives, the risk of fatal and non-fatal myocardial infarction is estimated to increase two to four fold. However, with lower dose preparations (those now used), the absolute increase in risk is small. On the positive side, oral contraceptives are associated with lowering ovarian cancer risk. However, concurrent smoking and oral contraceptive use substantially elevates the risk of myocardial infarction (Heart and Stroke Foundation of Canada 1995). Postmenopausal oestrogen replacement seems to lower the risk of fatal and non-fatal heart attacks by one-third to one-half. However, since oestrogen replacement can increase the risk of endometrial cancer, a low dose progestin should be combined with the oestrogen. An estimated 5,250 lives are saved annually per 100,000 oestrogen users aged from fifty to seventy-five, and 333 lives annually from ischaemic heart disease and stroke per 100,000 oestrogen users aged between sixty-five and seventy-five years (Heart and Stroke Foundation of Canada 1995).

Nutrition Risk Factors

Nutrition and diet are very important risk factors but remain one of the most uncertain with respect to specific details and mechanisms. The importance of nutrition is suggested by the large difference in international rates for various causes of mortality. However, other explanations such as genetic differences can confound interpretation of this information. Yet when people migrate to new countries, their disease and mortality patterns often begin to match those of the new country. Although environmental factors play some role in these findings, many studies point to the importance of nutrition.

This abstract of a recent article on nutrition and health provides a good summary of the issue:

Many recent studies have implicated dietary factors in the cause and prevention of important diseases, including cancer, coronary heart disease, birth defects and cataracts. There is strong evidence that vegetables and fruits protect against these diseases; however, the active constituents are incompletely identified. Whether fat per se is a major cause of disease is a question still under debate, although saturated and partially hydrogenated fats probably increase the risk of coronary heart disease. One clear conclusion is that many individuals in the United States have suboptimal diets and that the potential for disease prevention by improved nutrition is substantial (Willett 1994, 532).

Nearly 200 studies in the epidemiological literature show a consistent association of diet with cancer incidence. The lowest quarter of dietary intake for fruits and vegetables has roughly twice the cancer rate for most types of cancer (lung, larynx, oral cavity, oesophagus, stomach, colon and rectum, bladder, pancreas, cervix, and ovary). However, only 9% of Americans eat the recommended level of two fruits and three vegetables a day (Ames et al. 1995).

The National Research Council in the US made nine recommendations in its large report on diet and health, which focused on chronic disease risk (US NRC 1989). These recommendations are similar to, but more detailed than those outlined in Canada's Guide to Healthy Eating (Health Canada 1995).

- Reduce total fat intake to 30% or less of calories. Reduce saturated fatty acid intake to less than 10% of calories, and the intake of cholesterol to less than 300 mg daily. The intake of fat and cholesterol can be reduced by substituting fish, poultry without skin, lean meats, and low- or non-fat dairy products for fatty meats and whole-milk dairy products; by choosing more vegetables, fruits, cereals, and legumes; and by limiting oils, fats, egg yolks, and fried and other fatty foods.

- Every day eat five or more servings of a combination of vegetables and fruits, especially green and yellow vegetables and citrus fruits. Also, increase intake of starches and other complex carbohydrates by eating six or more daily servings of a combination of breads, cereals, and legumes.

- Maintain protein intake at moderate levels.

- Balance food intake and physical activity to maintain appropriate body weight.

- The committee does not recommend alcohol consumption. For those who drink alcoholic beverages, the committee recommends limiting consumption to the equivalent of less than 1 oz of pure alcohol in a single day. This is the equivalent of two cans of beer, two small glasses of wine, or two average cocktails. Pregnant women should avoid alcoholic beverages.

- Limit total daily intake of salt (sodium chloride) to 6 g or less. Limit the use of salt in cooking and avoid adding it to food at the table. Salty, highly processed, salt-preserved, and salt-pickled foods should be consumed sparingly.

- Maintain adequate calcium intake.

- Avoid taking dietary supplements in excess of the RDA (recommended daily allowance) in any one day.

- Maintain an optimal intake of fluoride, particularly during the years of primary and secondary tooth formation and growth.

The US NRC (1989) concluded that there was not enough information to quantify the contribution of diet to overall cancer risk or to determine whether following any of the recommendations would reduce this risk. The US NRC did note that the first recommendation, reducing fat intake, was likely to have the greatest impact. Willett (1994) observed that the type of fat is important (monounsaturated or polyunsaturated fats are preferable to

**Table 7.4 ◆ Estimated Effects of Dietary Actions
on Reducing Cancer Incidence**

Cancer Site	PAR	Action*
Colo-rectal	60%	Reduce fat and increase vegetable consumption
Breast	27%	Reduce fat and increase vegetable consumption
Prostate	20%	Reduce fat consumption
Stomach	80%	Reduce nitrite in cured meats and salt-preserved foods, and increase fruit and vegetable consumption
Oral	10%	Increase fruit and vegetable consumption
Pancreas	30%	Reduce sugar and increase vegetable consumption
Kidney	30%	Reduce fat consumption
Ovary	30%	Reduce fat consumption

Note: All PAR estimates are based on males except for breast and ovary cancers.
*Miller noted that these actions could not fully eliminate the cancer incidence to the PAR level stated.

Source: Adapted from Miller 1992, S36

saturated fat) and suggested that increased fruit and vegetable consumption could have a greater impact than lowering fat intake.

Miller (1992) provided an excellent overview of risk factors associated with cancer. Table 7.4 presents some PAR values that Miller assigned to diet-related risk factors for individual cancer sites. The PAR is the incidence (not mortality) of a disease in a population exposed to a risk factor.

Exercise Risk Factors

In 1994, 56% of Canadians reported they were inactive in leisure time, 27% were moderately active, and 17% had physically active leisure pursuits (Statistics Canada 1995B). The category of physical activity was based on the average hours of energy cost of the physical activity. Another survey found that 43% of Canadians were inactive in their leisure time (Heart and Stroke Foundation of Canada 1995).

Physical inactivity, whether occupational or recreational, is associated with an increased risk of CHD independent of other risk factors (WHO 1994). Most of these risks relate to heart disease, with some incidence of stroke (Heart and Stroke Foundation of Canada 1995). Regular exercise is associated with lower blood pressure and less obesity, which is linked to diabetes.

Weight Risk Factors

The body mass index (BMI) is often used as an index of an individual's weight. The BMI equals a person's weight in kilograms divided by the square of his or her height in metres. In a 1994 survey of Canadians aged between twenty and sixty-four, 23% were overweight (BMI 28 and over); 23% had some excess weight (BMI between 25 and 27); 43% were in the acceptable range (BMI between 20 and 24); and 9% were underweight (BMI less than 20). Of those overweight, 25% were male and 20% were female (Statistics Canada 1995B).

In an editorial in the New England Journal of Medicine, Byers (1995) asks and attempts to answer three questions about the relation between body weight and mortality:

1. *Is it harmful to be overweight? The answer is "yes," with some qualifications. Studies show an increase in mortality above a BMI 27. However, differences occur between sexes and the area of the body where the fat is located.*

2. *Within the range of "normal" weights, is it better to be thinner? The answer is "no."*

3. *Does it matter if weight changes over time? The answer is "yes" and "no." Over a few years, losses and variations in weight may be harmful, but small weight gains are not. However, over longer periods, moderate weight change (+/- 10 kg) is not harmful, but major weight gain (over 10 kg) is associated with increased mortality.*

A study on weight based on the Nurses Health Study cohort in the US found that among non-smokers, the RR of women with a BMI greater than 32 for cardiovascular diseases was 4.1 (95% CI 2.1–7.7), and for cancer was 2.1 (95% CI 1.4–3.2), compared with women with a BMI less than 19 (Manson et al. 1995).

There is a strong association between nutrition, exercise, diabetes, high blood pressure, cholesterol level, and smoking. Abdominal obesity can lead to an increased risk of ischaemic heart disease. Obesity and abdominal fat distribution are associated with an increased prevalence of diabetes, high blood pressure, and elevated plasma cholesterol. High blood pressure is more than doubled among individuals with abdominal obesity (Heart and Stroke Foundation of Canada 1995).

Sexual and Reproductive Risk Factors

Breast cancer is apparently hormonally related, with a late age of first birth or no births being strong risk factors. Sexual and reproductive factors are also linked to endometrial, ovarian, cervical, and colo-rectal cancer in women. Reducing the number of sexual partners and using barrier contraception should reduce the incidence of cervical cancer and reduce the risk of contracting AIDS (Miller 1995).

Avoiding Risk

Evidence of the toll of injury and death, particularly among young people, has promoted an increased awareness of safety in a variety of areas.

- Motor vehicle safety: choosing a safer mode of transport, and using seatbelts, airbags, ABS (anti-lock braking systems), and helmets (motorcycle and bicycle).

- Medical safety: regular checkups, blood pressure and cholesterol level testing (for cardiovascular disease), pap tests (for cervical cancer), mammograms (for breast cancer), and digital rectal exams (for prostate cancer).

- Fire safety: providing smoke detectors, sprinklers, and fire extinguishers.

- Recreational safety: using life jackets, harnesses, and protective clothing.

- Occupational safety: using protective equipment and safety devices.

An overriding safety theme is education. Most risks can be reduced with proper training in addition to using safety devices. Training includes defensive driving courses, courses on potentially high-risk recreational activities, occupational safety courses (e.g., WHMIS, the Workplace Hazardous Materials Information System), and health courses (e.g., CPR, cardiopulmonary resuscitation).

Personality Risk Factors

Those who race toward death
Those who wait
Those who worry
Jim Morrison of The Doors (1943–1971)

The degree and frequency of risk-taking is related to personality. Some people continually take large risks, while others avoid risks at all costs (which may itself lead to other risks). However, most people are somewhere in-between. Most people take high risks in some areas of their lives and avoid risks in others. Personality is one risk factor that could contribute to the high rates of motor vehicle accidents in young adults, especially young male adults.

Stress Risk Factors

Stress is widely suspected to be a health risk. It is difficult to study the effects of stress on health because stress is hard to define and measure. People in jobs with high stress but low individual control increase their risk of cardiovascular disease (WHO 1994).

Increased stress is associated with an increased heart rate and respiration, and elevated blood pressure, cholesterol, and fat levels. In an effort to cope with stress, people may turn to alcohol and drugs, and so increase their risks.

Multiple Risk Factors

This section looks at the effects of multiple lifestyle risk factors, based on information from a large cohort study.

> *...[W]e can control and modify our life span, the speed of ageing and the risk for major diseases simply by choosing an appropriate life-style* (Hirayama 1990, 1).

This quotation summarizes the results of a cohort study in Japan that followed 270,000 adults aged forty and above for sixteen years (1966–1982). Unlike many prospective studies that focused mostly on smoking, the Japanese study examined lifestyle issues as well.

Hirayama divided the causes of death into cancer deaths and all other deaths. A total of forty-four possible causes of death were analysed. Seven lifestyle variables were examined, including consumption of meat, fish, milk, green-yellow vegetables, soybean paste soup, cigarettes, and alcohol. RRs with 90% confidence intervals were calculated for each of the seven lifestyle variables, which compared daily vs non-daily exposure for each lifestyle variable. The choice of a 90% confidence level is weaker than the more conventional 95% confidence level, which demands a stronger association to conclude that any association is statistically significant.

Table 7.5 summarizes Hirayama's calculations and lists the number of causes of death that were significant at the 90% confidence interval level for each lifestyle variable. Cigarette consumption was associated with an increased RR in twenty-nine of the forty-four possible causes of death analysed. Green-yellow vegetables were associated with a decreased RR in fifteen of the forty-four possible causes of death and an increased RR in only one.

Table 7.6 shows mortality rates for people with different lifestyle variables (smoking, meat, green-yellow vegetables, and drinkers). The absence or presence of a dot indicates whether or not the person is a daily user of the variable. The most significant, but not surprising finding, is that the mortality rate for non-smokers (No.s 1–8) is lower than the mortality rate for smokers (No.s 9–16). A less substantial finding is that green-yellow vegetables lower the mortality rate, even in smokers.

Smoking, alcohol, and meat consumption actually shift the mortality rate upward at all ages by varying amounts. These habits do not only have an effect later in life, but also increase mortality earlier in life. However, because age is such a substantial risk factor, more people are affected later in life. The shift varies from five to fifteen (or more) years for selected causes. Eating green-yellow vegetables decreased the observed upward shift.

Table 7.5 ◆ Summary of RRs for Lifestyle Variables Found to be Statistically Significant for Affecting 44 Health Conditions

Daily Consumption of	RR Significance*	
	Below 1.0	Above 1.0
Cigarettes	0 of 44	29 of 44
Alcohol	3 of 44	18 of 44
Milk	8 of 44	10 of 44
Soybean Paste Soup	9 of 44	7 of 44
Meat	13 of 44	5 of 44
Fish	14 of 44	4 of 44
Green-Yellow Vegetables	15 of 44	1 of 44

* 10% Significance Level

Source: Hirayama 1990, Table 13

Table 7.6 ◆ Age-Standardized Mortality Rates for Combinations of Lifestyle Variables

No.	S	M	G	D	No. of Deaths	All Cancers Age-Standardized Rate	All Causes Age-Standardized Rate
1					1,006	306	1,542
2				◆	259	347	1,478
3			◆		2,738	324	1,482
4			◆	◆	916	357	1,507
5		◆			30	471	1,390
6		◆		◆	16	367	1,159
7		◆	◆		169	352	1,321
8		◆	◆	◆	98	450	1,629
9	◆				3,797	548	1,901
10	◆			◆	2,279	574	2,121
11	◆		◆		8,536	522	1,830
11	◆		◆	◆	5,569	595	2,064
13	◆	◆			187	586	1,937
14	◆	◆		◆	198	808	2,261
15	◆	◆	◆		596	508	1,644
16	◆	◆	◆	◆	595	542	1,834

Note: S-smoking; M-meat consumption; G-green-yellow vegetable consumption; D-drinking alcohol.

Source: Hirayama 1990, Table 31

Societal Risk Factors

Education Level Risk Factors

Individuals with a lower level of education (less than six years of education) are more likely to have one major risk factor for cardiovascular disease than those with a higher level (more than twelve years of education). Men who have less than six years of education have a 77% risk of having one of the major risk factors for cardiovascular disease vs 58% for men with a higher level of education. The figures for women are 86% vs 53% (Heart and Stroke Foundation of Canada 1995).

In a 1994 survey of Canadians' self-reported health, 72% of people with a post-secondary or diploma education reported excellent or very good health, while only 48% of people with less than a secondary education reported excellent or very good health (Statistics Canada 1995B). These results must be interpreted in relation to individual perceptions of satisfaction with personal circumstances.

The estimated percentage of current smokers over the age of fifteen divided by individual maximum education level in 1990 was elementary (34%), secondary (31%), college (27%), and university (18%) (Health Canada 1993). Clearly, smoking prevalence is lower with higher levels of education. The effects of smoking are likely to be a substantial contributor to any association between health status and education.

Economic Status Risk Factors

Socio-economic status is a widely studied risk factor, often in relation to education level and lifestyle/behavioural risk factors. An older report by Health and Welfare Canada looked at mortality by income level in urban Canada and concluded that "Despite the problems which arise in the interpretation of differential mortality by income level, it is clear that Canadians in lower income levels did experience substantially higher mortality rates for most diseases than persons with higher incomes" (Health and Welfare Canada 1980, 3).

The association between economic status and health is widely accepted and a causal linkage is supported by a variety of evidence. Economic status, usually measured by household or individual income, is the commonly used measure for dividing a population into groups based on socio-economic status. Studies in several countries have shown that higher household incomes are associated with a declining annual mortality risk, except at the highest incomes levels (Graham et al. 1992). Increased income is related to better nutrition, sanitation, health care, and education (Keeney 1990).

In the 1994 survey of Canadians' self-reported health mentioned above, 77% of males and 74% of females in the highest household income group reported excellent or very good health, while 52% of males and 51% of females in the lowest income group reported excellent or very good health (Statistics Canada 1995B).

Two articles looked at mortality and other health outcomes relating to the income level of Canadians (Wilkins et al. 1989; Wilkins et al. 1991). The articles used the metropolitan areas of Canada, account for approximately 60% of the population, and divided the areas by census tract into income quintiles (using 20% increments). Some of the results, based on 1986 information, were as follows:

- life expectancies 5.6 years greater for males and 1.8 years greater for females in the highest compared with the lowest income quintiles;

- for males, the age-standardized mortality rates per 10,000 by income quintile (highest to lowest) were: q1 (57), q2 (60), q3 (64), q4 (69), q5 (86);

- for females, the age-standardized mortality rates per 10,000 by income quintile (highest to lowest) were: q1 (49), q2 (50), q3 (49), q4 (50), q5 (56);

- for males, the RR of higher mortality between the lowest and highest income quintiles for the major causes of death were: infectious (1.90), cancer (1.40), cardiovascular (1.35), respiratory (1.67), external (1.88), and for all causes (1.52);

- for females, the RR of higher mortality between the lowest and highest income quintiles for the major causes of death were infectious (1.24), cancer (1.47), cardiovascular (1.11), respiratory (1.03), external (1.43), and for all causes (1.13);

- the RR for infant mortality and low birth weight between the highest and lowest income quintiles were 1.7 and 1.4, respectively.

In summary, there were consistent trends for several measures of health based on income level. These trends were strongest in males and for the lowest (poorest) income quintile.

The estimated percentage of current smokers over the age of fifteen divided by income in 1990 was as follows: very poor (36%), other poor (32%), lower middle (34%), upper middle (29%), and rich (25%) (Health Canada 1993).

Hirayama, whose work on lifestyle risk factors was summarized above, downplayed the importance of socio-economic factors: "In summary, although socioeconomic status is an important determinant of mortality from various causes of death, the influence of selected life-style variables on risk of dying from these causes is mostly independent of socioeconomic status" (Hirayama 1990, 120).

Race Risk Factors

Race is not recorded on death certificates in Canada. However, race is recorded in the US and most vital statistics include information by race: "Vital statistics in the U.S. report information by race in addition to age and gender... In the U.S., blacks have a higher mortality rate for most causes. Rates of mortality in blacks are greater than twice that of whites for diabetes, hypertension, homicide, maternal mortality and infant mortality. These differences are related to many other risk factors including diet, lifestyle, education, occupations, access to and use of health care, etc." (Lilienfeld and Stolley 1994, 93).

In Canada, the health of native people has been studied because of their higher overall mortality. The mortality rate for natives is approximately two to four times greater for those under the age of fifty than the Canadian average. Once again, other societal risk factors, for example, economic factors such as poor housing on reserves and other lifestyle/behavioural factors, are the main reasons for high mortality among Canadian natives (Shah 1994).

Unemployment Risk Factors

A good review of unemployment and health in Canada conducted by Jin et al. (1995) concluded that: "on an epidemiologic basis, the evidence suggests a strong, positive association between unemployment and many adverse health outcomes. Whether unemployment causes these adverse outcomes is less straightforward, however, because there are likely many mediating and confounding factors, which may be social, economic or clinical" (Jin et al. 1995, 529).

The types of events leading to adverse health effects from unemployment included the disruption of relationships, greater risk behaviour (alcohol consumption and poor diet), increased stress, and a bereavement-like reaction to the lack of employment.

Marital Status Risk Factors

There is accurate evidence on marital status, based on direct evidence recorded from death certificates. This information was reviewed earlier (Figures 3.16 and 3.17). The direct evidence showed that married people have death rates two to three times lower than single and widowed/divorced people. This finding was consistent between age categories and sexes.

The reasons behind this association are not well known. Single people may be less safety conscious than married people. (Some insurance companies will lower car insurance premiums for married males under twenty-five.) Being widowed or divorced may increase financial and emotional stress. However, caution must be used in making conclusions, as confounding can occur.

Occupational Risk Factors

Both accidental and chronic occupational risks will be considered in this section. We can gather an idea of occupational mortality caused by accidents from Workers' Compensation Board data combined with estimates of employment by occupation (Statistics Canada 1994A, 1995D). Table 7.7 summarizes evidence for 1993, not necessarily the year the deaths occurred, but the year the claims were accepted. However, barring large annual variations, the numbers should be similar from year to year. The overall annual mortality rate for occupational mortality caused by accidents was 7.3 deaths per 100,000. However, several occupations (e.g., agriculture and fishing) may under-report deaths.

An earlier Canadian study on occupation and mortality by Howe and Lindsay (1983) analysed mortality information for approximately 10% of the Canadian workforce between 1965 and 1973. Although this was a weak epidemiological study for several reasons, including the fact that it had no data on confounders such as smoking, it clearly showed what has been termed the healthy worker effect. Overall, this study group had a standard mortality ratio (SMR, a measure of RR) of 0.83 (90% CI 0.82–0.84) and for cancer, an SMR of 0.88 (90% CI 0.86–0.90).

Identifying occupational and environmental carcinogens is a major area of study in public health sciences. Part Three, Predictive Information, will discuss quantitative risk predictors for environmental carcinogens. Characterizing a substance as a human carcinogen requires the kind of human evidence produced by epidemiological studies. Currently, only a short list of environmental chemicals have been identified as human carcinogens. The evidence for most of these was based on studies of occupational exposures. One-half of the sixty chemicals and mixtures classified as human carcinogens by the WHO International Agency for Research on Cancer (IARC) came out of studies on occupational exposures (Ames et al. 1995). Occupational exposures allow better identification and characterization of individual exposures than other types of exposures. Likewise, occupational exposures generally involve higher levels of exposure than non-occupational exposures (Siemiatycki 1992).

Doll and Peto (1981) estimated that occupation contributed to 4% of cancers. However, Miller (1992) in a Canadian study, concluded that 9% of cancer deaths were attributable to occupation. Miller claimed that Doll and Peto's estimates were too low because they eliminated the overlap with tobacco, yet occupation and tobacco use are interactive.

Siemiatycki (1992) performed a large case-control study of occupational cancers in Montreal. Some of the cancer sites included gastro-intestinal, lung, genito-urinary, and lymphomas. For bladder cancer, Siemiatycki et al. (1994) estimated that 6.5% (95% CI 2.0–9.9) of bladder cancers were attributable to occupational exposures.

Table 7.7 ◆ Occupational Mortality, 1993

Occupation	Annual Fatalities*	Employment (thousands)	Mortality Rate (per 100,000)**
Agriculture and related services	15		
Fishing and trapping	17		
Logging and forestry	50	74.4	67.0
Mining, quarrying, and oil wells	106	118.1	90.0
Manufacturing	128	1,636.1	7.8
Construction	137	484.2	28.0
Transportation and storage	107	452.3	24.0
Communication and other utilities	21	389.3	5.4
Wholesale trade	29	602.1	4.8
Retail trade	19	1,366.3	1.4
Finance and insurance	3	479.1	0.6
Real estate operator and insurance agent	3	187.7	1.6
Business services	15	534.1	2.8
Government services	46		
Educational services	10	758.0	1.3
Health and social services	6	1,149.8	0.5
Accommodation, food, and beverage services	13	808.1	1.6
Other services	14		
Industry unspecified or undefined	19		
TOTAL	**758**	**10,369**	**7.3**

* Fatalities reported to be directly related to occupational activity.
** Rate is expressed per 100,000 individuals participating (employed) in the specified occupation.

Source: Statistics Canada 1994A and 1995D

Geographical Area/Regional Risk Factors

In Canada, it is common to distinguish information by province. As a risk factor, geographical location is generally weak. Provinces and governments have prepared cancer atlases that compare cancer incidence and mortality rates by geographical region (e.g., county). These atlases identify areas with abnormally high rates for more detailed epidemiological study. Many differences between regions are linked to lifestyle/behavioural risk factors (e.g., lower smoking rates in the western provinces).

Medical Risk Factors

The high quality of medical care in Canada has reduced mortality and prolonged life. Some methods used by the medical community to reduce health risks include immunization, antibiotics, chemotherapy, surgery, and radiation treatment. These interventions all carry some health risk, from very small to substantial.

We should recognize that in life-threatening situations, higher risks are taken to overcome the threat. For example, some cancer chemotherapeutic drugs, particularly alkylating agents, cause secondary malignancies, most commonly leukaemias, lymphomas, and sarcomas.

Transportation Risk Factors

This section will summarize the risks associated with various modes of transportation. In Motor Vehicle Accidents (p. 165), risk factors for motor vehicle accidents will be examined in more detail.

Table 7.8 summarizes some US values for the risks of various modes of transportation. The number of deaths per 100 million miles travelled is shown as well as the RR compared with the safest mode-bus travel. Walking and bicycles were not included because of a lack of data. The risk of these modes of transportation depend almost entirely on what other transportation modes they must mix with (most people killed walking or biking are struck by a motor vehicle) (Halperin 1993).

Recreational Risk Factors

Risk is sometimes partly associated with a level of enjoyment. Often an increased challenge involves an increased level of risk (e.g., canoeing on a lake vs canoeing down rapids).

Cohen (1991) summarized the risks of several recreational activities (Table 7.9). Though based on US data, the information is applicable to Canada. Cohen used loss of life expectancy (LLE), described above (p. 111), and probability to quantify the risks. Wilson and Crouch (1982) have comparable numbers for recreational activities.

Table 7.8 ◆ **Risk by Various Modes of Transportation**

Mode of Travel	Deaths/100 million miles (Risk relative to safest mode)			
	Inter-urban		Intra-urban	
Eighteen-year-old males, no seat belts, intoxicated, driving light cars on rural interstates	49.0	(1,600)	93.0	(9,300)
Motorcycle (aggregate)	29.0	(970)	29.0	(2,900)
Roadway/Automotive (aggregate)	2.1	(70)	2.1	(210)
Average drivers	0.67	(22)	1.3	(130)
Forty-year-old females, wearing seat belts, sober, driving heavy cars on rural interstates	0.080	(2.7)	0.15	(15)
Airline passengers	0.061	(2.0)		
Train (Amtrak) passengers	0.052	(1.7)		
Bus passengers	0.03	(1.0)	0.01	(1)

Source: Halperin 1993, Tables 1 and 2

Table 7.9 ◆ **Risks Associated with Various Recreational Activities**

Activity	Annual Probability of Death*	Loss of Life Expectancy (LLE) per Year of Participation (days)
Mountain Climbing (dedicated)	1 in 167	110.0
Mountain Climbing (all climbers)	1 in 1,750	10.0
Hang Gliding	1 in 560	25.0
Parachuting	1 in 570	25.0
Sail Planing	1 in 1,710	9.0
Professional Boxing	1 in 2,200	8.0
Scuba Diving (amateur)	1 in 2,400	7.0
Snowmobiling	1 in 7,600	2.0
Mountain Hiking	1 in 15,700	0.9
Football (college)	1 in 33,000	0.6
Skiing (racing)	1 in 40,000	0.5

* These risks are expressed for participants in the specified activity.

Source: Cohen 1991, Table 7

Other Risk Factors

There are several risks that are significant in other parts of world, but, fortunately, not in Canada. These include wars, famine, and epidemics. Though violence is a meaningful risk to life in Canada (e.g., there were 498 homicide deaths in 1994), it is significantly lower than in the US.

Environmental Risk Factors

Environment is a word that has multiple meanings in different contexts. In one context, the environment and genetics are the only factors that cause disease. Everything not already encoded in one's genes comes from the environment. The body is exposed to environmental factors through air, food, and water. Much confusion surrounds the meaning of environment in relation to health risk. However, this book uses a much narrower definition of environmental risk, i.e., the unintentional exposure to specific environmental agents. There are four exposure routes that connect the environment and the human body: inhalation (air), eating (food), drinking (water), and skin (several) (Hrudey et al. 1996).

People commonly separate environmental risks into two broad categories-natural and human. Natural risks include natural disasters and chemicals originally present in the environment (e.g., arsenic in drinking water). Human risks include human-made or mass-produced chemicals, such as car exhausts, industrial emissions, and pesticide use. Agent-specific environmental risk factors are generally weak and highly confounded by other factors.

Air Pollution Risk Factors

The following quote summarizes one of the recent issues in epidemiological studies of air pollution: "Are small particles in the air killing people? Dozens of studies conducted in the past five years suggest that they are. Even more disturbing, the studies show statistical associations between airborne particulate matter (PM) and increased mortality and sickness, even at levels well within current national air quality standards. Although the implied risks to individuals are small compared with health factors such as smoking, they are large compared with typical environmental risks from toxic compounds and carcinogens in the air and water" (Reichhardt 1995, 360A).

Reichhardt's statement includes two important observations, that air pollution from particulate matter may be one of the largest environmental risks we face, but that the risks are small compared with other health factors. There are still many uncertainties associated with air pollution and mortality. Some important uncertainties include whether the particle itself or some other pollutant attached to the particle causes the health problem, the nature of the biological mechanism, the lack of accurate individual and indoor/outdoor exposure data, and the degree of association between specific causes of death. Another question is whether air pollution affects the mortality of healthy people or only those already weak and susceptible from other conditions. It may be that air pollution is linked with mortality at the end of life, but may have less effect on overall life expectancy.

Small particles have shown stronger associations with mortality than specific air pollutants like ozone, nitrous oxide, sulphur dioxide, and carbon monoxide. Lipfert and Wyzga (1995) examined results from thirty-one (mostly time-series) epidemiological studies and estimated the joint daily mortality from various air pollutants as approximately 5% of daily mortality. Once again, the association is with daily mortality rates rather than lifetime mortality.

Water Pollution Risk Factors

The most direct health risk related to water pollution is drinking water. A more indirect concern is for people who eat large quantities of fish from polluted water.

In drinking water there are two general concerns. Pathogens are not usually a health issue when the water has had full conventional treatment and adequate disinfection. However, some rural locations' adequacy of water treatment is questionable. Pathogens include bacteria (e.g., campylobacter), viruses (e.g., Norwalk), giardia and cryptosporidium. The latter two pathogens are protozoan parasites that are harder to treat than the bacterial pathogens.

Some inorganic chemicals, like arsenic, are naturally present in water at elevated concentrations and can pose a health risk. Chlorination by-products from disinfecting drinking water have been associated with excess bladder cancer.

Food Additives and Contaminants Risk Factors

Most of the work with food additives and contaminants has been with quantitative risk assessment, discussed in Part Three, Predictive Inference. The main groups of food additives include processing aids, texturing agents, preservatives, flavoring and appearance agents, and nutritional supplements. As any food additives will affect humans directly, they are very highly regulated. Similarly, residual pesticides are a concern, but apart from occupational exposures, their risks must be estimated using quantitative risk assessment (Amdur et al. 1991).

Chemical Risk Factors

Vainio and Wilbourn (1993) have summarized the chemicals associated with human cancer. The summary is based on International Agency for Research on Cancer (IARC) documents. Of the 742 chemicals considered, the fifty-seven that have been judged by experts to cause human cancer are shown in Table 7.10. The RR of the different chemicals listed and the

Table 7.10 ◆ Chemicals and Exposures Associated with Human Cancer

Agents	Complex Mixtures	Exposure Circumstances
• Aflatoxins • 4-Aminobiphenyl • Arsenic and arsenic compounds • Asbestos • Azathioprine • Benzene • Benzidine • Bis (chloromethyl) ether and chloromethyl methyl ether • Chlorambucil • Chlornaphazine • Chromium [VI] compounds • Cyclophosphamide • Cyclosporin • Diethylstilbestrol • Erionite • Melphalan • Methoxsalen plus UV • Methyl-CCNU • MOPP • Mustard gas • Myleran • 2-Naphthylamine • Nickel compounds • Oestrogen replacement therapy • Oestrogens—nonsteroidal and steroidal • Oral contraceptive—combined and sequential • Radon and its decay products • Solar radiation • Talc containing asbestiform fibres • Thiotepa • Treosulfan • Vinyl chloride	• Alcoholic beverages • Analgesic mixtures containing phenacetin • Betel—quid with tobacco • Coal-tar pitches • Coal-tars • Mineral oils—untreated and mildly treated • Shale-oils • Soots • Tobacco products—smokeless (chewing tobacco, oral snuff) • Tobacco smoke	• Aluminum production • Auramine—manufacture of • Boot and shoe manufacture repair • Coal gasification • Coke production • Furniture and cabinet making • Haematite mining (underground) with exposure to radon • Iron and steel founding • Isopropanol manufacture (strong-acid process) • Magenta—manufacture of • Painter (occupation exposure as) • Rubber industry • Strong inorganic acid mists containing sulphuric acid (occupational exposure to)

Source: Vainio and Wilbourn 1993, Tables 2, 3, and 4

circumstances of exposure vary greatly (e.g., tobacco smoke and furniture and cabinet making). The public is only exposed to trace levels, if any, for all but the consumer products (tobacco, alcohol, and pharmaceuticals) listed.

Bruce Ames is an award-winning biochemist noted for discovering the Ames test for mutagenicity: a means for rapidly testing substances for their mutagenic potential. Ames is a controversial speaker on the issue of natural vs synthetic chemicals, and has stated: "There are more natural carcinogens by weight in a single cup of coffee than potentially carcinogenic synthetic pesticide residues in the average US diet in a year, and there are still a thousand known chemicals in roasted coffee that have not been tested" (Ames et al. 1995, 5262).

Radiation Risk Factor

Risk factors for skin cancer include a light skin and hair, tendency to sunburn, and possibly sunburning incidents as a child (Miller 1995). Doll and Peto (1981) have estimated that UV light causes 90% of lip cancer, 50%+ of melanomas, and 80% of other skin cancers. Macneill et al., have stated: "The only well established causal factor for melanoma is sun exposure. Severe, intermittent exposure increases the risk of melanoma while continued regular exposure produces no increase and may even reduce the incidence. This is presumably because the protection against UVR provided by natural tanning and skin thickening associated with continued exposure is sufficient to more than compensate for the carcinogenic effects of the UVR itself" (Macneill et al. 1995, 837).

Another important type of radiation exposure is radon. Ames et al. (1995) claim that radon is likely the most important indoor air pollution concern. Based on estimates from underground miners, radon exposure likely contributes to 15,000 lung cancers per year (in the US), mostly in smokers due to synergistic effects. However, epidemiological studies of radon have failed to demonstrate convincingly any excess risk at domestic exposure levels (Letourneau et al. 1994).

Natural Disaster Risk Factors

Cohen (1991) summarized the risks of several natural disasters in the US (Table 7.11). Canada will have similar values, but they may be lower for some disasters (e.g., hurricanes) and higher for others (e.g., excessive cold). Cohen used the loss of life expectancy (LLE) described above (p. 111) to quantify the risks. Table 7.12 summarizes the five worst tornadoes in Canada.

Lightning is the only natural disaster listed on a death certificate. The following number of Canadians have died after being struck by lightning: 1991, five; 1992, four; 1993, one; 1994, eleven. Note the variability from year to year, despite the relatively constant size of the population. Other natural hazards that kill Canadians include forest fires and weather-induced accidents.

Table 7.11 ◆ Risks Associated with Various Natural Disasters

Natural Disaster	Loss of Life Expectancy (LLE) (days)
Hurricanes	0.3
Tornadoes	0.8
Excessive Heat	0.6–0.7
Excessive Cold	1.0–2.1
Lightning	0.7–1.1
Floods	0.4
Earthquakes	0.2
Tsunami	0.15

Source: Cohen 1991, Table 8

Table 7.12 ◆ Worst Tornadoes in Canada

Date	Location	Deaths	Injured
1912, June 12	Regina	28	100s
1987, July 31	Edmonton	27	300
1946, June 17	Windsor to Tecumseh	17	100s
1888, August 16	Lancaster Town to Valleyfield, Quebec	9–11	14
1974, April 3	Windsor	9	30

Source: Colombo 1996, 23

8 Risk Factors by Cause of Death

Infectious Diseases

The section Infection Disease in Part One, Direct Evidence, highlighted the significant decline in mortality from infectious diseases. Barrett (1992) identified four factors associated with the mortality decline: sanitary reforms, changing disease patterns, improved medicine and health care, and improvements in living standards.

1. **Sanitary Reforms**. The aim of sanitary reforms is to reduce contact with infectious micro-organisms. This measure requires a knowledge of the conditions that promote the spread of micro-organisms. There are five major routes by which humans can be infected: water (e.g., cholera, typhoid), food (e.g., dysentery, gastro-enteritis), vectors/carriers (e.g., rabies, malaria, bubonic plague), air (e.g., pneumonia, respiratory tuberculosis), and personal contact (e.g., sexually transmitted diseases). Drinking water has proven the easiest to control with appropriate technological measures.

2. **Changing disease patterns**. These are changes in the nature of the disease itself. Scarlet fever has been a minor disease, then a major cause of death, and then changed again to become less of a threat.

3. **Improved medicine and health care**. People used to assume that the mortality decline in nineteenth-century Europe was the result of medical advances. However, there is now a lively debate on this subject. Improved medicine and health care have been much more influential in recent declines in the third world. Most of the tuberculosis decline took place before the introduction of antibiotics, but the decline was greater after antibiotics were introduced. Diphtheria, however, was decreased following the introduction of anti-toxins, and then significantly decreased following immunization. In addition, smallpox has been eradicated by means of effective immunization.

4. **Improvements in living standards**. The incidence of many diseases declines with rising standards of living. Nutritional status affects an individual's resistance to influenza, pneumonia, bronchitis, diarrhoea, and tuberculosis.

HIV infection has several risk factors relating to how it spreads, i.e., through sexual contact, sharing contaminated needles, from an infected mother to her baby, transfusion of infected blood, and accidental handling of infected blood. The first and second categories are the most common ways that HIV is spread. The last two categories currently carry very small risks, although the effects of tainted blood transfusion are still current. More than 1400 Canadians were infected with HIV by blood transfusions in the early 1980s; more than three-quarters were hemophiliacs (CBC National News, 9 December 1996). Unlike most other types of health risks, there are several easy safety measures that can significantly reduce the probability of developing HIV infection. These measures include sexual practices (e.g., abstinence, monogamous relationships, safe sex practices) and not sharing needles.

Cancer

Risk factors for a particular disease or outcome are often labelled "sufficient" or "necessary." A sufficient risk factor will inevitably produce or initiate a disease and often includes several components. A necessary risk factor must be present for a disease to develop. Vainio and Wilbourn describe the difficulty in studying the causes of cancer in terms of sufficient and necessary factors: "In human cancer, there is probably no such thing as a 'sufficient' and 'necessary' cause; all what we are studying are 'contributory' causes, active in some stages of the multistep (and multifactorial) process of carcinogenesis ... Therefore, for pragmatic purposes, an agent is considered carcinogenic when a change in the frequency or intensity of exposure to the agent is accompanied by a change in the frequency of occurrence of cancer of a particular type(s) at a later time" (Vainio and Wilbourn 1993, s4).

In 1981, Doll and Peto published a review of the causes of cancer that is still widely used as a reference. Two earlier publications in the same journal where Doll and Peto originally published their article were similar but less comprehensive (Wynder and Gori 1977; Higginson and Muir 1979).

Doll and Peto (1981) submitted four pieces of evidence that some human cancer is avoidable.

1. **Differences in incidence between countries**. Doll and Peto included a table that lists nineteen common cancers with a cumulative incidence of greater than 1% in any area. For each of the nineteen causes, they listed the ratio of the highest to the lowest incidence rate. These ranged from a ratio of six to over 100, indicating that large geographical variations existed.

2. **Changes in incidence following migration**. Studies have shown that immigrants to new countries have developed cancer rates similar to those of the population in the new country. Studies have generally attributed this trend to lifestyle (avoidable) factors and have tended to downplay the importance of genetics (at least between races). This finding may change with the rapid advances in genetic typing that illuminate the specific role of genes in cancer.

3. **Changes in incidence over time**. Changing rates of cancer incidence in the same country indicate that external factors affect those cancers. In the United States, the mortality rate from stomach cancer has decreased 61%, while the mortality rate for lung cancer has increased 148% between 1950 and 1975.

4. **Identification of causes**. Avoidability of cancer can be demonstrated if specific causes can be identified. If a particular chemical's removal from an occupational setting is followed by decreases in cancer, there is evidence of causation.

Doll and Peto claim that luck determines the differences between actual and expected outcomes (based on observation and theory). Doll and Peto point out that luck plays a role in determining exactly who will develop any cancer. However, for the population as a whole, this luck is averaged out and becomes a negligible factor (e.g., only 17% of current male smokers are expected to develop lung cancer, Villeneuve and Mao 1994).

Table 8.1 summarizes Doll and Peto's estimates. Miller (1992) has developed a list similar to Table 8.1 for Canada, using more recent information and categories similar to Doll and Peto (Table 8.2). Unlike Doll and Peto, Miller did not propose an uncertainty range for his estimates, but the uncertainty in his estimates is probably similar to Doll and Peto's. Miller's study also included a table of estimates for the potential effects of prevention or early detection on cancer incidence (Table 8.3). These estimates do indicate that a large percentage of cancers are potentially preventable.

A recent study on breast cancer could only attribute an estimated 41% (95% CI 1.6%–80%) of cases in the US to the major risk factors: later age at first birth, nulliparity, family history of breast cancer, and higher socio-economic status (Madigan et al. 1995).

Table 8.1 ◆ Estimated Proportion of Cancer Deaths Attributed to Various Factors

Factor or Class of Factors	Best Estimate (%)	Range of Acceptable Estimates (%)
Tobacco	30	25–40
Alcohol	3	2–4
Diet	35	10–70
Food Additives	<1	0.5–2
Reproductive and Sexual Behaviour	7	1–13
Occupation	4	2–8
Pollution	2	<1–5
Industrial Products	<1	<1–2
Medicines and Medical Procedures	1	0.5–3
Geophysical Factors	3	2–4
Infection	10 ?	1–?
Unknown	?	?

Source: Doll and Peto 1981, Table 20

Table 8.2 ◆ Estimated Causes of Cancer Deaths in Canada

Factor	Percentage
Tobacco	29
Diet	20
Occupation	9
Family History	8
Alcohol	6
Parity (given birth)	4
Sexual Activity	3
Sunlight	1
Drugs	1
Radiation	1

Source: Miller 1992, S26

Table 8.3 ◆ Estimates of Potential Effects of Prevention or Early Detection on Cancer Incidence

Cancer Site	Action	PAR
Lung	Eliminate smoking	90%
	Reduce occupational exposure to carcinogens	20%
Colo-rectal	Reduce fat and increase vegetable consumption	60%
Breast	Reduce fat and increase vegetable consumption	27%
	Reduce obesity (postmenopausal women)	12%
	Screen women aged 50 to 69	25%*
Prostate	Reduce fat consumption	20%
Lymphoma	Reduce exposure to herbicides and pesticides	?
Bladder	Eliminate smoking and reduce dietary cholesterol	60%
	Reduce occupational exposure to carcinogens	27%
Body of the uterus	Reduce obesity	30%
	Protective effect of oral contraceptives (ages 20 to 54)	28%
Stomach	Reduce nitrite in cured meats and salt-preserved foods, and increase fruit and vegetable consumption	80%
Leukaemia	Reduce exposure to radiation and benzene	?
Oral, etc.	Eliminate smoking and reduce alcohol	80%
	Increase fruit and vegetable consumption	10%
Pancreas	Eliminate smoking	40%
	Reduce sugar and increase vegetable consumption	30%
Melanoma of the skin	Reduce unprotected exposure to sunlight	20%
Kidney	Eliminate smoking	40%
	Reduce fat consumption	30%
Brain	Reduce occupational exposure to carcinogens	?
Ovary	Reduce fat consumption	30%
	Protective effect of oral contraceptives (ages 20 to 54)	26%
Cervix	Eliminate smoking	23%
	Encourage use of barrier contraceptives	?
	Screen women aged 20 to 69	60%

Note: Estimates are for males except for breast, body of uterus, ovary and cervical cancer.
*Effect on mortality, not incidence.

Source: Miller 1992, Table 4

Cardiovascular Disease

There are several major risk factors relating to cardiovascular disease: blood pressure, hypertension, blood cholesterol (lipids, LDL, HDL), smoking, alcohol, weight, amount of exercise, diabetes, stress, heredity, oral contraceptives (combined with smoking), menopause (taking estrogen), previous heart attack, and atrial fibrillation.

As cardiovascular disease is the leading cause of death, its risk factors have been extensively studied. Strikingly, however, there are few overall quantitative predictions available, highlighting the difficulty in providing them. One of the few predictions for cardiovascular disease estimated that as much as 30% of cardiovascular disease mortality is attributable to high blood pressure, 19% to diabetes, 17% to smoking, and 15% to elevated serum cholesterol (Heart and Stroke Foundation of Canada 1995).

It has been estimated that 54% of the decline in ischaemic heart disease in North America is due to changes in lifestyle and 40% to medical intervention, leaving 6% unexplained. Medical intervention is needed thousands of times annually for cardiovascular disease. In the fiscal year 1992–1993 there were 15,034 coronary artery bypass surgeries and 14,299 angioplasties, and both are increasing in number (Heart and Stroke Foundation of Canada 1995). In addition, an estimated 65,000 Canadians have pacemakers.

A limiting factor in determining who is at high risk is the difficulty in detecting them. Screening for major risk factors (serum cholesterol, blood pressure, and smoking) will leave undetected about half of those who will develop cardiovascular disease (WHO 1994).

Respiratory Disease

Smoking is one of the largest risk factors for non-cancer respiratory disease. Illing and Kaiserman (1995) compared estimates of smoking-attributable mortality (SAM) with total deaths. They found that approximately 50% of male and 35% of female respiratory disease deaths were related to smoking. Respiratory failure is often the result of lifelong cumulative damage to lung function. This relates to Figure 1.1, Disability vs Impairment, which shows impairment continuing, causing increasing, permanent disability, and eventually death.

In terms of cause of death, respiratory disease is often the underlying cause of deaths that could be considered "natural."

External Causes

External causes are different from other major causes of death. These deaths occur from fatal injuries, and because they occur rapidly, the contributing causes are more easily determined. However, similar to other causes of deaths, multiple risk factors are often associated with external cause deaths. In this Section, the two largest external causes of death are reviewed, suicide and motor vehicle accidents.

Suicide

Identifying risk factors for suicide is important because it can be used to educate others about warning signs. Risk factors for suicide include depression, previous attempted suicide, substance abuse, stressful life events, perceived or actual lack of family support, rural (isolated) residence, exposure to media reports on suicide, and alienation (Hayes 1994).

Blumenthal and Kupfer (1990) identified five overlapping domains for suicide.

1. **Psychiatric diagnosis**. More than 90% of adults who commit suicide have an associated psychiatric illness.

2. **Personality traits**. These include aggression, impulsiveness, and hopelessness, as well as the combination of antisocial and depressive symptoms.

3. **Psychosocial factors, social supports, life events, and chronic medical illness**. These factors, combined with a recent humiliating life experience, were an indicator.

4. **Genetic and familial factors**. The genetics of suicide may be independent of family history disorders such as alcoholism.

5. **Neurochemical and biochemical variables**. Under investigation is whether there are biological variables associated with psychiatric and personality traits.

Motor Vehicle Accidents

Though accidents are different from most other causes of death, Gordon (1949) demonstrated that accidents had properties similar to infectious disease and could be studied using epidemiological methods (e.g., there are variations by time, age, race, geographical distribution, and socio-economic distribution). Millar (1995) and Riley and Paddon (1989) have reviewed accidents in Canada, including information on motor vehicle accidents.

In the past twenty years, there has been a reduction of over 50% in the annual number of motor vehicle fatalities. If the number of vehicles registered is factored in (a form of standardization), then the reduction has been approximately 70% (Transport Canada

1995B). However, motor vehicle accidents remain an important cause of death, especially of young adult males.

Motor vehicle accidents differ from many other accidents in that a large amount of information is recorded in addition to that on the death certificate. This additional information, based on police collision reports, is summarized provincially and then nationally. The national report published by Transport Canada is entitled Traffic Collision Statistics in Canada (Transport Canada 1994). Some of the information included is sex, age, province, time, light condition, road surface, road condition, road type, weather condition, place of occurrence (rural/urban), road user class, vehicle type, vehicle condition, vehicle manoeuvre, model year, driver condition, driver action, pedestrian action, and pedestrian collision site.

Motor vehicle accidents are a good example of multiple risk factors interacting to produce fatalities. Table 8.4 shows risk factors related to the vehicle, human, and road. In addition, the risk factors are separated into those occurring before, during, and after an accident. Table 8.4 highlights the many factors involved in any motor vehicle accident, each contributing to the final outcome.

In 1993, 45% of fatally injured drivers had used alcohol. For males, alcohol use was involved in 50% of the cases, while in females, alcohol was involved in only 26% of the cases (Transport Canada 1995A).

Table 8.4 ◆ Risk Factors for Motor Vehicle Accidents

	Vehicle	Human	Road
BEFORE (Primary prevention)	**Design** • Stability • Road holding • Power • Visibility • Brakes • Lights • Tires **Maintenance** • Regular service • Competent mechanics • Training of mechanics	**Drivers** • Adequate training • Psychology • Attitude • Physical fitness • Fatigue • Emotional stress • Alcohol • Drugs **Pedestrians** • Training • Awareness • Physical fitness (age) • Fatigue • Emotional stress • Alcohol • Drugs	**Design and Construction** • Carriageway • Surface • Visibility • Intersections • Corners • Traffic control equipment • Signs • Maintenance
DURING (Secondary prevention)	**Design** • Stability • Braking efficiency • Steering control • Tires **Built-in protection** • Strong passenger compartment • "Crumple zones" • Triplex glass • Seat belts • Door locks	• Reflexes • Training • Psychology • Physical fitness	• Weather • State of surface • Space • Presence of "escape route"
AFTER (Tertiary prevention)	**Design** • Ease of ingress for rescue • Fire resistance	• Psychology • Training (first aid) • Medical and rescue services	• Communications • Space of access to accident

Source: Rowland and Cooper 1983, Table 7.8

Part 1

Predictive Inference

three

Predictive inference involves risk assessment and is based on toxicological studies of specific chemicals and compounds. Estimates of health risk are developed from knowledge of chemical properties and laboratory studies with experimental animals. Although these studies generate considerable evidence about the hazards of chemical substances, translation of these findings into human health risk involves interpreting the meaning of animal results. Frequently, laboratory experiments at high levels of exposure are used to predict human risks at much lower levels of exposure. Thus, although toxicology can identify hazards of chemical substances, human health risk assessment is primarily an exercise in predictive inference. The risk predictions are used to develop guidelines to protect human health by limiting exposure to various hazardous substances.

Risk assessment and toxicology are closely connected. Human health risk estimates are generated using risk assessment that itself requires toxicological evidence. Toxicology is both an art and a science (Amdur et al. 1991). The science relates mainly to the observations and experimental evidence collected on the effects of poisons. The art comes in the interpretation of this evidence for purposes such as risk assessment.

Although the uncertainties of predictive inference are enormous compared with risk judgements based on indirect and, especially, direct evidence, predictive inference has several advantages. First, there is a substantial link between health effects in animals and humans because of common metabolic and physiological processes. The laboratory environment allows many factors to be rigorously controlled, helping to establish causation between a chemical and an effect. Mechanisms of toxic action can be studied through invasive monitoring and post-mortem examination. Laboratory experiments allow new drugs and chemical compounds to be tested before widespread human exposure. For example, the tragic consequences of the drug thalidomide could have been avoided with appropriate evidence from animal experiments. Despite the inherent and enormous uncertainties of risk assessment by predictive inference, there is no better way to predict health risks before they affect human populations.

Predictive inference studies have mainly focused on estimating the probability of developing cancer from long-term exposure to carcinogens and on judging tolerable levels of exposure to non-carcinogens. Direct evidence from human incidents provides insight about high level acute exposures to poisonous substances. Likewise, higher level chronic exposures, often in occupational exposure settings, have provided epidemiological evidence and inference about human health risk.

Risk Assessment

Humans have always informally assessed the risk of things that may be poisonous or cause disease. However, our industrial-scale production and increasingly complex use of pharmaceuticals, cosmetics, food additives, and pesticides mean that we now need to make formalized, societal judgements about the health risks of individual substances. Accordingly, different regulatory agencies have developed their own ways to assess the risks of specific substances.

The rapid growth of risk assessment and management in several regulatory agencies in the United States, each with its own approach and perspective, led to a landmark study by the US National Academy of Sciences, a comprehensive generic guide for risk assessment and management (US NRC 1983). Although this is an American document, its approach applies to most regulatory agencies involved in risk assessment. This document defines risk assessment as an evaluation of: what is known of the hazardous (toxic) properties of a substance; the quantitative relationship between substance exposure and toxic effect; and the level and conditions of human exposures to the substance. All of these elements are combined to evaluate the nature and character of the substance's risk to human populations. These activities are typically described as hazard identification, dose-response or toxicity assessment, exposure assessment, and risk characterization.

Four Stages of Risk Assessment

Hazard Identification
Hazard identification seeks to determine whether the substance has any important toxic effects that are relevant to humans. Any available and relevant information from both epidemiology and toxicology is used to determine the associations between exposure to the chemical and its effect. Relevant effects include mortality, reproductive or developmental effects, neurotoxicity, specific organ damage, and cancer (Amdur et al. 1991).

Dose-Response Assessment
Dose-response assessment seeks to determine the relationship between the dose of a substance and the toxic response in humans. Dose-response assessment is often the most controversial aspect of risk assessment because data is rarely available for doses experienced

by the general human population. Consequently, dose-response assessment involves judging this relationship between a substance's dose and a human toxic response using data from much higher than normal exposure levels. For a limited number of chemicals, data from human exposure, often occupational exposures, are available. In most cases, data from animal experiments must be used. In either case, extrapolations from high to low doses are required, involving several assumptions that are discussed later. More common predictions derived from animal experiments involve extrapolations from animals to humans.

Exposure Assessment

Exposure assessment tries to determine what routes of exposure, if any, are relevant for humans and (based on monitoring evidence or modelling predictions) what doses of the substance humans may experience from these exposures. For many substances, no adequate exposure information is available for the general population, which means that risk assessment can only use models to estimate exposure. Dimensions of exposure include intensity, frequency, schedule, route, and duration, and the nature, size and make-up of the exposed population. Difficulties include competing exposures, interactions with other chemicals, and special populations (e.g., old, young, pregnant). Major exposure routes for humans are through air, food, and water (Hrudey et al. 1996).

Risk Characterization

Risk characterization combines the dose-response and exposure assessments to estimate the incidence of the adverse effects in humans. This estimate may be achieved in two major ways: as a prediction of the probability of the adverse outcome, or as an estimated ratio of the actual exposure levels to a tolerable exposure level. This second method is based on the exposure assessment and the level judged to produce no adverse effects in humans using the dose-response assessment. The latter ratio is commonly referred to as a margin of exposure or an exposure ratio.

Risk characterization must also provide some insight into the uncertainty of risk predictions. There has been increasing recognition that expressing risk probability (based on the highly uncertain processes involved in risk assessment) as a single value or point estimate is not justified and is inherently misleading (US NRC 1994). Rather, risk characterization should reveal the variability of both exposures and responses and the confidence limitations on the accuracy of the risk estimates. Recently, there has also been growing recognition that risk characterization must also involve potentially affected parties, because of the many ways to characterize risk. The choice of risk characteristics cannot be determined strictly on scientific grounds, but rather requires judgement about what aspects of a risk are most important to the potentially affected parties (US NRC 1996).

Prediction of the Probability of an Adverse Outcome

The two approaches to quantitative risk characterization have very different perspectives on risk. The first approach has commonly been used for carcinogens, generally by comparing actual exposure levels to a risk-specific dose, i.e., a dose level predicted to yield a specified level of cancer risk (e.g., a lifetime cancer risk of one in a 100,000). This method may also be used to predict the number of hypothetical cancer cases that would arise for actual exposure levels. In either approach, the calculations depend on a dose-response model, which will extrapolate from observed data down to the much lower risk levels normally used for risk characterization. The first approach is only valid for toxic substances that may exhibit no threshold in their dose-response relationship, i.e., substances that may involve some level of risk at any level of exposure.

As this low-dose extrapolation process involves many assumptions that cannot be experimentally verified, the resulting calculations are subject to enormous uncertainty. Concern over the uncertainty of these estimates has caused some risk assessors and regulatory agencies, including Health Canada, to reconsider their reliance on these methods for quantitative cancer risk assessment (Hrudey 1995; Meek and Long 1996).

Despite these very serious limitations and valid concerns, the quantitative extrapolation approach currently is the only basis for calculating probability estimates for cancer occurrence at the levels of exposure that human populations normally experience. This approach has been widely used, particularly in the United States. Currently, most North American estimates for cancer occurrence from individual substance exposures are based upon this method. These estimates commonly appear in popular articles on risk. As these types of estimates are so prevalent in the literature, we have also used them, but only as a way to compare these hypothetical cancer risk predictions with other risk data. These comparisons are useful if you remember that quantitative extrapolations are intended to overestimate the number of cancer cases caused by any specific substance at the evaluated exposure levels.

Margin of Exposure or Exposure Ratio

The second quantitative risk characterization approach, which has most commonly been used for non-carcinogens, is not discussed to any extent in this book, because it cannot estimate, even cautiously overestimate, the number of cases of illness arising from a specified level of exposure to a substance. This approach tries to determine the level of exposure in toxicological experiments that causes no significant adverse effect, the so-called no observed adverse effect level or NOAEL. This approach assumes that the substance exhibits a threshold in its dose-response relationship, i.e., there is a level below which no harmful effects will occur. This level must be selected after a rigorous evaluation of all published toxicology studies and requires substantial judgment. Using a value taken from a review of toxicology experiments, uncertainty factors are applied to reduce the NOAEL exposure level to what is called a tolerable daily intake (TDI) in Canada or a reference dose (RfD) in the

United States. These uncertainty factors (generally in the range of one to ten) are derived on a case-by-case basis, and take into account (Meek et al. 1994):

- the variability of sensitivity within the population to account for more sensitive individuals;

- the extrapolation from an experimental animal species to humans;

- inadequacies in the experimental data, including, but not limited to, lack of adequate data on developmental, chronic or reproductive toxicity, and reliance on a lowest observed effect level rather than a NOAEL;

- evidence of an enhancing interaction with another substance in the environment;

- in exceptional cases, the severity of effect, such as a capability to cause birth defects.

Collectively, the uncertainty factors may typically reduce the TDI from the NOAEL by 100 to 1,000-fold. Uncertainty factors greater than 10,000 indicate that the toxicology data is too incomplete or unreliable to set a TDI.

This margin of exposure or exposure ratio approach is now the one most commonly used to set exposure guidelines for non-carcinogenic substances.

Toxicology

Toxicology is concerned with the adverse effects of specific agents on living systems. Professional toxicologists may be primarily descriptive, mechanistic, or regulatory. Descriptive toxicologists perform toxicity testing on experimental animals. This information is normally used to evaluate risks to humans and the environment. Mechanistic toxicologists research the mechanisms of action of toxic effects. Regulatory toxicologists use the data provided by descriptive toxicologists and, increasingly, the findings of mechanistic toxicologists to evaluate the health risks associated with a substance.

The next sections will focus on descriptive toxicology. The following sections on interpreting cancer data focus on regulatory toxicology.

Substances and Chemicals

Toxicological risk assessment usually begins by identifying an agent or hazard rather than an adverse effect (see Figure 1.2) This process, beginning with hazard identification, focuses on specific compounds and sometimes elements. Unfortunately, actual human exposure always involves a mixture of compounds and elements. Depending on the concentrations, common exposures involve hundreds or thousands of different chemicals simultaneously, at different concentrations. If one could detect exposures down to individual molecules of a substance, the variety of substances we are exposed to in a lifetime would be too numerous to count.

There are an estimated 70,000 to 75,000 distinguishable chemical substances used in society, with over 40,000 used in commercially significant quantities (Health and Welfare Canada 1991). About 1,000 new or replacement chemical substances are introduced into commerce each year. Most commercial chemical substances will contain at least one biologically significant impurity. This inventory of chemical substances is in addition to the almost infinite number and variety of naturally occurring chemicals that are not commercially used. The numbers for natural substances are almost infinite because many biological molecules are complex polymers, with infinite variety in their specific monomer sequence and resulting overall structure. This enormous diversity is evident in the variety of unique structures for protein and DNA molecules.

Some Principles of Toxicology

Toxicology, the study of poisons, has been practised for centuries. However, the scientific investigation of how substances act as poisons in human systems has only matured in the last half of this century, in part because of the need to assess the risks associated with the growing number of substances we use. The relatively recent development of toxicology as a discipline has been accompanied by a recognition of various principles.

Perhaps the most fundamental concept in toxicology is that the dose makes the poison. Any substance given in a large enough dose will be harmful to humans and ultimately capable of causing death. However, the range of doses needed to cause harm or death for different substances varies enormously.

One measure of the range is the dose required to cause death in one-half (50%) of an exposed population of animals. This dose is termed the median lethal dose, commonly abbreviated as LD_{50}. The LD_{50} typically equals the mass of the substance administered divided by the body mass of the exposed animal. Ethyl alcohol has a LD_{50} value of 10,000 mg/kg, while botulinum toxin has a LD_{50} value of 0.00001 mg/kg, a lethal toxic range of nine factors of ten (1,000,000,000-fold). Clearly, in evaluating the risk of any substance, two pieces of information are required: the toxicity of the substance (e.g., LD_{50} for acute toxicity) and the level of exposure (the actual dose administered).

Not only does the dose make the poison, but, generally, as the exposure to a substance increases within its harmful range, the probability and/or severity of adverse effects will increase, forming the basis for the quantitative dose-response relationship. Increasing harm is expected within the harmful exposure range because a deficiency of many substances, although they may be essential at low doses, will cause harmful effects (e.g., vitamin D, zinc).

Knowledge of the exposure (dose) of an agent and the dose-response relationship of an agent is essential for any quantitative prediction of adverse health effects. This requirement is imbedded in the risk assessment framework as the dose-response assessment stage.

As much toxicological insight is derived from animal experiments, interpretations rely on the fact that humans are animals. Although much can be learned from the study of toxic effects in animals exposed to a substance, important anatomical and physiological similarities and differences between experimental animals and humans must be recognized and reconciled.

A common misunderstanding about toxic substances is that the toxicity shown by a substance in one form can be generalized to a wide variety of toxic effects. Experience generally shows that adverse effects of agents will not be universal, but will lead to one or more specific adverse effects.

Adverse effects resulting in toxicity occur via molecular level chemical reactions and/or physical processes. Although these effects are classified as adverse because of their outcome on the function of the affected host, most of these chemical reactions are not otherwise distinguishable from normal life processes. The disruption of normal function generally reveals the toxicity. A toxic effect does not require some form of unique chemical reaction.

There are many possible toxic effects from chemical substances. These effects include cancer, reproductive effects (fertility, birth defects, or teratogenic), neurotoxic effects, immune system effects, and damage to specific organs like the lungs, liver, and kidneys. Effects can also be distinguished according to whether they are immediate or delayed, reversible or irreversible, or local or systematic.

Immediate effects are evident within a short time after exposure to the causative substance, while delayed effects may not be evident for a long time (perhaps years) after exposure. Cancer caused by exposure to a carcinogenic substance is an example of an observable effect delayed by decades after causative exposure.

The body can repair the damage caused by reversible effects with no apparent loss of function. Reversible effects include recoveries like the complete healing of a minor cut, burn, or skin irritation. An irreversible effect's damage cannot be repaired to restore complete function; some residual damage remains. This damage from irreversible effects can accumulate over time to create an increasing loss of function. The cumulative damage to lung function associated with emphysema is an example of an irreversible effect. For some types of reversible effects, a tolerance can be developed and the body will respond to toxic challenges (see Figure 1.1).

Local effects occur at or near the point of contact with an irritant substance, such as a skin or respiratory tract irritation. In contrast, systemic effects require distribution of the substance via the circulatory system to affect various internal organs.

Four Categories of Chemical Interactivity

As toxic agents do not occur in isolation, exposures must consider the ways chemicals interact with one another to modify their toxic effects. Four categories of interaction can be described: additivity, synergism, potentiation, and antagonism (Amdur et al. 1991).

In additivity, the integrated effects of two toxic substances are the arithmetic sum of the quantitative effect of each substance alone. For example, the effect of nerve poisoning when two organophosphate pesticides act simultaneously is additive in that the total response is the sum of the responses that each substance would cause if acting independently.

For synergism, the integrated effects of two toxic substances is greater than the arithmetic sum of the quantitative effect of each substance alone. For example, the combination of acute poisoning by carbon tetrachloride and ethanol will produce more severe liver damage than each substance independently.

Potentiation is where a more toxic effect occurs because an essentially non-toxic agent adds to or enhances the effect of a toxic agent. For example, the non-hepatotoxic (non-liver toxic) agent, isopropanol, when given with the hepatotoxic agent, carbon tetrachloride, will cause greater liver damage than acute poisoning by carbon tetrachloride alone.

Antagonism occurs when the combined quantitative effect of two toxic substances is less than the arithmetic sum of the effect of each substance acting alone. This antagonism includes the concept of an antidote, an agent that works in opposition to the effects of a toxic substance to reduce its toxic effect.

Although all of these interactions are possible, synergism is usually the greatest concern in risk assessment. Normally, mixtures of toxic substances acting by the same mechanism will be additive (Meek et al. 1994). If substances act synergistically, then risk assessment protocols may not be as protective as intended. However, substantial synergism among toxic substances has not been documented in a large number of cases of environmental exposures. It is not practical to assume synergism as a default position without evidence.

All of these characteristics of toxicity challenge basing the predictive assessment of toxic effects strictly on laboratory animal evidence. The reliability of predicting toxic effects is limited by the complexity of real toxic substance exposure and health outcomes.

Absorption, Distribution, Metabolism, and Excretion

In risk assessments, human exposure is usually determined by calculating the substance concentrations in air, food, or water, and determining the consumption rates for breathing, drinking water, and food consumption. However, what actually happens to the human (or experimental animal) when exposed to a substance varies tremendously, depending on the substance, exposure scenario, animal species, and human individual. Interaction between a substance and the body depends on a sequence of processes: absorption, distribution, metabolism, and excretion. These processes help to explain many of the differences in the resulting toxic effects for different substances, the same substance in different species, and the different responses within a species (Hrudey et al. 1996).

Absorption determines the amount of a substance that crosses an exchange boundary in an organism. The three main exchange boundaries are the gastrointestinal tract, lungs, and skin. Substances may enter the body or touch the skin without consequences if they are not absorbed. An exception would be local irritants that affect the point of contact. The gastrointestinal tract controls how much of ingested substances in food and water will be absorbed into the blood stream. Many factors affect the amount of a substance absorbed, including the chemical and physical characteristics of the substance and the species of animal. Likewise, differences exist between individuals of the same species due to variable sensitivity.

A substance is distributed throughout the body in the bloodstream following absorption. Once in the bloodstream, the substance can move to various parts of the body. The substance may be stored in fat tissue or in the bone. Two natural barriers exist in the body, the blood-brain barrier, which prevents many non-essential substances from entering the brain, and the placenta, which separates the mother from the developing fetus.

Once in the bloodstream, the substances can be metabolized by several organs. The liver is the main metabolic organ, but the skin, lungs, intestines, and kidneys also metabolize substances. Metabolism is performed by enzymes that transform parent substances into metabolites. Often the metabolism of non-essential substances changes them into metabolites that promote excretion of the substance from the body. In some cases, the metabolism can create metabolites that are more dangerous than the original substance. For example, some substances become carcinogenic after the first stage of metabolism. The efficiency of metabolism is a significant factor in the different effects of substances on individuals and species.

Excretion of substances takes place primarily through the urine, feces, and exhaled air. Substances are excreted to a lesser extent through sweat and saliva. In the fecal and exhalation excretion routes, the chemicals may have never been absorbed into the circulatory system. In other cases, excretion involves a transfer back from the bloodstream (e.g., alcohol in exhaled breath as a measure of blood alcohol levels).

Types of Toxicological Investigation

Experimental toxicology studies the adverse effects of chemicals on health and the conditions under which those effects occur. Generally, animal bioassays are used to determine dose-response relationships for specific chemicals or mixtures. Bioassays range from short-term acute testing to long-term chronic testing. The adverse effects monitored depend on the substance being tested.

There are three general types of toxicological investigations (Amdur et al. 1991).

1. **Animal bioassays**. Animal bioassays may be further classified according to duration as acute, subchronic, and chronic. Acute bioassays normally use high doses over a short time to determine clinical signs of toxicity or types of adverse reactions. The quantitative relationship between dose and effect reveals the relative potency of the chemical. Acute bioassays cannot predict consequences for chronic, low-level human exposures, but are useful for characterizing high-level exposures and selecting doses for longer term studies. Subchronic bioassays generally range from one to three months and are used to confirm appropriate dose levels and suggest likely effects for longer term chronic studies. Chronic bioassays take longer than three months and include cancer bioassays, which typically last the majority of the test animal's lifespan (e.g., two years in rodents).

2. **Genotoxicity studies**. As chemicals may cause genetic damage leading to consequences ranging from cancer to birth defects, many short-term studies measure genetic and chromosomal mutations in bacteria, fungi, plants, insects, cultured mammalian cells, or small mammals.

3. **Metabolic, pharmacokinetic, or mechanistic studies**. Bioassays that only measure adverse effects for different dose levels may provide little insight into what mechanisms are involved with the substance causing the adverse effect. Consequently, a better understanding of the mechanism of toxic action involves measuring the characteristics and rates of absorption, distribution, and elimination. These compare test results from different species and help to determine how much chemical actually reaches the target organ and differentiate between an external level of exposure and the dose of chemical that reaches the tissue where effects may be caused. The resulting insights allow a more detailed investigation of the mechanisms of toxic action.

Cancer Bioassays

A specific type of chronic test, common in health risk assessment, is the cancer bioassay. Some of the many decisions and procedures involved in conducting a cancer bioassay are briefly summarized. These illustrate the sources of uncertainty in interpreting the results that are the basis for predicting cancer risk in humans. Although performing a cancer bioassay is a rigorous scientific exercise, the design of the bioassay depends on both scientific principles and a range of scientific and regulatory policy choices.

Good laboratory practices include a protocol stating the purpose of the study, how it will be achieved, and a list of staff and their qualifications. Procedures are required for the care of the animals, including cage washing, temperature maintenance, humidity, lighting, and weighing equipment. Additional procedures are required for preparing slides and performing pathological assessments of the tissue (e.g., evidence of tumors). Both an internal and external group should monitor the performance of a bioassay. Several million items of data can be generated from one of these studies, and a single study can cost approximately 2.5 million dollars (Health and Welfare Canada 1991). These financial and intellectual demands limit the number of substances that can be subjected to such testing. Such practical limitations restrict our collective state of knowledge about the carcinogenic properties of substances.

A brief review of the design of a cancer bioassay is presented to highlight the complexity and difficulties involved. Major aspects involved in the design of the bioassay include the following (Health and Welfare Canada 1991).

- **Test substance**. The substance used in the bioassay is usually the same as that to which the public will be exposed. The substance must be checked for any impurities or suspected carcinogens. The protocol must ensure that animals are exposed only to the intended substance and not to products of decomposition or other impurities.

- **Choice of animal species and strain**. Routinely, two animals species are used. In practice, rats and mice are most common. Hamsters, dogs, and primates can be used, but dogs and primates require a very long, and thus extremely expensive, experiment. One problem with rats and mice is that these species have a high incidence of naturally occurring cancer in some tissues, so that any effect of the test substance must be measured against this high background rate of spontaneous tumor occurrence. Another is the existence of different metabolic mechanisms in rodents than in humans.

- **Routes of administration of the test substance**. The dosage route should resemble the major route of human exposure to the test substance. Routes include water, food ingestion, air inhalation, skin application, and direct injection into the bloodstream or the abdominal cavity. The dosage route affects the amount and distribution of the chemical in the animal's body.

- **Number of animals to be used**. Usually fifty animals of each sex are needed for each dose (exposure level) to the substance, with an equal or greater number of control animals. The number of animals is a compromise between providing useful information and the affordability of the entire procedure. Clearly, the basic procedure is already expensive. By limiting the number of test animals at each dose level to only fifty, the minimum detectable response is one out of fifty, or 2%. As the results must be statistically analysed as a single result in relation to the control response, such a minimal response can not establish a 2% response rate with any confidence. These numbers highlight the difficulty in trying to predict dose levels that may pose a much smaller (and therefore more tolerable) risk for humans.

- **Dose selection**. A major problem in a chronic cancer bioassay is to select the maximum tolerated dose (MTD), i.e., the maximum possible dose that does not produce substantial non-tumour effects, affect the longevity of the animals, or reduce the animals' weight by more than 10% compared with the controls. Subchronic studies of ninety days or less are normally performed to establish the MTD. The danger in only selecting doses well below the MTD is that a carcinogenic effect may actually be caused by the substance at a higher dose, but may not be observed within the limited test population at the maximum dose tested. Frequently, two additional doses have been used at one-half and one-quarter of the MTD in addition to the controls. Krewski et al. (1993) suspected that the use of MTD in cancer bioassays has contributed to results for carcinogenesis that may not be meaningful at lower doses. They explored the correlation between estimates of carcinogenic potency and the MTD for 263 full carcinogen bioassay data sets. Krewski et al. (1993) found a highly significant negative correlation between the values of the extrapolation model slope of the dose-response line (introduced on p. 189, as q_1^*) and the MTD (r = -0.94). They attributed their findings to the narrowness of the range of possible carcinogenic dose-response slope values once the limited number of dose levels were fixed as fractions of the MTD. Krewski et al. estimated that once the MTD was established as a dose level that produced a carcinogenic response, the experimental carcinogenic slope could vary over only a range of twenty-two-fold if other doses as low as MTD/4 were used. These findings show that the MTD (which is more of a measure of acute toxicity) strongly determines the quantitative cancer bioassay results and provide compelling grounds for questioning the meaning of quantitative cancer risk estimates, which are calculated using the extrapolation model slope factor.

- **Diet**. Different types of diet can be used. In cancer bioassays, the animals are usually allowed free access to their food. However, restricting access to food reduces the amount of cancer and increases the animals' longevity. Questions are now being asked about the role of excess feeding in causing cancer (Hart et al. 1995).

- **Avoidance of bias**. Even though animals are chosen for genetic similarity, differences still exist between individual animals. Randomization must be used in selecting animals for the different doses of the chemical and conducting the study. The location of the cages can be periodically and randomly switched to avoid biases like lighting and drafts. In addition, keeping animals in separate cages avoids competition over food supply, which can alter the tumour rates (e.g., restricting access to food as mentioned above).

- **Study duration**. The study must cover an appreciable proportion of the animal's lifetime, enough to allow cancer to develop before an otherwise natural death. Typically, two years have been used for rats, and one-and-a-half to two years for mice. Over the past decade, laboratory rat strains have on average increased their body weight and, concurrently, decreased their longevity.

- **Special protocols**. Additional or alternative study goals can be pursued with this bioassay. One of the most difficult is a two-generation study, where animals are exposed to a chemical for two months or more, then mated, and the offspring raised in a similar manner to the conventional bioassay. A different study design can test whether the substance is a tumour promoter, first by providing exposure to a substance known to initiate tumours, and then observing whether ongoing exposure to the test substance will increase the tumour rate.

Other considerations in animal bioassays are the care of animals, post-mortem and pathological examination of tissues, and, finally, statistical analysis and dose-response modelling.

Quantitative Interpretation of Cancer Data

Once the animal data has been generated, it must be interpreted. There are three key issues associated with using animal data to predict human effects: the accuracy of inferring human responses from animal outcomes; whether or not a dosage threshold exists; and inferring low-dose response from high-dose experiments. Although the results of a chronic cancer bioassay are certainly evidence for an effect, estimating effects at low exposure levels in humans involves a level of inference far exceeding the direct evidence that can be derived from the animal data.

Interspecies Comparisons

A concern in toxicological risk assessment is the validity of using laboratory animals to calculate the risk to humans. In a review of genetically related (phylogenetic) animal studies, a 74% agreement on observed carcinogenicity was observed. Obviously, experimental animals and humans are not genetically identical; strict reliance on animal results raises concerns about their validity for human risk assessment. However, nearly all substances that exhibit carcinogenicity in humans (using epidemiological studies) have been eventually found to be carcinogenic in one or more animal models (Health and Welfare Canada 1991).

Some important differences between animals and humans include the following elements.

- **Life span**: rodents typically have life spans of two or three years vs over seventy-five for humans.

- **Genetic homogeneity**: laboratory animals are bred to be genetically similar.

- **Body mass and size**: the mass of a human is 3,500 times greater than that of a mouse, and a human's surface area is only about 390 times greater-approximately a ten-fold difference in the two size ratios.

- **Metabolic processes and rates**: rodents exhibit much higher metabolic rates.

- **Exposure**: the route of exposure used in an animal study may differ from the exposure route of greatest concern for humans.

One interesting similarity between rodents and humans is the probability of developing cancer over their lifetimes. Both have a cumulative cancer risk that increases with age to approximately the fourth power. Approximately 30% of rats and mice will have cancer by the end of their two to three year lifespan if not tested with any chemicals or killed prematurely (Ames 1989). Humans have a 30% chance of developing cancer by the age of eighty (33% in males, 28% in females) (National Cancer Institute of Canada 1996).

Threshold vs Non-Threshold for Carcinogenic Chemicals

One of the most controversial debates in risk assessment is whether or not carcinogenic chemicals have a threshold in their dose-response relationship. If there is not a threshold, then any exposure to a carcinogen poses some risk, even if that risk is negligible. Theoretically, a single molecule of a carcinogenic substance could, under ideal circumstances, react with the DNA in a cell to produce a mutated cell that could subsequently replicate and lead to a cancerous tumour. The probability of this example is extremely small, but not zero (Hrudey and Krewski 1995).

The following analogy attempts to illustrate how the "no threshold hypothesis" might be understood quantitatively. Assume that 1 million people are randomly scattered along an elevated ledge 100 m wide. Crossing the exact edge of the ledge by any finite distance will lead to a fall off the ledge and will cause the person who fell to develop cancer. If everyone must move toward the edge by 90 m from where they were standing, 90% (or 900,000 people) will get cancer. However, if everyone must move toward the edge by only 1 m, 1% (or 10,000 people) will get cancer. Even if the distance for moving toward the edge is reduced to 1 mm, 0.001% (or ten people) will get cancer. No matter how small the distance, the no-threshold hypothesis predicts a probability that someone will develop cancer, even if the estimated probability corresponds to less than one person.

A cautious and protective policy for carcinogens makes the assumption that carcinogenic chemicals do not have a threshold. Many chemicals show measurable evidence of a threshold, while some other chemicals do not. As it is not possible to prove a negative, it is not possible to scientifically prove the absence of a threshold. However, assuming the absence of a threshold does not mean that there is no "safe" level of exposure to a carcinogen, because safety does not equate with zero risk in practical terms (Hrudey and Krewski 1995).

Several complex issues are involved in the debate over thresholds for carcinogens.

- **Mechanisms of carcinogenesis**. The existence of several stages in the development of cancer is widely accepted. The basic stages are initiation, promotion, and progression. Carcinogenic substances may be involved in any one or all of these stages. Theoretically, only initiators should have no threshold, while promoters should exhibit a threshold.

- **Relevance of animals studies**. As most animal studies involve testing only fifty animals at two or three doses, they are not capable of answering the threshold debate. These studies can only detect effects in the region of a 10% response. However, a large study involving a total of over 23,000 mice has been used to observe the shape of the dose-response curve below the 1% response level. The results were inconclusive because the development of bladder tumours seemed to indicate a threshold, but the liver tumours did not (Amdur et al. 1991).

- **Repair mechanisms**. The human body has about 10^{14} cells with 4×10^9 DNA base pairs per cell, which go through 10^{16} division cycles in a normal human life. The estimated error rate for DNA replication is about 10^{-10} mutations per base pair per cell generation. These estimates suggest that natural spontaneous errors will usually be substantially greater than the probability of DNA damage arising from very low level exposure to carcinogenic substances from the environment (Koshland Jr. 1994).

- **Ubiquitous exposure**. Everyone on earth is exposed to known carcinogens. A quantitative foundation of chemistry, Avogadro's number, indicates that there are 6.02×10^{23} molecules per mole of a pure substance (e.g., one mole of benzene is 78 g and will contain 6.02×10^{23} molecules of benzene). As benzene occurs naturally in petroleum and vegetation, exposure to many molecules of benzene (and countless other chemicals) in a lifetime is an inevitable consequence of being alive and cannot be avoided.

Extrapolation from High to Low Dose

Whether or not carcinogenic chemicals have thresholds, extrapolation is still required because human doses are usually several factors of ten smaller than the lowest experimental animal dose. Even when human exposure data are available, the concentrations commonly experienced by the public are significantly lower than the human exposures (usually occupational) found in many epidemiological studies. Extrapolation to lower environmental doses is still usually necessary.

Extrapolation models may be statistical or mechanistic. Statistical models will make some basic assumptions about the dose-response relationship, and then focus on fitting the experimental data. Mechanistic models are similar, but may attempt to establish the assumptions using the conceptual mechanisms of carcinogenesis. But neither model type is currently based on direct measurement of contributing mechanistic parameters, rather, both seek to fit observed patterns or responses in the animal bioassays. Consequently, in both kinds of extrapolation models, the mechanistic basis is still empirically applied, and the models' extrapolation remains without validation and is inherently uncertain.

The most widely used model for extrapolating animal carcinogen bioassay data has been the linearized multistage model (US EPA 1986). This model assumes that there is no threshold for response for exposure to a carcinogen. Although this assumption cannot be verified, this assumption reflects a public health protection policy of caution to avoid underestimating the carcinogenic risk. Thus, the quantitative predictive inference process intentionally seeks an upper limit to the risk estimate. As the US EPA put it: "It should be emphasized that the linearized multistage procedure leads to a plausible upper limit to the risk that is consistent with some proposed mechanisms of carcinogenesis. Such an estimate, however, does not necessarily give a realistic prediction of the risk. The true value of the risk is unknown, and may be as low as zero" (US EPA 1986, 33997).

Another factor intended to make this procedure conservative is the choice of the most sensitive of all study results for use in the extrapolation.

This model generates a linear slope from a zero dose up towards the actual animal exposure data. The slope of this line is called the q_1^*, or the carcinogenic potency slope value. The steeper the slope, the more potent the carcinogen. Not all potency slope values are calculated using the linearized multistage model. When a dose-response relationship can be derived from human epidemiology studies (e.g., inorganic arsenic, benzene, cadmium), other methods of extrapolation are used to estimate the slope value. However, for most substances, quantitative human epidemiological studies that can provide dose response slopes are not available.

These potency slope values are often translated into a unit risk factor. This involves selecting a lifetime risk level, typically one in a million, then using the q_1^* values together with default assumptions about intake rates (breathing rate or water ingestion) to calculate an environmental medium (air or water) concentration that would correspond to the specified risk level.

Other Methods

Although the focus of Part Three, Predictive Inference, is on quantitative risk assessment, other methods are also used to evaluate cancer data. Two of these methods are the human exposure dose/rodent potency dose (HERP) index and the exposure/potency indices (EPIs). The latter is also described as a tumorigenic dose 05 (TD_{05}), which taken together with a suitable margin of exposure, establishes tolerable exposure levels (Meek and Long 1996). Although both methods result in a quantitative estimate of cancer potency from bioassay data, they do not estimate the risk probability to humans. These two methods can be used as guides in comparing the results for several different chemicals.

The HERP index, as it name suggests, compares an estimate of human exposure with rodent potency (in the form of the TD_{50}), expressed as a percent. This method was developed by Ames et al. (1987) as an alternative to quantitative risk assessment, which the authors argued was not scientifically credible because of the numerous uncertainties. Ames et al. point out that their index is not a direct estimate of the human hazard, but can be used to rank relative priorities of concern about carcinogens.

The EPIs are currently used by Health Canada to characterize risk for carcinogens. The potency in this case is the "concentration or dose which induces a 5% increase in the incidence of, or deaths due to, tumours or heritable mutations considered to be associated with exposure" (Meek et al. 1994, 114). The potency is based either on epidemiological studies or more commonly on cancer bioassays. A dose-response model is required to estimate the 5% level, but the uncertainties are small compared with the high to low dose and the animal to human extrapolations. Suitable margins of exposure must be applied to reduce the target exposure to a tolerable level below the 5% response level extracted from the bioassay evidence (Meek and Long 1996).

Exposure Assessment

Once the toxicological information is available, human exposure information is required to complete the risk assessment. Although, in theory, obtaining exposure information should be much easier than performing a toxicological investigation on a chemical, the amount of valid exposure information is surprisingly limited. Just as there is a lack of toxicological information for many chemicals, there is also a lack of exposure information.

There are many factors involved in estimating exposure to humans, including the following.

- **Population**: size, age structure, gender, special risk groups.

- **Exposure pathways**: groundwater, surface water, soil, air, food chain, sediments.

- **Exposure routes**: ingestion, inhalation, dermal contact.

- **Populations at risk**: activity, location, age, high-risk populations (elderly, pregnant women, infants, hypersensitive individuals, personal habits), magnitude and frequency of exposure.

- **Exposure estimation**: concentration, duration, frequency, fluctuation, bioavailability.

Most of the reliable exposure information has been obtained for occupational settings. These exposures are usually greater than the general population's exposure, which makes exposure easier to detect. Monitoring a specific workforce is usually more practical than monitoring the entire population. Often, exposure information for the general public relies on a few measurements taken in one or two major urban centres. Usually, only point estimates of exposure are available, even though large variabilities can exist with time and location. Ideally, some personal monitoring information should be available in addition to the general monitoring of environmental media (air, water, food), but this is rarely the case.

Exposure vs Dose

Distinguishing between exposure and dose is important. Exposure is the contact with the outer boundary of the organisms and is expressed in terms of a concentration. Dose, however, has several possible definitions, including exposure. Rhomberg (1995) provided several definitions based on increasingly smaller, but more relevant, levels of dose as a substance is absorbed, metabolized, and ultimately reaches the target organ:

- exposure -> applied dose and never consumed;

- applied dose -> absorbed dose and not absorbed;

- absorbed dose -> metabolized dose and not activated;

- metabolized dose -> target organ dose and not reaching target organ;

- target organ dose.

Risk Estimates

The risk estimates in this discussion are for only one small part of risk assessment. To compare with the other risk probabilities presented, estimates can only be done for substances classified as carcinogens, having a published potency factor (which implies that suitable toxicological or epidemiological data exist and that a model was used to extrapolate the data), and having some published estimates for typical human exposure. All of these requirements can be met for only a small number of substances. This fact should not be interpreted as evidence that there are countless human carcinogens to which Canadians are exposed in the environment. Rather, those substances that have met all of these requirements tend to be those considered the highest carcinogenic risks.

Levels of Human Exposure

Accurate data on levels of human exposure are difficult to find. As an example, suitable exposure information was required for a quantitative risk assessment for Canadians. Instead of selecting chemicals at random, or attempting to collect all suitable exposure information in Canada, the chemicals reviewed under the Canadian Environmental Protection Act (CEPA) provided a useful summary of exposure information for substances of priority concern. While this list does not include all chemicals that are of concern, it does include many important ones.

The CEPA was proclaimed in June 1988, and allowed the Ministers of the Environment and Health to investigate substances that may adversely affect the environment or human health.

Each CEPA study was supposed to decide whether or not any chemical or substance was "toxic." "Toxic" in this legal definition included three categories:

- harm to the environment;

- danger to the environment on which human life depends; or

- danger to human life or health.

In February 1989, the first Priority Substances List was published, and included forty-four substances (later reduced to forty-three). All assessments had to be published within five years after the publication of the list, a feat that was accomplished. Forty-one reports were prepared (dioxin and furans, and bis (chloromethyl) ether and chloromethyl methyl ether were each combined in one report). These reports and a summary of thirty-five of the substances in the journal Environmental Carcinogenesis & Ecotoxicology Reviews (Meek et al., 1994) have been used in preparing the following summary.

Table 9.1 is a summary of the forty-one reports that shows their classification for human toxicity, carcinogenicity, and whether or not there was exposure data. Only two of the chemicals classified as toxic did not have exposure data, benzidine and mineral fibres.

Health Canada assumed that there was no threshold for carcinogens and automatically classified a level I or II substance as "toxic" to humans. Of the forty-one reports, fifteen were reported as toxic for humans (third category), and all fifteen were carcinogens of level III or greater (but not all level III carcinogens were classified as toxic). Therefore, no non-carcinogens were classified as toxic. Of greater concern was the carcinogen rating. As potency values are only generated for carcinogens, only those chemicals given a rating of I, II, or III were considered. The overall uncertainty in the validity of the hypothetical cancer predictions increases from the I to III ratings.

The exposure evidence collected was meant to be an average for the general population of Canada. The first criterion in selecting the chemicals for quantitative calculations was the presence of exposure data. Of the forty-one CEPA reports, twenty-seven contained some form of exposure data. Most of the exposure data was in the form of tables, but for two chemicals (3,3'-dichlorobenzidine and methyl methacrylate), the data were presented in the text.

The second criterion in selecting chemicals was their carcinogenicity. Of the twenty-seven reports with exposure data, only chemicals with a carcinogenicity rating of I, II, or III were selected. These criteria reduced the number of chemicals to seventeen.

The seventeen chemicals were then reduced to ten for the following reasons.

- Chlorobenzene, 1,4-dichlorobenzene, nickel, styrene and trichloroethylene were either withdrawn from the Integrated Risk Information System (IRIS) database for

Table 9.1 ◆ Summary of CEPA Chemicals for Toxicity, Carcinogenicity, and Exposure Data

No.	Chemical	Tox.	Carcinogen	Exposure Data
1.	Aniline	●	III	No
2.	Arsenic and its Compounds	◆	I (inorg.)	Yes
3.	Benzene	◆	I	Yes
4.	Benzidine	◆	I	No
5.	Bis (2-Chloroethyl) Ether	●	–	No
6.	Bis (2-Ethylhexyl) Phthalate	◆	III/IV	Yes
7.	Bis (Chloromethyl) Ether and Chloromethyl Methyl Ether	–	I	No
8.	Cadmium	◆	II (inorg.)	Yes
9.	Chlorinated Wastewater Effluents	●		No
10.	Chlorinated Paraffins	●	II/III/VI	No
11.	Chlorobenzene [monochlorobenzene]	–	III	Yes
12.	Chromium and its Compounds	◆	I (hex.)	Yes
13.	Creosote-Impregnated Waste Materials	●		No
14.	Di-n-Octyl Phthalate	●	VI	No
15.	Dibutyl Phthalate	–	VI	Yes
16.	1,2-Dichlorobenzene	–	V	Yes
17.	1,4-Dichlorobenzene	–	III	Yes
18.	3,3'-Dichlorobenzidine	◆	II	Yes (text)
19.	1,2-Dichloroethane	◆	II	Yes
20.	Dichloromethane	◆	II	Yes
21.	3,5'-Dimethylaniline	●		No
22.	Dioxins and Furans	◆	III	Yes
23.	Hexachlorobenzene	◆	II	Yes
24.	Inorganic Fluorides	–	–	Yes
25.	Methyl Methacrylate	–	VI	Yes (text)
26.	Methyl Tertiary-Butyl Ether (MTBE)	–	VI	No
27.	Mineral Fibres (Man-Made Vitreous Fibres)	◆	II/III/IV/VI	No
28.	Nickel	◆	I	Yes
29.	Non-Pesticidal Organotin Compounds	●		No
30.	Pentachlorobenzenes	–	VI	Yes
31.	Polycyclic Aromatic Hydrocarbons	◆	II	Yes
32.	Pulp Mill Effluents	–		No
33.	Styrene	–	III	Yes
34.	Tetrachlorobenzenes	–	IV	Yes
35.	1,1,2,2-Tetrachloroethane	●	III	Yes
36.	Tetrachloroethylene	–	IV	Yes
37.	Toluene	–	IV	Yes
38.	Trichlorobenzenes	–	VI	Yes
39.	Trichloroethylene	◆	II	Yes
40.	Waste Crankcase Oils	●		No
41.	Xylenes	–	IV	Yes

CEPA Toxicity

◆ Toxic (legal definition)
● Inadequate Information (legal definition)
– Not Toxic (legal definition)

Carcinogenicity Related to Humans

I Carcinogenic
II Probably carcinogenic
III Possibly carcinogenic
IV Unlikely to be carcinogenic
V Probably not carcinogenic
VI Unclassifiable with respect to carcinogenicity

Source: Environment Canada, CEPA documents

Table 9.2 ◆ Estimated Daily Food Intake (µg/kg.bw/day) by Age Categories

No.	Compound	Age Categories (years)				
		0-0.5	0.5-4	5-11	12-19	20-70
1.	Arsenic (inorganic)	0.20	0.30	0.20	0.10	0.08
2.	Benzene	0.06	0.06	0.05	0.03	0.02
3.	Bis (2-Ethylhexyl) Phthalate	7.90	18.00	13.00	7.20	4.90
4.	Cadmium	0.62	0.64	0.51	0.29	0.21
5.	Chromium (VI)	<0.90	<1.00	<0.70	<0.40	<0.30
6.	3,3'-Dichlorobenzidine					
7.	1,2-Dichloroethane					
8.	Dichloromethane	0.03	0.11	0.09	0.05	0.05
9.	Hexachlorobenzene	0.2100	0.0180	0.0098	0.0048	0.0027
10.	1,1,2,2-Tetrachloroethane					

Source: Environment Canada, CEPA documents

Table 9.3 ◆ Exposure Values

No.	Compound	Food (µg/kg.bw/day)	Drinking Water (µg/L)	Air (µg/m³)
1.	Arsenic (inorganic)	0.11	5	0.0005–0.017
2.	Benzene	0.027	1	7.4
3.	Bis (2-Ethylhexyl) Phthalate	6.8	1–3	3.1
4.	Cadmium	0.28	<0.01–0.09	0.001–0.004
5.	Chromium (VI)	<0.4	0.3–4.3	0.003–0.009
6.	3,3'-Dichlorobenzidine	–	3.4E–10	7.6E–16
7.	1,2-Dichloroethane	–	<0.05–0.139	0.1
8.	Dichloromethane	0.06	0.2–2.6	16.3
9.	Hexachlorobenzene	0.0061	0.0001	0.00015
10.	1,1,2,2-Tetrachloroethane	–	0.05–1	0.1–0.25

Source: Environment Canada, CEPA documents

further review or were not available. Potency values for these chemicals were not available.

- Dioxins and furans were removed because of the difficulty in having exposure data in toxic equivalents and because there were no equivalent IRIS data.

- Polycyclic aromatic hydrocarbons (PAHs) were not included. The exposure data for the specific chemical to be evaluated, benzo[a]pyrene, were for air, while the IRIS database only contained potency values for oral ingestion.

Exposure information was divided into three categories: food, drinking water, and air. Nine of the ten chemicals had tables of the estimated daily intake that were broken into several age groups. The estimated daily intake values for food are shown in Table 9.2. In most cases, the largest daily intake is during the early years; only using the twenty to seventy year age category would underestimate the mean intake over seventy years. Therefore, for the oral category, the estimated intake for food was taken as the weighted mean over the age categories. In the case of hexachlorobenzene, this more than doubled the mean compared only with the intake from twenty to seventy, because of the much greater estimated intake in the early years of life.

Exposure values are shown in Table 9.3. For both drinking water and air, the estimated intake was not compatible with the potency factors, which are expressed in media concentrations to the negative power. Therefore, the concentrations (μg/L for drinking water and μg/m^3 for air) were taken from the footnotes and placed in the estimated intake tables. As exposure concentrations do not depend on age, no adjustments or additional calculations were required.

Several simplifications were made in selecting the exposure values for the calculations in this book.

- Only estimates for the general population were used (some chemicals had separate estimates if they were found near a point source).

- Soil/dirt exposure was not used. However, the daily intake from soil/food exposure was less than the daily intake from food.

- Only indoor air was used (in all but one case, the indoor air had a higher concentration). Overall exposure was greatest indoors as it was assumed that twenty hours per day were spent indoors. In addition, some chemicals had a separate listing for smoking, which contributed significantly to the daily intake. However, for simplicity's sake, these additional exposure variables were not included in the calculations.

Carcinogenic Potency

Carcinogenic potency data were taken from the IRIS registry, which contains reviews of toxicity data for several hundred chemicals. Each review is separated into four sections:

I - Chronic Health Hazard Assessments for Non-Carcinogenic Effects

II - Carcinogenicity Assessment for Lifetime Exposure

III - Health Hazard for Varied Exposure Duration

IV - US EPA Regulatory Actions

For this book, section II was the most important, because it contained the carcinogenic slope potency estimates. These were contained in two subsections: oral exposure, which contained the oral slope factor and drinking water unit risk; and inhalation exposure, which contained the inhalation unit risk. The IRIS registry was assessed on CD-ROM at the Alberta Environmental Protection library in Edmonton. The data was current to June 1996.

Table 9.4 presents the slope factors for the ten chemicals selected from the CEPA documents. As mentioned, several chemicals have been withdrawn from the database for further review or were not available. Although the slope factors for the withdrawn chemicals were available from US Agency for Toxic Substances and Disease Registry documents, we did not use any values currently under review or deleted from the IRIS registry.

Table 9.5 summarizes the basis for the slope factors shown in Table 9.4. Four of the ten chemicals used human data for their extrapolation (arsenic, benzene, cadmium, and chromium), and used several different models. All but the oral arsenic value for these four chemicals were based on occupational exposures. The other six chemicals were based on rodent bioassay data and used the linearized multistage model for extrapolation.

Calculation of the Estimated Lifetime Cancer Risk

The calculation of the estimated lifetime cancer risk is mathematically very simple. The risk, expressed as the lifetime risk of developing cancer, is calculated by multiplying the estimated average exposure by the slope factor. Table 9.6 summarizes these calculations, which used exposure values from Table 9.3 and slope factors from Table 9.4. To help in interpreting the results, they can be expressed as ratios (e.g., 0.00016 is the same as 1 in 6,100). To calculate the annual risk, the reported values must be divided by seventy.

One way to interpret these cautious estimates of lifetime cancer risk is to calculate the upper bound for the annual number of predicted cancers. By dividing the Canadian population by seventy, there are on average 400,000 people in each age category. This assumes a fixed, stable population of 28 million who all live seventy years, but the population is currently greater than 28 million and the life expectancy is greater than seventy years. Multiplying the values in Table 9.6 by 400,000 provides an estimate of the plausible maximum annual number of predicted cancers for each chemical. These estimates are shown in Table 9.7.

Table 9.4 ◆ Carcinogen Slope Factors and Unit Risk Factors

No.	Compound	Carcinogenic Potential*	Oral $(mg/kg/day)^{-1}$	Drinking Water $(\mu g/L)^{-1}$	Air $(\mu g/m^3)^{-1}$
1.	Arsenic (inorganic)	A	1.5E + 0	5E-5	4.3E-3
2.	Benzene	A	2.9E-2	8.3E-7	8.3E-6
3.	Bis (2-Ethylhexyl) Phthalate	B2	1.4E-2	4.0E-7	NA
4.	Cadmium	B1	NA	NA	1.8E-3
5.	Chromium (VI)	A	NA	NA	1.2E-2
6.	3,3'-Dichlorobenzidine	B2	4.5E-1	1.3E-5	NA
7.	1,2-Dichloroethane	B2	9.1E-2	2.6E-6	2.6E-5
8.	Dichloromethane	B2	7.5E-3	2.1E-7	4.7E-7
9.	Hexachlorobenzene	B2	1.6E + 0	4.6E-5	4.6E-4
10.	1,1,2,2-Tetrachloroethane	C	2.0E-1	5.8E-6	5.8E-5

*Note:
A. Known Human Carcinogen
B1. Probable Human Carcinogen
B2. Probable Carcinogen
C. Possible Human Carcinogen
D. Not Classifiable as to Human Carcinogenicity
E. Evidence of Non-Carcinogenicity in Humans

Source: US EPA, IRIS database June 1996

Table 9.5 ◆ Basis for Carcinogen Slope Factors

No.	Compound	Type	Extrapolation Method	Tumour Type, Tested on Humans or Animals, and Exposure Route
1.	Arsenic (inorganic)	Oral	Time- and dose-related formulation of the multistage model	Skin cancer; human (Taiwanese); drinking water
		Inhalation	Absolute-risk linear model	Lung cancer; human (occupational); inhalation
2.	Benzene	Oral	One hit (pooled data)	Leukaemia; human (occupational); inhalation
		Inhalation	One-hit (pooled data)	Same as above
3.	Bis (2-Ethylhexyl) Phthalate	Oral	Linearized multistage procedure, extra risk	Hepatocellular carcinoma and adenoma; mouse, male; diet
		Inhalation	NA	NA
4.	Cadmium	Oral	NA	NA
		Inhalation	Two stage; only first affected by exposure; extra risk	Lung, trachea, bronchus, cancer deaths; human (workplace); inhalation
5.	Chromium (VI)	Oral	NA	NA
		Inhalation	Multistage, extra risk	Lung cancer deaths; human (occupational); inhalation
6.	3,3'-Dichlorobenzidine	Oral	Linearized multistage procedure, extra risk	Mammy adenocarcinoma; rat, female; diet
		Inhalation	NA	NA
7.	1,2-Dichloroethane	Oral	Linearized multistage procedure with time-to-death analysis, extra risk	Hemangiosarcomas; rat, male; gavage
		Inhalation	Linearized multistage procedure, extra risk	Same as above, assuming 100% absorption and metabolism at the low dose
8.	Dichloromethane	Oral	Linearized multistage procedure, extra risk	Hepatocellular adenomas or carcinomas and hepatocellular cancer and neoplastic nodules; mouse, male and female; inhalation and drinking water
		Inhalation	Linearized multistage procedure, extra risk	Combined adenomas and carcinomas; mouse, female; inhalation
9.	Hexachlorobenzene	Oral	Linearized multistage, extra risk	Hepatocellular carcinoma; rat, female; diet
		Inhalation	Linearized multistage, extra risk	Same as above
10.	1,1,2,2-Tetrachloroethane	Oral	Linearized multistage procedure, extra risk	Hepatocellular carcinoma; mouse; gavage
		Inhalation	Linearized multistage procedure, extra risk	Same as above

Source: US EPA, IRIS database June 1996

Table 9.6 ◆ Estimated Lifetime Cancer Risk

Caution: These are upper bound risk estimates based on hypothetical exposures using a highly uncertain extrapolation model. These point estimates should not be used for anything other than rough comparisons with the other health risk data in this book.

No.	Compound	Oral (Food)	Drinking Water	Air
1.	Arsenic (inorganic)	1.6E-4	2.5E-4	2.2E-6 to 7.3E-5
2.	Benzene	7.8E-7	8.3E-7	6.1E-5
3.	Bis (2-Ethylhexyl) Phthalate	9.6E-5	4.0E-7 to 1.2E-6	
4.	Cadmium			1.8E-6 to 7.2E-6
5.	Chromium (VI)			3.6E-5 to 1.1E-4
6.	3,3'-Dichlorobenzidine		4.4E-15	
7.	1,2-Dichloroethane		1.3E-7 to 3.6E-7	2.6E-6
8.	Dichloromethane	4.3E-7	4.2E-8 to 5.5E-7	7.7E-6
9.	Hexachlorobenzene	9.8E-6	4.6E-9	6.9E-8
10.	1,1,2,2-Tetrachloroethane		2.9E-7 to 5.8E-6	5.8E-6 to 1.4E-5

Source: Based on values from Tables 9.3 and 9.4

Table 9.7 ◆ Maximum Plausible Annual Number of Predicted Cancers

Caution: These are upper bound risk estimates based on hypothetical exposures using a highly uncertain extrapolation model. These point estimates should not be used for anything other than rough comparisons with the other health risk data in this book.

No.	Compound	Oral (Food)	Drinking Water	Air
1.	Arsenic (inorganic)	66	100	0.86 to 29
2.	Benzene	0.31	0.33	25
3.	Bis (2-Ethylhexyl) Phthalate	38	0.16 to 0.48	
4.	Cadmium			0.72 to 2.9
5.	Chromium (VI)			14 to 43
6.	3,3'-Dichlorobenzidine		0.0000000017	
7.	1,2-Dichloroethane		0.052 to 0.14	1
8.	Dichloromethane	0.17	0.017 to 0.22	3
9.	Hexachlorobenzene	3.9	0.0018	0.028
10.	1,1,2,2-Tetrachloroethane		0.12 to 2.3	2.3 to 5.8

Source: Based on multiplying values in Table 9.6 by 400,000

Several assumptions have been used to generate Table 9.7. The sole purpose for the Table's numbers is to compare and contrast them with estimates from Parts One and Two, Direct and Indirect Evidence and Inference. Even though the estimates in Table 9.7 are relatively low, they used a method designed to provide cautious upper bound estimates, so that the expected risks from the carcinogen exposures are likely to be much lower.

Uncertainty

Different risk assessment assumptions can change the risk probability estimates by several factors of ten. Differences in estimates based on the model selected for the high-to low-dose extrapolation can be very large. One article compared four types of models for estimates at a 10^{-6} risk level. The most extreme difference was between the one-hit and multi-hit models. For vinyl chloride, the multi-hit model estimated a risk 200 million times smaller than the one-hit model at the same dose level. For nitriloacetic acid, the multi-hit model estimated a risk 400,000 times greater than the one-hit model (Food Safety Council 1980).

Another example of uncertainty is in the risk assessment of N-nitrosodimethylamine (NDMA) to develop a drinking water guideline value. Four separate risk assessments were performed by different agencies, all using the same animal bioassay data (ACES 1992). Three different models were used to estimate the potency slope factor. Of these three models, the highest estimate was eighty times greater than the lowest. After considering further reasonable assumptions, the difference between the highest and lowest proposed guideline values for tolerable exposure to NDMA was over 5,000-fold. This range indicates the uncertainty possible in interpreting the same toxicological information from a single cancer bioassay for a specific chemical.

The uncertainties of predictive inference in quantitative cancer risk assessment far exceed those of epidemiological studies' indirect evidence and inference. Both these kinds of information are dramatically more uncertain than direct evidence for causes of death. However, predictive inference of risk assessment is important despite its inherent uncertainty. The controlled experimental conditions in animal experiments can yield evidence of causation, at least in theory, and biological mechanisms of toxic action can be determined. Unlike direct and indirect evidence gathering, which measures the effects of past exposures, predictive inference can estimate outcomes prior to human exposures (for new drugs and chemicals). The predictive approach evaluates levels of risk far lower than those measured using the epidemiological approach. However, the substantive meaning of the quantitative cancer risk probability predications at extrapolated low doses remains controversial, and any numerical estimates should be used with great caution and a healthy scepticism.

Part four

Discussion and Summary Observations

10 Discussion

The three previous parts of this book have summarized three kinds of health risk information. Direct evidence is based on information collected from individuals, and direct mortality evidence is based on death certificates or other individual investigations of causes of death (e.g., autopsy or fatality inquiries). Indirect evidence and inference come from information collected from individuals, which is analysed for causal inferences using epidemiological methods. Predictive inference is largely based on information from experimental animals studies, which are extrapolated to estimate human health risk. Quantitative predictions by toxicological risk assessment of the number of fatalities can currently only be made for carcinogenic chemicals. Risk assessment methods can only make quantitative predictions about the number of cases of a disease if the human exposure levels are known and if the dose-response relationships are extrapolated from high-dose animal experiments down to the lower documented human exposure levels. In a limited number of cases, quantitative dose-response relationships are available from epidemiological studies (usually for occupational exposures). As none of the extrapolation models available can verify their quantitative risk predictions at lower human exposure levels, using these models is a public health policy choice, not a decision dictated by scientific evidence.

Comparisons Between Categories

Direct Evidence to Epidemiology (Indirect Evidence)

Many studies that generate indirect evidence and inference rely on direct evidence, in addition to other information. An example is the Illing and Kaiserman (1995) study, which used the causes of death from the International Classification of Disease (ICD) codes and RRs from a cohort epidemiological study to estimate smoking-attributable mortality (SAM). Ultimately, direct evidence is the foundation for all health risk estimates. Some indirect studies have sufficient scope and resources to collect their own direct evidence for their population sample. In such cases, the validity of the cause of death evidence will usually be better than that available from strict reliance on death certificate data. This is especially true for the more subtle causes of death.

Direct Evidence to Toxicological Risk Assessment (Predictive Inference)

There is a very limited tangible relationship between direct evidence and predictive inference. Both are used to estimate the health risk from chemicals. An example of direct evidence would be acute accidental or intentional poisoning by chemicals using historical observations. The estimate of the number of accidental poisonings this year would be based on the most recent poisoning data plus historical poisoning data. For predictive inference, the quantitative risk estimates are based on exposure estimates and extrapolated dose-response models for chronic (seventy-year) exposure to chemical carcinogens. Health risk estimates use knowledge of exposure concentrations and chemical potencies. Direct evidence estimates can be verified by future observations. Predictive inference estimates cannot be truly verified because they presume a causal link that will remain uncertain.

Predictions of disease may be invalidated by future experience, for example, predicting more deaths from a particular disease than subsequently arise from all causes of that disease. But, if the total disease toll exceeds that predicted for a specific cause, we are not able to know directly what proportion of this disease can be attributed to a specific cause.

Epidemiology (Indirect Evidence) to Toxicological Risk Assessment (Predictive Inference)

Some of the most interesting comparisons occur between epidemiology and toxicological risk assessment. The overlap between these two sources of knowledge is small, but important. The chemical risks, and specifically the carcinogenic chemical risks, studied in toxicological risk assessment address one small part of epidemiology. However, most of the chemicals studied for predictive inference have no equivalent or comparable human-based information. The overlap occurs where both epidemiology and toxicological risk assessment have been used to evaluate the risk posed by a chemical.

Nelson (1988) summarized some of the limitations and advantages of epidemiology and toxicological risk assessment (Table 10.1). The major advantage of epidemiology is its human relevance. However, there are many limitations in epidemiological studies of environmental chemicals. The major disadvantage of toxicological risk assessment is its limited relevance to humans; however, there is very good control of many variables.

Most of the substances identified as human carcinogens, based on epidemiological evidence, are also experimental animal carcinogens. Of the fifty-seven substances and exposures listed by the IARC as associated with human cancer (see Table 7.10), only five have not been carcinogenic in animal studies. These five are alcoholic beverages (ethanol), oral contraceptives (sequential), smokeless tobacco products, talc containing asbestiform fibres, and treosulfan (Vainio and Wilbourn 1993). These findings link animal study to human cancer causation. However, this link does not mean that any individual substance that is carcinogenic in animal studies will cause cancer in humans.

Table 10.1 ◆ Comparison of Epidemiology and Toxicological Risk Assessment

Factor	Epidemiology	Toxicological Risk Assessment
Relevancy	Excellent	Uncertain
Control of Variables (exposure, environment and confounding factors)	Poor	Excellent
Identifying Causal Factors	Poor	Excellent
Size of Population	Can be large	Limited
Sensitivity	Poor	Poor
Genetic Diversity	Broad	Normally deliberately narrow
Intercurrent Disease	Not controllable	Controllable
Study of Mechanisms	Ethical hindrances, but directly relevant	Easily accessible, but uncertain relevancy
Diagnostic Tests	Severely restricted	Unrestricted

Source: Nelson 1988, Table 4-1

Higginson points out the difficulty of using epidemiology to detect the relatively low risks of most chemical health risks, as well as the inability of "negative" studies to refute chemical risks: "Even under favorable conditions, analytical epidemiological studies usually are insufficiently sensitive to detect cancer increases or decreases below 1 in 1000, except for certain rare tumors. A 'negative study', even with large numbers, will usually be compatible with a 20% increase in risk. The interpretation of 'negative' or weak associations in epidemiological investigations requires considerable scientific judgment and expertise..." (Higginson 1992, 150).

The nature of these problems is illustrated in Table 10.2, adapted and modified from a table originally in McMichael (1991). Table 10.2 compares different environmental levels of human exposure to substances with the much higher levels normally required for a 50% response in animal experiments. Table 10.2 illustrates what RR would theoretically arise if these comparative levels were allowed to occur in a human population (with some background level of disease from other causes) if a perfect epidemiology study could be performed (with no bias, misclassification, or confounding).

Table 10.2, which is a little intimidating at first, is best understood by following a few examples. Consider first Exposure Level A, equivalent to the exposure that caused a 50% response in animal toxicology experiments. Using this knowledge, we could assume an equivalent incidence level of 500 per 1,000 humans exposed (Incidence Level A, lower in the same column). If the background rate for the resulting disease were very high in the population, say fifty per 1,000 (Background Level I), the total observed rate in an exposed population would be 550 per 1,000. This would lead to an RR calculation (incidence in

Table 10.2 ◆ **Comparison of the Quantitative Capabilities of Human Epidemiological Studies with Toxicological Risk Assessment Predictive Levels**

		Usual range of maximum environmental exposures to humans		
	Background level of cumulative (lifetime) incidence of any specific disease in the human population which is not exposed to the test causative agent	**Level of human exposure to a test causative agent expressed as a multiple of the dose of that agent found experimentally to induce a given specific disease in 50% of laboratory animals**		
		Exposure Level A 1	Exposure Level B 0.01	Exposure Level C 0.0001
		Predicted or expected excess incidence of the specified disease in humans at the above Exposure Level, yielding the resulting Relative Risks (RR) shown below for each resulting Incidence Level		
		Incidence Level A 500/1000	Incidence Level B 5/1000	Incidence Level C 0.05/1000
	Background Level I 50/1000	11	1.1	1.001
Typical range of background lifetime risks of specific diseases or disorders	Background Level II 10/1000	51	1.5	1.005
	Background Level III 5/1000	101	2.0	1.01
	Background Level IV 1/1000	501	6.0	1.05

The above Relative Risks (**RR**) may be detectable by epidemiological study. Although a **RR = 1.1** could conceivably be detectable in a large closely controlled study, with high statistical power, in practice, a **RR < 2 to 3** from a single risk factor epidemiology study will have limited meaning (Taubes 1995)

Source: Adapted and modified from McMichael 1991

exposed population/incidence in unexposed population) of 550/50 or an RR = 11. This RR is certainly high enough to be detectable in a good epidemiological study. However, these numbers would not be found for any relevant environmental exposure.

More realistic is the right-hand column of Table 10.2, where the human exposure level from the environment is only 0.0001 (Exposure Level C) of the level that causes a 50% response in an animal toxicology experiment. In this case, direct translation of the animal results to humans would predict a human response of 0.05 cases per 1,000 exposed (Incidence Level C). For a background disease level of fifty per 1,000 (Background Level I), the RR would be 50.05/50 = 1.001, a level that could never be discriminated in even the largest and most sophisticated epidemiological study. Even for a rarer disease with a much lower background level (1 in 1,000 or Background Level IV), the RR would be 1.05, beyond a level that could be discriminated in any environmental epidemiology study. In fact, a critical commentary on risk factors or environmental epidemiology has stated (as have many leading epidemiologists) that there is limited practical meaning in RR levels of less than two or three from a single epidemiology study, unless there is substantial supporting evidence from experimental toxicology and clinical investigations to support causal inference for the RR (Taubes 1995).

The product sought in toxicological risk assessment is often a de minimis risk level of one in 100,000, or one in 1 million lifetime risk. Such risk levels will correspond to a very small RR unless a rare disease (extremely low background rate in the population) is involved. These observations highlight the discrepancy between the level of quantitative risk predictions of epidemiological studies and the extrapolation models commonly used in quantitative risk assessment.

Of the ten chemicals used in Part Three, Predictive Inference, to generate risk estimates in humans, four were based on potency factors that used human data (based on extrapolation from epidemiological studies), not extrapolation for laboratory animal carcinogen bioassay results. We have this relatively high number of human-based potency factors because the first priority substances list sensibly focused on chemicals of greatest concern to humans. However, only a handful of the hundreds of chemicals tested for carcinogenicity have any supporting epidemiological information on human health risk.

One of the most relevant comparisons of indirect and predictive information was provided by Gough (1989). Gough compared the Doll and Peto (1981) estimates of cancer deaths relating to environmental factors using epidemiological information with the US EPA estimates of cancer incidence relating to environmental factors (derived from quantitative risk assessment that used low-dose extrapolation models). Table 10.3 presents the comparison. A conversion is needed because the US EPA estimates were for developing cancer (incidence), while the Doll and Peto estimates were for cancer mortality. Gough converted the cancer incidence to mortality by dividing the incidence by two, because on average across all forms of cancer, approximately 50% of people die within five years of cancer diagnosis.

Table 10.3 ◆ Annual Cancer Mortality Associated with Environmental Exposures

Study	Pollution*	Geophysical Factors*	Occupation*	Consumer Products*
Doll and Peto (range)	2% (<1–5%)	3% (2–4%)	4% (2–8%)	<1% (<1–2%)
U.S. EPA	1–3%	3–6%	<1–4%	<1%

Note: *Doll and Peto (1981) definitions:
Pollution—cancer from air pollution, water pollution, and pesticide residues on food;
Geophysical factors—cancer from UV radiation and ionizing radiation;
Occupation—cancer from occupational exposures;
Consumer Products—cancer from industrial products (e.g., detergents, paints, dyes).

Source: Gough 1989, Table 4

Table 10.4 ◆ Summary of Statistics Related to Mortality, 1994

Parameter	Males	Females
Deaths	109,742	97,335
Mortality Rate	7.7 deaths per 1,000	6.6 deaths per 1,000
Infant Mortality	6.3 per 1,000 live births	
Life Expectancy at Birth	75.1 years	81.1 years

Source: Statistics Canada 1996A

Table 10.5 ◆ Summary of Major Causes of Death, 1994

Cause of Death	Total Annual Deaths Males	Females	% of Total Annual Deaths Males	Females
Infectious Diseases	2,300	897	2.1	1.5
Cancer	31,496	26,815	28.7	28.2
Cardiovascular Diseases	39,885	38,688	36.3	37.9
Respiratory Diseases	10,087	8,255	9.2	8.9
External Causes	9,046	4,150	8.2	6.4
Other	16,928	18,530	15.4	17.1
All Causes	109,742	97,335	100.0	100.0

Source: Statistics Canada 1996A

Gough concluded that both epidemiological and toxicological risk assessment methods generate similar estimates for the major sources of cancer risk. Despite the vastly different methods used, in a broad comparison, the estimates yielded from these two different approaches were very similar.

Summary of Health Risk Evidence and Inference

This section will highlight some of the health risks that are based on direct evidence, indirect evidence and inference, and predictive inference.

Health Risks Based on Direct Evidence

Table 10.4 is a summary of mortality-related statistics in Canada for 1994. Deaths, mortality rates, infant mortality, and life expectancy are included. There were approximately 205,000 deaths in Canada in 1994, which averages out to approximately 560 deaths per day. Males continue to have a greater number of deaths and mortality, and, consequently, a lower life expectancy by approximately six years than females.

Table 10.5 is a summary of the major causes of death in Canada in 1994. Cardiovascular disease, cancer, respiratory diseases, and external causes (fatal injuries from accidents, suicides, and homicides) are the four leading causes of death for both sexes. Infectious disease is no longer a leading cause of death in Canada, but was a major factor until earlier this century. Figures 4.5 and 4.6 show the age-standardized death rates for the five major causes of death from 1930 to 1990. These Figures, based on thousands of pieces of information, summarize trends in mortality and health in recent Canadian history.

Cardiovascular disease has remained the leading cause of death, with two dramatic changes. Mortality increased for cardiovascular disease until approximately 1950, and then, gradually for males and immediately for females, mortality began to decrease substantially by approximately two-fold. Cancer mortality rates have been increasing slightly for males, while staying constant for females. Infectious diseases, which had already declined significantly before 1930, continued to decline to current low levels. The impact of HIV infection has begun to increase infectious disease mortality levels, mostly in males to date. External causes have remained relatively stable over time, with a small decrease starting around 1975.

Table 10.6 is a summary of the 1994 causes of death for Canadians, using the seventeen categories from the ICD-9 code. Three methods rank and compare the size of the various causes of death: percentage of total deaths, percentage of the potential years of life lost (the PYLL @ seventy-five), and the loss of life expectancy (the LLE). The PYLL and LLE compare the differential between the actual age at death for each death with a specified life expectancy age. The PYLL places much greater weight on early deaths than the LLE. The

Table 10.6 ◆ Causes of Death, 1994

Cause of Death	Total		The PYLL (@75 yrs)		The LLE	
	Males	Females	Males	Females	Males	Females
Infectious Diseases	2.1%	0.9%	5.6%	1.9%	2.4%	1.1%
Cancer	28.7%	27.5%	23.0%	38.0%	28.7%	33.7%
Endocrine and Others	2.9%	3.5%	2.4%	2.8%	2.5%	3.2%
Blood Diseases	0.3%	0.4%	0.3%	0.3%	0.3%	0.3%
Mental Disorders	1.8%	2.8%	1.2%	0.8%	1.3%	1.6%
Nervous System Diseases	2.4%	3.4%	2.2%	3.1%	2.1%	3.1%
Cardiovascular Diseases	36.3%	39.7%	20.2%	15.6%	34.5%	33.6%
Respiratory Diseases	9.2%	8.5%	3.3%	3.5%	6.9%	6.4%
Digestive Diseases	3.6%	3.9%	3.3%	3.1%	3.2%	3.4%
Genito-Urinary Diseases	1.5%	1.7%	0.6%	0.8%	1.1%	1.4%
Pregnancy-Related	–	<0.1%	–	0.1%	–	<0.1%
Skin Diseases	0.1%	0.1%	<0.1%	0.1%	<0.1%	0.1%
Musculo-Skeletal Diseases	0.2%	0.7%	0.2%	0.6%	0.2%	0.6%
Congenital Anomalies	0.6%	0.5%	3.6%	5.1%	1.5%	1.8%
Perinatal Conditions	0.5%	0.5%	3.9%	5.9%	1.6%	2.0%
Ill-Defined	1.5%	1.5%	4.1%	3.4%	2.0%	1.7%
External Causes	8.2%	4.3%	26.2%	14.9%	11.5%	6.1%

Source: Statistics Canada 1996A

leading causes of deaths using the PYLL for males were external causes, cancer, and cardio-vascular diseases. For females, the leading causes of death using the PYLL were cancer, external causes, and cardiovascular disease. The LLE shifted the various percentages, but cardiovascular disease and cancer remained the most significant for both sexes. The LLE's numerical estimates may be more insightful for the individual than the PYLL, because the LLE approximates the potential increase in life expectancy across the population if the specified cause of death were eliminated, assuming it was not interactive with any other causes of death.

Table 10.7 summarizes the annual risk of dying by age and sex in Canada based on 1994 information. To aid in interpretation, the annual mortality rate values (deaths per 100,000) have been converted to chance or odds of death per year, and are displayed in adjacent columns. Expressing this information as odds makes it more individual than the population rates. For example, an annual mortality rate of 509 deaths per 100,000 for males aged fifty to fifty-four equals a one in 196 chance of dying in that year for a male in that age category. Of course, every individual male in Canada will have countless individual risk factors that modify his risk above or below the average for that category.

As we would expect, age is strongly and consistently associated with the risk of dying. In the early years of life (ages 5–9), the annual chance of dying is less than one in 5,000, while for later years (85+) the annual chance becomes greater than one in ten. Obviously, we know that our chances of death increase dramatically as we age, given the inevitability of death. However, the actual numerical levels may not be widely understood, beyond what one might see in increasing life insurance premiums. For example, males advancing from the fifty to fifty-four category to the fifty-five to fifty-nine category can see their average annual risk of death from all causes increase from one in 196 to one in 116, almost doubling the total annual risk of death. Of course, the apparent sharp increase at fifty-five is an artifact of grouping the data in five-year categories. The chances will increase smoothly as one ages, not in five-year steps.

Table 10.8 combines Tables 10.5 and 10.7. Table 10.8 shows the annual risk of dying by selected age, sex, and major cause of death in Canada for 1994. Six age categories present the range in mortality with age. Both the death per rate 100,000 and chance of dying are presented. Table 10.8 highlights the substantially greater mortality risk for males from some causes of death (e.g., infectious diseases because of AIDS, and external causes because of accidents and suicides).

Table 10.7 ◆ Annual Risk of Dying by Age and Sex, 1994

Age Categories	Deaths per 100,000 Males	Females	Chance of Dying Males	Females
<1	694	558	1 in 140	1 in 180
1–4	35	28	1 in 2,800	1 in 3,500
5–9	18	14	1 in 5,500	1 in 7,300
10–14	24	17	1 in 4,100	1 in 6,000
15–19	84	31	1 in 1,200	1 in 3,200
20–24	102	34	1 in 980	1 in 2,900
25–29	107	38	1 in 940	1 in 2,700
30–34	128	50	1 in 780	1 in 2,000
35–39	168	79	1 in 600	1 in 1,300
40–44	229	119	1 in 440	1 in 840
45–49	310	197	1 in 320	1 in 510
50–54	509	319	1 in 200	1 in 310
55–59	865	523	1 in 120	1 in 190
60–64	1,484	804	1 in 67	1 in 120
65–69	2,372	1,279	1 in 42	1 in 78
70–74	3,721	2,045	1 in 27	1 in 49
75–79	6,011	3,446	1 in 17	1 in 29
80–84	9,636	5,924	1 in 10	1 in 17
85–89	14,942	10,336	1 in 7	1 in 10
90+	23,007	19,783	1 in 4	1 in 5
All Ages	757	660	1 in 130	1 in 150

Source: Statistics Canada 1996A

Table 10.8 ◆ Annual Risk of Dying by Selected Age, Sex, and Major Cause of Death, 1994

Infectious Diseases (Annual Risk)

Age Categories	Deaths per 100,000		Chance of Dying	
	Males	Females	Males	Females
<1	9.6	6.4	1 in 10,000	1 in 16,000
5–9	0.5	0.7	1 in 200,000	1 in 140,000
25–29	10.9	1.3	1 in 9,200	1 in 76,000
45–49	23.3	3.8	1 in 4,300	1 in 26,000
65–69	19.5	10.0	1 in 5,100	1 in 10,000
85–89	122.9	75.6	1 in 810	1 In 1,300
All Ages	15.9	6.1	1 in 6,300	1 in 16,000

Cancer (Annual Risk)

Age Categories	Deaths per 100,000		Chance of Dying	
	Males	Females	Males	Females
<1	3.5	1.6	1 in 28,000	1 in 62,000
5–9	3.6	2.6	1 in 28,000	1 in 39,000
25–29	8.6	7.0	1 in 12,000	1 in 14,000
45–49	88.2	112.6	1 in 1,100	1 in 890
65–69	942.4	585.3	1 in 110	1 in 170
85–89	3,009.0	1,480.5	1 in 33	1 in 68
All Ages	217.3	181.7	1 in 460	1 in 550

Cardiovascular Diseases (Annual Risk)

Age Categories	Deaths per 100,000		Chance of Dying	
	Males	Females	Males	Females
<1	13.6	10.2	1 in 7,300	1 in 9,800
5–9	0.5	0.4	1 in 200,000	1 in 240,000
25–29	4.7	3.2	1 in 21,000	1 in 32,000
45–49	81.2	26.4	1 in 1,200	1 in 3,800
65–69	875.7	378.0	1 in 110	1 in 270
85–89	6,555.5	5,298.4	1 in 15	1 in 19
All Ages	275.2	262.2	1 in 360	1 in 380

Respiratory Diseases (Annual Risk)

Age Categories	Deaths per 100,000		Chance of Dying	
	Males	Females	Males	Females
<1	14.6	6.4	1 in 6,800	1 in 16,000
5–9	0.3	0.6	1 in 340,000	1 in 160,000
25–29	1.5	1.2	1 in 65,000	1 in 81,000
45–49	6.6	4.7	1 in 15,000	1 in 21,000
65–69	172.8	88.2	1 in 580	1 in 1,100
85–89	2,267.1	1,014.2	1 in 44	1 in 99
All Ages	69.6	55.9	1 in 1,400	1 in 1,800

External Causes (Annual Risk)

Age Categories	Deaths per 100,000		Chance of Dying	
	Males	Females	Males	Females
<1	15.7	17.7	1 in 6,400	1 in 5,700
5–9	8.5	5.1	1 in 12,000	1 in 20,000
25–29	67.2	17.5	1 in 1,500	1 in 5,700
45–49	59.8	18.9	1 in 1,700	1 in 5,300
65–69	66.8	28.8	1 in 1,500	1 in 3,500
85–89	400.2	280.7	1 in 250	1 in 360
All Ages	62.4	28.1	1 in 1,600	1 in 3,600

Source: Statistics Canada 1996A

Health Risks Based on Indirect Evidence and Inference

The discussion above has addressed only direct information. The large number of Tables and Figures in Part One, Direct Evidence, indicate the substantial body of information available. Unfortunately, similar extensive data summaries are not readily available for indirect evidence and inference. The following summary details some available indirect health risk information, judged sufficiently valid for a meaningful comparative discussion.

- Age is the overriding risk factor for most diseases. For example, assume that any hypothetical risk factor doubles your chances of dying from cardiovascular disease at all ages (i.e., a relative risk of two). For a male aged 25–29, the annual risk of dying from cardiovascular diseases is approximately one in 21,000 (see Table 10.8), so that doubling the risk yields approximately one chance in 10,500. For a male aged 65–69, the annual risk of dying from cardiovascular disease is approximately one in 110, so that doubling that risk is approximately one in fifty-five. The increased risk between the two age categories varies by a factor of twenty, vs an increase of two for the hypothetical risk factor. As noted in the discussion of Table 10.7, males moving from the 50–54 to the 55–59 age category will see their total annual risk of death from all causes almost double. Although a hypothetical risk factor with an RR of two may seem substantial, age is a dominant factor, with much greater certainty of effect averaged across the entire population.

- Approximately 26% of all male and 15% of all female mortality has been attributed to smoking. Of all the sources of epidemiological (indirect) evidence for any major health risk, the evidence for smoking and mortality is the most extensive and convincing. Cancer and cardiovascular disease account for roughly equal proportions of smoking-attributable mortality (approximately 40% each) while non-cancer respiratory diseases account for approximately 20% (Illing and Kaiserman 1995).

- Diet has been shown to be an important determinant of health risk, but, unfortunately, reliable quantitative estimates of health risk associated with the Canadian diet were not found.

- The major factors in cancer causation have been quantitatively summarized by Doll and Peto (1981), and these estimates appear consistent with more recent estimates. Miller (1992) identified some of the principal factors associated with several types of cancer (Table 8.2).

- The major risk factors for cardiovascular disease have been estimated as follows: 30% of mortality is attributable to high blood pressure; 19% to diabetes; 17% to smoking; and 15% to elevated serum cholesterol (Heart and Stroke Foundation of Canada 1995).

- The overwhelming risk factor for external causes is the influence of alcohol on accidental deaths. Approximately 40% of all motor vehicle fatalities were associated with blood alcohol levels over the legal limit, and reasonable inferences suggest that alcohol impairment plays a contributory role in many other types of fatal injuries.

Health Risks Based on Predictive Inference

Toxicological risk assessment (predictive inference) provides very little information on major human health risks. The uncertainty of estimating those risks is extremely large. Table 9.7 estimates the cancer risk (intentionally cautious over-estimates) for Canadians of ten chemicals at average exposures. At these average chemical exposure levels, the overall impact on Canadians' health should be very low, even using cautious upper limit estimates. Specific individual exposures, however, may have significantly higher exposures, which would increase risk for a small segment of the population. Such localized situations do not substantially affect regional or national health risk statistics.

Table 10.9 is a summary of annual mortality risks from the three different categories: direct evidence, indirect evidence and inference, and predictive inference. Ideally, Table 10.9 should have a big red Caution stamped on it because of all the qualifications that surround it. The differences in evidentiary basis for the different estimates are very large, as are the differences in uncertainty.

Method

The sections of Table 10.9 were constructed as follows.

1. Direct evidence.

    a. The first four entries were taken from Tables 10.7 and 10.8; motor vehicle fatalities was based on approximately 3,500 deaths in 1994; lightning was based on an average of approximately five deaths/year for 1991–1994.

2. Indirect evidence and inference.

    a. Occupation. This section was based on values from Table 7.7, both the total occupation and the occupations with the highest and lowest mortality rates.

    b. Recreation. This section was based on values from Table 7.9, and used recreations that covered the range of mortality rates.

    c. Smoking. This section was based on the mortality rate (already expressed as deaths per 100,000) from Table 7.2.

Table 10.9 ◆ Annual Mortality Risks From Several Sources

Caution: These values should normally not be compared unless a complete explanation is included of how the estimates were generated and of the relative uncertainty in different estimates. All of these annual risks are highly age dependent. When no age category is included in the estimate, variations of several factors of ten can be hidden.

Source		Deaths per 100,000	Chance of Dying
1. Direct Evidence (1994)			
All Ages, All Causes of Death	Males	760	1 in 130
	Females	660	1 in 150
Ages 5–9, All Causes of Death	Males	18	1 in 5,500
	Females	14	1 in 7,300
Ages 85–89, All Causes of Death	Males	15,000	1 in 7
	Females	10,000	1 in 10
All Ages, All Cancer Deaths	Males	220	1 in 460
	Females	180	1 in 550
Motor Vehicle (All)		12.5	1 in 8,000
Lightning		0.017	1 in 5,900,000
2. Indirect Evidence and Inference Occupation			
Total Occupation		7.3	1 in 13,700*
Mining, quarrying, and oil wells		90.0	1 in 1,100*
Health and social services		0.5	1 in 200,000*
Recreation			
Mountain Climbing—dedicated		600	1 in 170*
Parachuting		180	1 in 570*
Scuba Diving—amateur		42	1 in 2,400*
Snowmobiling		13	1 in 7,600*
Mountain Hiking		6.4	1 in 15,700*
Skiing—racing		2.5	1 in 40,000*
Smoking			
	Males	210	1 in 480
	Females	100	1 in 1,000
3. Predictive Inference (Risk Assessment Low Dose Extrapolation Models)			
Arsenic (inorganic)		0.35	<1 in 290,000
Benzene		0.045	<1 in 2,200,000
Dichloroethane		0.0017	<1 in 59,000,000

* These chances expressed for those participating in the activity.

Source: Statistics Canada 1995; Halperin 1993; Cohen 1991; Illing and Kaiserman 1995

3. Predictive inference.

    a. This section was based on Table 9.7. As the values were for cancer incidence, they were divided by two to estimate the mortality, as discussed earlier. The highest and lowest of the ten chemicals in Table 9.7 were selected, in addition to benzene, which is between the extremes. These estimates were derived from quantitative risk assessment low-dose extrapolation models. These models use cautious upper bound assumptions to overestimate what is likely to happen.

All values were rounded to two significant figures for consistency, despite our recognition that predictive risk estimates are not reliable to more than one significant figure. Not only are there substantial differences in uncertainty between the estimates, many of these estimates should more logically be expressed in terms of lifetime risks. Ideally, all the estimates should also include age categories. The occupational, recreational, and possibly lightning categories may be the most insensitive to the effects of age. These first two groups also express the chance of dying only for those participating in the activity. Other risks, like cancer, smoking, and the chemical-specific cancer risk estimates (based on a risk over a seventy-year lifetime), must be interpreted with great caution, as we have noted.

Summary of Uncertainty

Table 10.10 summarizes the uncertainty estimates for the three categories of health risks. Care should be taken in using these uncertainty estimates, since they may not completely portray all of the uncertainty for some health risks, especially for the more specific parameters.

For indirect evidence and inference, the statistical confidence limits do not account for bias and confounding. It has been estimated that the actual range of the confidence limits should be at least twice as large as commonly reported in studies to account for bias and confounding (Shlyakhter et al. 1993). Estimates of motor vehicle, recreational, and occupational (acute) fatalities are more certain because they are based on direct evidence, unlike most other risk factor estimates that rely on greater inference.

Uncertainty is related to how well and consistently an outcome can be measured. If everyone is included (direct evidence) and the measures are direct and do not need substantial judgement, then estimates with low uncertainty are possible. When only a subset of the population is measured (indirect evidence and inference), the uncertainty of the estimated risk increases. This is especially true when exposure situations or population characteristics are different, for example, using laboratory animals to predict human health risks (predictive inference). Even though these estimates are highly uncertain, they do evaluate health risks in a predictive manner, which is better than having no information at all. Preventing harm from new substances or new exposures to substances is only possible using predictive risk assessment methodologies.

Table 10.10 ◆ Summary of Uncertainty

Caution: Care should be taken in interpreting the uncertainty estimates, since they may not accurately portray the uncertainty for some health risks, especially for the more specific ones.

Category	Parameter	Appraisal of the Minimum Level of Uncertainty in Estimates
Direct	Total number of deaths (including separation by sex and age)	Less than 0.1%
	Population-based rates (not by cause of death)	Less than 5% (overall population); less than 10% (age-specific)
	Cause of death	Less than 5% (major category level); less than 10% to greater than 50% (three-digit ICD codes)
Indirect Evidence and Inference	Motor vehicle, recreational, occupational (acute)	Less than 10%
	Smoking	Plus or minus 15% for estimating total annual mortality; greater than 15% for specific causes of death (among diseases, lung cancer would be most certain)
	Smoking—second-hand smoke	Greater than ten fold (i.e., +/-1000%) for lung cancer and significantly larger for other cancers
	Diet	Plus or minus 100% for estimating contribution to total cancer mortality (less for some specific cancers); significantly larger for non-cancer mortality
	Societal factors	Less than 25% (quantitative estimates of education, level of income); greater than 100% (occupation); stress-currently unknown
	Environmental factors	Less than 25% for extremely well-documented risks to several factors of ten
Predictive Inference	Selection of low-dose extrapolation model	From two factors of ten (100) to over eight factors of ten (100,000,000)
	Overall toxicological risk assessment	Larger than uncertainty in selection of model, because of additional uncertainty from variable exposures and susceptibilities

Source: Estimates based on Parts One, Two, and Three of this book

Summary Observations

Direct Evidence

A large and relatively reliable source of health risk information is available from the Statistics Canada mortality statistics. Overall, very low uncertainty is associated with direct information, especially compared with other sources of health risk information. Although there are well recognized inaccuracies in reporting subtle causes of death, the comprehensiveness of direct evidence makes it invaluable for evaluating major causes of death in the entire population. This source provides detailed knowledge of recent health outcomes and reliable evidence on historical trends.

Age is the single most significant risk factor relating to mortality. As obvious as this is, many discussions of health risk do not explicitly mention age, an oversight that ignores vitally important insights. Annual mortality rates vary over one thousand fold with age. An exponential increase in mortality related to age starts after the first few years of life. Infant mortality (under the age of one), though significantly lower than in the past, still has a mortality rate comparable with adults in their fifties. Overall life expectancy has significantly increased in Canada over the last sixty-five years. A large part of this increase can be attributed to substantial decreases in infant mortality. The change in life expectancy for those who reach eighty has not increased substantially over this period.

A dramatic decline in infectious disease mortality occurred over this century. This decline has allowed chronic diseases (cancer and heart disease) to assume a progressively larger proportion of total mortality. The recent rise in mortality from AIDS, primarily among men, runs counter to this trend, but the numbers have not been large enough to influence substantially the major categories of mortality.

There are consistent and often large differences in the mortality rates between the sexes; males have a substantially higher mortality rate for most causes of death compared with females. These statistics demonstrate that the sex of an individual, along with the influence of age, are the dominant risk factors for death from all causes which apply to any individual. There is also evidence that marital status is associated with substantially different risks of mortality.

The percentage of total deaths from any cause is commonly used to summarize the causes of death. However, two measures, potential years of life lost (PYLL) and loss of life expectancy (LLE), provide important additional information in death statistics. These measures incorporate the age at death relative to a predefined life expectancy or reference age, and give greater weighting to early or premature deaths.

Epidemiology (Indirect Evidence and Inference)

The extensive data provided by direct evidence fails to provide evidence on the underlying causes of death. Although there is ample data documenting Canadian fatal diseases, these statistics do not tell us what caused those diseases. Epidemiology explores the outcome (disease) evidence and attempts to link it with causal or risk factors. This is a much more complex undertaking than compiling and sorting mortality statistics. Although epidemiological studies can address more closely the questions for which we are really seeking answers, there are few comprehensive quantitative summaries of the health risks associated with major risk factors. This deficiency reflects a number of substantial difficulties, including interpreting the interactions between major risk factors and individual risk factors.

Smoking is by far the most significant modifiable fatality risk factor. A large fraction of all cancer, cardiovascular disease, and respiratory disease mortality is associated with smoking. The epidemiological evidence for tobacco-related mortality is the most comprehensive and convincing risk factor evidence available for chronic, non-infectious diseases.

A diet high in fruits, and especially vegetables, has been linked consistently with lower mortality for several causes of death. Lowered fat intake, especially saturated fat, is also associated with a lower mortality risk. Despite the consistent nature of these observations, no overall quantitative summary of the impact of dietary risk factors on Canadian mortality was located.

Alcohol is consistently associated with many types of accidents, including almost half of motor vehicle fatalities. Alcohol consumption is a substantial modifiable risk factor for a major cause of fatalities, particularly in the younger age groups. There are also many societal risk factors (such as level of income and education) that are related to lifestyle/behavioural risk factors. The link between socio-economic factors and risk factors like alcohol consumption are complex and not amenable to simple quantitative analysis.

Compared with the major identifiable causes of death and established risk factors, specific environmental risk factors (e.g., chemical contamination in air, water, or food) show small and relatively weak associations with mortality in Canada. Analysis on a national or regional scale, where average environmental contaminant exposures are small, cannot isolate the possible effects on small groups of individuals exposed to high levels of contaminants and at higher risk.

An individual exposed to multiple risk factors may significantly increase his or her RR of mortality, but the quantitative interactions of these risk factors are largely unknown. On the other hand, many people die from particular causes of mortality without exhibiting any of the major known risk factors, other than age or sex.

Uncertainty varies tremendously among different risk factors because of the differing quality of evidence and strength of association. Failing to consider uncertainty in risk estimates makes any resulting risk comparisons misleading, because such comparisons fail to elaborate fully the evidentiary basis for the risk estimates.

Quantitative Risk Assessment (Predictive Inference)

The estimates of lifetime cancer risks for the ten chemicals on the CEPA priority substances list are very low for currently estimated background human exposure levels. Although the extrapolation models used for these cancer risk estimates provide upper bound (cautiously high) estimates of the number of cancer cases, the cancer cases predicted from these priority chemical exposures are less than one-quarter of 1% of the total number of annual Canadian cancer cases. The reliability of this estimate is low because of its many assumptions. However, predictive risk assessment on these priority chemicals indicates that environmental chemicals do not cause more cancer risk in Canada than previously estimated by Gough (1989) or Doll and Peto (1981) for the United States. These estimates were that from <1% up to 5% (best estimate of 1 to 2%) of all cancers might be attributed to environmental pollution.

These national estimates mask specific high contaminant exposure situations (e.g., certain occupations), which may produce substantially higher risk estimates in small populations. As the exposed populations are small, unless exposures are massive, the influence on the total number of cases will still be small.

The enormous uncertainties of low-dose extrapolation methods mean that little credence should be given to the resulting estimates of the total number of cancer cases. Rather, quantitative risk assessment should be used to compare and interpret the RR of carcinogenic chemicals to most effectively apply risk management resources.

General Observations

Numerical risk estimates are commonly misused in risk debates to support individual or expert claims about the "real risks." As we noted in the Preface, the mortality risk information in this book informs readers about the major sources of our knowledge about risk. This book's data should not be used to defeat the concerns of any individual about an imposed, individual risk. Those types of risk conflicts are primarily about fairness and equity, and will not be resolved using risk statistics.

Probability estimates (chances of death) are often only one component involved in making personal decisions about risk. This text is intended to allow any individual to know more about what is known and how it is known. Everyone is assaulted with competing health claims that are often misleading and/or unjustified. Health risk estimates are likely to misinform if their source and method of determination are not understood. Only with such information can one judge the validity of any health risk estimate, taking into account the evidentiary basis, inferential logic used, and remaining uncertainty. Understanding the source or character of the evidence and the inferential process used in processing the evidence clarifies the uncertainty in the risk estimate.

Due to the growing interest in health risk in society, there will be a greater need for more dissemination of and access to understandable Canadian health risk information. Although there are many gaps and deficiencies in our summary of the risks of death in Canada, our analysis may encourage more constructive discussion and debate about health risk information and contribute to greater knowledge among Canadians about their own health.

Additional Information Sources

Popular Literature

Popular books are specifically written for and marketed to the general public, rather than academics or some other group of professionals. This book rarely refers to popular books because they do not provide original and reliable data. In most cases, these popular references highlighted the difficulty of presenting health risk information in an accessible, understandable, and accurate way.

Living with Risk by M. Henderson (1987). *Living with Risk* has a very similar purpose to this book. It is one of the best and most accurate popular books that keeps the presentation at a level suitable for the public. The main causes of death are reviewed, as well as some of the major risk factors. Chapters on occupational, transportation, recreational, and chemical risks are included. Likewise, information on the nature of risk and the perception of risk is provided. However, the evidentiary basis and uncertainty associated with each primary source of risk information are not extensively developed. Furthermore, the health risk data is based on United Kingdom information prior to 1985 and is not entirely applicable to Canadians in the 1990s.

The Book of Risks by L. Laudan (1994). This book, subtitled *Fascinating Facts about the Chances We Take Every Day*, includes chapters on the risks of accidents, travel, health, crime, sin, nature, and technology. Numerous Figures and tables are included, but the book primarily provides single-line statements for specific risks, followed by a single probability estimate.

Beating Murphy's Law by B. Berger (1994). This book takes a different approach from the *The Book of Risks*. The risk probability numbers are embedded within a fictionalized, often humorous, story to provide some context for the risks.

Risk Watch by J. Urquhart and K. Heilmann (1984). This older book written by two doctors is more academic and goes into much more detail than the other books in this section. *Risk Watch* starts out by tracing the decline in mortality in the twentieth century and describes the major causes of death. These sections are followed by information on major voluntary hazards, and medical, surgical, and food risks.

Governmental and Non-Profit Health Agencies

There are governmental and non-profit health agencies concerned with all major and many minor diseases in our society. These agencies supply information about the risk from the particular disease to the public as brochures or booklets. This information usually describes what the disease is, how common it is, and what, if any, preventive actions can be taken to reduce the risk. We mainly used these information sources to check that important information (e.g., major risk factors) were addressed. These sources rarely contained quantitative data that could be referenced. Two particularly useful annual publications that do contain quantitative information are the *Canadian Cancer Statistics* and *Heart Disease and Stroke in Canada*.

Textbooks

Textbooks provided some of the most relevant information for this book because they often summarize the most important knowledge that is available. The following is a list of some of the main ones we used.

Basic Epidemiology by R. Beaglehole, R. Bonita, and T. Kjellstrom (1993). A good, relatively concise overview of the different types of epidemiology.

Mortality, Morbidity and Health Statistics by Michael Alderson (1988). This book was one of the main references for Part I, Direct Evidence, especially for the uncertainties involved in reporting direct evidence.

Public Health and Preventive Medicine in Canada by C. P. Shah (1994). This book provides an overview of health in Canada from a public health perspective. This source was used to identify and describe several of the risk factors in our book.

Casarett and Doull's Toxicology edited by M. O. Amdur, J. Doull, and C. D. Klaassen (1991). This is a widely used introductory text on toxicology, which was used for developing Part Three, Predictive Inference, and for some of the environmental risk factors discussed in Part Two, Indirect Evidence and Inference.

Scientific Journal Articles

Journal articles include the majority of current information available on health risk. However, only articles of a summary or more general nature were directly useful for this book. Most of the risk factors addressed in Part Two, Indirect Evidence and Inference, could each fill a book just by including a review of all available literature. Two specific journal articles that were particularly useful were the following.

The Causes of Cancer: Quantitative Estimates of Avoidable Risks of Cancer in the United States Today by R. Doll and R. Peto (1981). This article remains the most widely recognized summary of the risk factors associated with cancer. Doll and Peto used epidemiological information to develop estimates of the major causes of cancer and included ranges to identify the uncertainty associated with their estimates.

Estimating Cancer Mortality by Michael Gough (1989). This article established a link between some of the estimates from the Doll and Peto (1981) study based on epidemiology and estimates from the US EPA based on toxicological risk assessment.

Government Publications

Government publications are often the best source for information specific to Canada. Most of the information in Part One, Direct Evidence, is from government publications and many of the Canadian references in the other sections are also from government publications.

Statistics Canada. An enormous volume of information is published annually by Statistics Canada on all aspects of Canada. For this book, the annual publications on mortality served as data for most of the Figures and Tables in Part One, Direct Evidence. Information on population and occupational information was taken from additional publications. A quarterly publication entitled Health Reports supplied several articles used in this book for information in Parts One and Two.

Health Canada. Several key articles for this book from Health Canada were on health risk determination and carcinogen assessment. The Canadian Environmental Protection Act documents published by Environment Canada supplied the exposure information for the Part Three, Predictive Inference, results. (The US EPA provided potency values from their IRIS database.) Health Canada also publishes the bimonthly *Chronic Diseases in Canada*.

Transport Canada. Transport Canada publishes annual documents that summarize motor vehicle injuries and fatalities. A document on motor vehicle use and alcohol consumption was also used.

Contacts

The first way to identify contacts for specific health-related issues is to check your local phone book (blue pages for government). For major health agencies, each province has local offices that can provide most of the information available from the national offices. (This information is current at the time of publication.)

Government of Canada

Reference tel. no.: 1 (800) 667-3355
Government of Canada
Links to federal departments:
http://canada.gc.ca/

Health Canada

Health Canada's main Web page is called The Canadian Health Network:
http://www.hwc.ca/

Health Canada's main link page is a very good spot to start looking for information on a specific topic; most Canadian pages are included:
http://www.hwc.ca/links/english.html

Statistics Canada

Little of the vast amount of Statistics Canada's data is available on-line (most major publications should be available in university libraries or main branches of public libraries):
http://www.statcan.ca/

Environment Canada

Information on environmental issues and risks:
http://www.doe.ca/

Other Sites

The Canadian Cancer Society

The National Office is in Toronto and the Public Issues Office is in Ottawa. Each province has its own Society.

National Office:
10 Alcorn Avenue, Suite 200
Toronto, Ontario M4V 3B1
Phone: (416) 961-7223
Fax: (416) 961-4189
For information on cancer,
call 1 (888) 939-3333.
Web site:
http://www.cancer.ca/

Heart and Stroke Foundation

The National Office is in Ottawa. Each province has its own Foundation.
National Office:
160 George Street, Suite 200
Ottawa, Ontario K1N 9M2
Phone: (613) 241-4361
Fax: (613) 241-3278
Web site:
http://www.hsf.ca

Canadian Institute for Health Information

The CIHI operates from its head office in Ottawa and offices in Toronto, Vancouver, Edmonton, and Halifax.

Head Office:
377 Dalhousie Street, Suite 200
Ottawa, Ontario K1N 9N8
Phone: (613) 241-7860
Fax: (613) 241-8120
Web site:
http://www.cihi.ca/

Canadian Red Cross
Web site:
http://www.redcross.ca/

Yahoo Health Site
Web site:
The Yahoo Health Site contains links to thousands of health related sites and has a "Canadian sites only" feature:
http://www.yahoo.ca/Health/

Appendix

Detailed Causes of Death, 1994

one

Appendix 1 ◆ Detailed Causes of Death, 1994

Class	ICD–9 #	Name	Male	Female	Total
I	**001–139**	**Infectious & Parasitic Diseases**	**2,300**	**897**	**3,197**
	001–009	Intestinal Infectious Diseases	17	22	39
	010–018	Tuberculosis	72	46	118
	020–027	Zoonotic Bacterial Diseases	5	7	12
	030–041	Other Bacterial Diseases	441	456	897
	036	–Meningococcal Infection	15	16	31
	038	–Septicaemia	400	421	821
	042–044	Human Immunodeficiency Virus (HIV) Infection	1,489	139	1,628
	045–049	Polio, Non-Arthropod-Borne Viral Diseases Central Nervous System	29	25	54
	050–057	Viral Accompanied by Exanthem	22	28	50
	060–066	Arthropod-Borne Diseases	0	0	0
	070–079	Other Diseases Due to Viruses & Chlamydiae	122	85	207
	080–088	Rickettsioses & Other Arthropod-Borne Diseases	0	0	0
	090–099	Syphilis & Other Venereal Diseases	4	2	6
	100–104	Other Spirochaetal Diseases	0	0	0
	110–118	Mycoses	40	16	56
	120–129	Helminthiases	0	0	0
	130–136	Other Infectious & Parasitic Diseases	37	39	76
	135	–Sarcoidosis	10	17	27
	137–139	Late Effects of Infectious & Parasitic Diseases	22	32	54
	137	–Late Effects of Tuberculosis	14	18	32

Appendix 1 ◆ Detailed Causes of Death, 1994 (continued)

Class	ICD–9 #	Name	Male	Female	Total
II	140–239	**Neoplasms**	**31,496**	**26,815**	**58,311**
	140–149	Malignant Neoplasms of Lip, Oral Cavity, & Pharynx	709	279	988
	141	–Malignant Neoplasm of Tongue	159	71	230
	150–159	Malignant Neoplasm of Digestive Organs & Peritoneum	8,397	7,010	15,407
	150	–Malignant Neoplasm of Oesophagus	837	310	1,147
	151	–Malignant Neoplasm of Stomach	1,237	801	2,038
	153	–Malignant Neoplasm of Colon	2,378	2,285	4,663
	154	–Malignant Neoplasm of Rectum, Rectosigmoid Junction, & Anus	805	551	1,356
	155	–Malignant Neoplasm of Liver & Intrahepatic Bile Ducts	683	389	1,072
	157	–Malignant Neoplasm of Pancreas	1,406	1,458	2,864
	160–165	Malignant Neoplasm of Respiratory System	10,453	5,407	15,860
	161	–Malignant Neoplasm of Larynx	424	91	515
	162	–Malignant Neoplasm of Trachea, Bronchus, & Lung	9,898	5,261	15,159
	170–175	Malignant Neoplasm, Bone, Connective Tissue, Skin, & Breast	753	5,471	6,224
	172	–Malignant Melanoma of Skin	373	237	610
	174	–Malignant Neoplasm of Female Breast	–	4,995	4,995
	175	–Malignant Neoplasm of Male Breast	31	–	31
	179–189	Malignant Neoplasm of Genito-urinary Organs	5,339	3,334	8,673
	183	–Malignant Neoplasm of Ovary & Other Uterine Adnexa	–	1,343	1,343
	185	–Malignant Neoplasm of Prostate	3,624	–	3,624
	188	–Malignant Neoplasm of Bladder	915	427	1,342
	189	–Malignant Neoplasm of Kidney & Other & Unspecified Urinary Organs	726	451	1,177
	190–199	Malignant Neoplasm of Other & Unspecified Sites	2,566	2,505	5,071
	191	–Malignant Neoplasm of Brain	755	594	1,349
	199	–Malignant Neoplasm without Specification of Site	1,603	1,637	3,240
	200–208	Neoplasms of Lymphatic & Haematopoietic Tissue	2,797	2,304	5,101
	201	–Hodgkin's Disease	83	47	130
	202	–Other Malignant Neoplasm of Lymphoid & Histiocytic Tissue	1,023	896	1,919
	203	–Multiple Myeloma & Immunoproliferative Neoplasms	558	480	1,038
	204	–Lymphoid Leukaemia	359	244	603

	205	—Myeloid Leukaemia	380	326	706
	208	—Leukaemia of Unspecified Cell Type	299	230	529
	210–229	Benign Neoplasms	71	93	164
	225	—Benign Neoplasm of Brain & Other Parts of Nervous System	45	63	108
	230–234	Carcinoma In Situ	3	1	4
	235–238	Neoplasm of Uncertain Behaviour	213	191	404
	239	Neoplasm of Unspecified Nature	195	220	415
	239.6	—Brain	121	140	261

Class	ICD–9 #	Name	Male	Female	Total
III	240–279	**Endocrine, Nutritional, & Metabolic Diseases & Immunity Disorders**	**3,194**	**3,416**	**6,610**
	240–246	Diseases of Thyroid Gland	26	84	110
	250–259	Diseases of Other Endocrine Glands	2,529	2,698	5,227
	250	—Diabetes Mellitus	2,509	2,656	5,165
	260–269	Nutritional Deficiencies	90	116	206
	270–279	Other Metabolic Disorders & Immunity Disorders	549	518	1,067
	276	—Disorders of Fluid, Electrolyte, & Acid-Base Balance	181	261	442

Class	ICD–9 #	Name	Male	Female	Total
IV	280–289	**Diseases of Blood & Blood-Forming Organs**	**336**	**377**	**713**
	280–285	Anaemias	173	255	428
	284	—Aplastic Anaemia	47	48	95
	286–289	Other	163	122	285

Class	ICD–9 #	Name	Male	Female	Total
V	290–319	**Mental Disorders**	**1,963**	**2,710**	**4,673**
	290–294	Organic Psychotic Conditions	684	1,289	1,973
	290	—Senile & Presenile Organic Psychotic Conditions	612	1,261	1,873
	295–299	Other Psychoses	440	830	1,270
	295	—Schizophrenic Psychoses	26	43	69
	300–316	Neurotic, Personality, & Other Non-Psychotic Mental Disorders	804	569	1,373
	303	—Alcohol Dependence Syndrome	463	115	578
	310	—Specific Non-psychotic Mental Disorders Following Organic Brain Damage	189	344	533
	317–319	Mental Retardation	35	22	57

Appendix 1 ◆ Detailed Causes of Death, 1994 (continued)

Class	ICD–9 #	Name	Male	Female	Total
VI	320–389	**Diseases of the Nervous System & Sense Organs**	**2,643**	**3,331**	**5,974**
	320–326	Inflammatory Diseases of the Central Nervous System	44	49	93
	330–337	Hereditary & Degenerative Diseases of Nervous System	1,879	2,619	4,498
	331.0	–Alzheimer's Disease	859	1,685	2,544
	332	–Parkinson's Disease	585	477	1,062
	335	–Anterior Horn Cell Disease	251	258	509
	340–349	Other Disorders of Central Nervous System	562	560	1,122
	340	–Multiple Sclerosis	129	184	313
	345	–Epilepsy	152	120	272
	350–359	Disorders of the Peripheral Nervous System	154	100	254
	359	–Muscular Dystrophies & Other Myophapthies	90	53	143
	360–379	Disorders of the Eye & Adnexa	0	2	2
	380–389	Diseases of the Ear & Mastoid Process	4	1	5

Class	ICD–9 #	Name	Male	Female	Total
VII	390–459	**Diseases of the Circulatory System**	**39,885**	**38,688**	**78,573**
	390–392	Acute Rheumatic Fever	5	8	13
	393–398	Chronic Rheumatic Heart Disease	152	383	535
	401–405	Hypertensive Disease	520	817	1,337
	410–414	Ischaemic Heart Disease	24,514	19,661	44,175
	410	–Acute Myocardial Infarction	12,929	9,324	22,253
	414.0	–Coronary Atherosclerosis	5,526	5,649	11,175
	415–417	Diseases of Pulmonary Circulation	365	512	877
	420–429	Other Forms of Heart Disease	5,061	5,728	10,789
	427	–Cardiac Dysrhythmias	1,441	1,637	3,078
	428	–Heart Failure	1,750	2,537	4,287
	430–438	Cerebrovascular Disease	6,442	8,864	15,306
	436	–Acute but Ill-Defined Cerebrovascular Disease	3,803	5,540	9,343
	440–448	Diseases of Arteries, Arterioles, & Capillaries	2,623	2,467	5,090
	440	–Atherosclerosis	717	1,200	1,917
	441	–Aortic Aneurysm	1,355	734	2,089
	451–459	Diseases, Veins, Lymphatics, Other Diseases of the Circulatory System	203	248	451

Appendix 1 ◆ Detailed Causes of Death, 1994 (continued)

Class	ICD–9 #	Name	Male	Female	Total
VIII	460–519	**Diseases of the Respiratory System**	**10,087**	**8,255**	**18,342**
	460–466	Acute Respiratory Infections	42	53	95
	470–478	Other Diseases of Upper Respiratory Tract	10	5	15
	480–487	Pneumonia & Influenza	3,447	3,855	7,302
	485	–Bronchopneumonia, Organism Unspecified	653	753	1,406
	486	–Pneumonia, Organism Unspecified	2,551	2,821	5,372
	487	–Influenza	83	150	233
	490–496	Chronic Obstructive Pulmonary Disease & Allied Conditions	5,546	3,374	8,920
	492	–Emphysema	689	363	1,052
	493	–Asthma	190	264	454
	496	–Chronic Airways Obstruction, NEC	4,296	2,432	6,728
	500–508	Pneumoconiosis, Other Lung Diseases Due to External Agents	303	234	537
	*** 500	–Coalworkers' Pneumoconiosis	0	3	3
	*** 501	–Asbestosis	24	1	25
	*** 502	–Pneumoconiosis Due to Other Silica or Silicates	33	2	35
	507.0	–Due to inhalation of food or vomit	237	230	467
	510–519	Other Diseases of Respiratory System	739	734	1,473
	515	–Postinflammatory Pulmonary Fibrosis	321	273	594

*** *Included for interest.*

Class	ICD–9 #	Name	Male	Female	Total
IX	520–579	**Diseases of the Digestive System**	**3,912**	**3,767**	**7,679**
	520–529	Diseases of Oral Cavity, Salivary Glands, & Jaws	10	6	16
	530–537	Diseases of Oesophagus, Stomach, & Duodenum	423	431	854
	540–543	Appendicitis	29	16	45
	550–553	Hernia of Abdominal Cavity	82	91	173
	555–558	Noninfective Enteritis & Colitis	360	588	948
	560–569	Other Diseases of Intestines & Peritoneum	528	926	1,454
	560	–Intestinal Obstruction without Mention of Hernia	221	379	600
	570–579	Other Diseases of Digestive System	2,480	1,709	4,189
	571	–Chronic Liver Disease & Cirrhosis	1,489	719	2,208
	578	–GI Haemorrhage	419	406	825

Appendix 1 ◆ Detailed Causes of Death, 1994 (continued)

Class	ICD–9 #	Name	Male	Female	Total
X	580–629	**Diseases of the Genito-Urinary System**	**1,670**	**1,691**	**3,361**
	580–589	Nephritis, Nephrotic Syndrome, & Nephrosis	1,258	1,222	2,480
	585	–Chronic Renal Failure	355	332	687
	586	–Renal Failure, Unspecified	717	697	1,414
	590–599	Other Diseases of Urinary System	333	446	779
	600–608	Diseases of Male Genital Organs	79	–	79
	600	–Hyperplasia of Prostate	59	–	59
	610–611	Disorders of Breast	–	1	1
	614–616	Inflammatory Diseases of Female Pelvic Organs	–	7	7
	617–629	Other Disorders of Female Genital Tract	–	15	15

Class	ICD–9 #	Name	Male	Female	Total
XI	630–676	**Complications of Pregnancy, Childbirth, & the Puerperium**	–	**14**	**14**
	630–639	Pregnancy with Abortive Outcome	–	2	2
	640–648	Complications Mainly Related to Pregnancy	–	6	6
	642	–Hypertension Complicating Pregnancy, Childbirth, & the Puerperium	–	2	2
	650–659	Normal Delivery, & Other Indications for Care in Pregnancy, Labour, & Delivery	–	0	0
	660–669	Complications Occurring in Labour & Delivery	–	2	2
	670–676	Complications of the Puerperium	–	4	4

Class	ICD–9 #	Name	Male	Female	Total
XII	680–709	**Diseases of the Skin & Subcutaneous Tissue**	**76**	**112**	**188**
	680–686	Infections of Skin & Subcutaneous Tissue	24	34	58
	690–698	Other Inflammatory Conditions, Skin & Subcutaneous Tissue	12	17	29
	700–709	Other Diseases of Skin & Subcutaneous Tissue	40	61	101
	707	–Chronic Ulcer of Skin	39	60	99

Appendix 1 ◆ Detailed Causes of Death, 1994 (continued)

Class	ICD–9 #	Name	Male	Female	Total
XIII	710–739	**Diseases of the Musculo-Skeletal System & Connective Tissue**	**259**	**664**	**923**
	710–719	Arthropathies & Related Disorders	164	484	648
	710	–Diffuse Diseases of Connective Tissue	54	145	199
	714.0	–Rheumatoid Arthritis	44	202	246
	720–724	Dorsopathies	22	14	36
	725–729	Rheumatism, Excluding the Back	12	22	34
	730–739	Other Diseases of the Musculo-Skeletal System	61	144	205

Class	ICD–9 #	Name	Male	Female	Total
XIV	740–759	**Congenital Anomalies**	**630**	**527**	**1,157**
	740–742	Nervous System	80	91	171
	745–747	Circulatory System	286	219	505
	746	–Other Congenital Anomalies of Heart	156	101	257
	748–749	Respiratory System	67	36	103
	750–751	Digestive System	15	10	25
	752–753	Genito-urinary System	38	32	70
	754–756	Limbs & Musculo-Skeletal System	26	35	61
	757–759	Other	118	104	222
	758	–Chromosomal Anomalies	69	70	139

Class	ICD–9 #	Name	Male	Female	Total
XV	760–779	**Certain Conditions Originating in the Perinatal Period (Excluding Stillbirths)**	**572**	**487**	**1,059**
	761	–Fetus or Newborn Affected by Maternal Complications of Pregnancy	69	55	124
	762	–Fetus or Newborn Affected by Complications of Placenta, Cord, & Membranes	61	70	131
	765	–Disorders Relating to Short Gestation & Unspecified Low Birthweight	101	89	190
	770	–Other Respiratory Conditions of Fetus or Newborn	86	63	149

Appendix 1 ◆ Detailed Causes of Death, 1994 (continued)

Class	ICD–9 #	Name	Male	Female	Total
XVI	780–799	**Symptoms, Signs, & Ill-Defined Conditions**	**1,673**	**1,434**	**3,107**
	780–789	Symptoms	55	91	146
	785.5	–Shock without Mention of Trauma	22	36	58
	790–796	Nonspecific Abnormal Findings	1	1	2
	797–799	Ill-Defined & Unknown Causes of Morbidity & Mortality	1,617	1,342	2,959
	798.0	–Sudden Infant Death Syndrome	176	93	269
	799.9	–Other Unknown & Unspecified Cause	1,273	893	2,166

Class	ICD–9 #	Name	Male	Female	Total
E XVII	E800–E999	**External Causes, Injury, & Poisoning**	**9,046**	**4,150**	**13,196**
	E800–E807	Railway Accidents	32	8	40
	E805	–Hit by Rolling Stock	29	8	37
	E810–E819	Motor Vehicle Traffic Accidents	2,121	928	3,049
	E810	–Motor Vehicle Traffic Accident Involving Collision with Train	31	12	43
	E812	–Other Motor Vehicle Traffic Accident Involving Collision with Another Vehicle	776	422	1,198
	E814	–Motor Vehicle Traffic Accident Involving Collision with Pedestrian	230	159	389
	E816	–Motor Vehicle Traffic Accident Due to Loss of Control, without Collision on the Highway	391	110	501
	E819	–Motor Vehicle Traffic Accident of Unspecified Nature	365	134	499
	E820–E825	Motor Vehicle Non-traffic Accidents	102	13	115
	E820	–Non-traffic Accident Involving Motor-Driving Snow Vehicle	50	4	54
	E826–E829	Other Road Vehicle Accidents	15	8	23
	E826	–Pedal Cycle Accident	11	4	15
	E828	–Accident Involving Animal Being Ridden	2	4	6
	E830–E838	Water Transport Accidents	124	11	135
	E830	–Accident to Watercraft Causing Submersion	47	2	49
	E840–E845	Air & Space Transport Accidents	54	8	62
	E841	–Accident to Powered Aircraft, Other, & Unspecified	48	8	56
	E846–E848	Vehicle Accidents Not Elsewhere Classifiable	1	0	1
	E850–E858	Accidental, Poisoning, Drugs, Medicaments, Biologicals	474	194	668

E850.0	—Opiates & Related Narcotics	181	34	215
E860–E869	Accidental Poisoning by Other Substances	155	41	196
E860	—Accidental Poisoning by Alcohol, NEC	78	19	97
E868	—Accidental Poisoning by Other Utility Gas & Other Carbon Monoxide	58	10	68
E870–E876	Misadventures to Patients during Surgical & Medical Care	12	23	35
E870	—Accidental Cut, Puncture, Perforation, or Haemorrhage during Medical Care	9	19	28
E878–E879	Complication of Medical Procedures without Mention of Misadventure	98	79	177
E880–E888	Accidental Falls	1,055	1,291	2,346
E887	—Fracture, Cause Unspecified	397	697	1,094
E888	—Other & Unspecified Fall	333	416	749
E890–E899	Accidents Caused by Fire & Flames	196	103	299
E890	—Conflagration in Private Dwelling	152	89	241
E900–E909	Accidents Due to Natural & Environmental Factors	118	42	160
E901	—Excessive Cold	66	18	84
*** E907	—Lightning	9	2	11
E910–E915	Accidents, Submersion, Suffocation, & Foreign Bodies	507	222	729
E910	—Accidental Drowning & Submersion	255	63	318
E916–E928	Other Accidents	422	104	526
E916	—Struck Accidentally by Falling Object	66	4	70
E919	—Accidents Caused by Machinery	113	8	121
E922	—Accident Caused by Firearm Missile	35	3	38
E925	—Accident Caused by Electric Current	35	0	35
E929	Late Effects of Accidental Injury	71	32	103
E930–E949	Substances Causing Adverse Effects in Therapeutic Use	8	14	22
E950–E959	Suicide & Self-inflicted Injury	2,969	780	3,749
E950	—... poisoning by solid or liquid substances	262	246	508
E952	—... poisoning by other gases & vapours	376	87	463
E953	—... by hanging, strangulation, & suffocation	1,033	237	1,270
E954	—... by submersion	87	45	132
E955	—... by firearms & explosives	916	59	975
E956	—... by cutting & piercing instruments	61	15	76
E957	—... by jumping from high place	134	56	190

Appendix 1 ◆ Detailed Causes of Death, 1994 (continued)

E960–E969	Homicide & Injury Purposely Inflicted by Other Persons	327	171	498
E965	–Assault by Firearms & Explosives	136	36	172
E966	–Assault by Cutting & Piercing Instrument	97	39	136
E970–E978	Legal Intervention	5	0	5
E980–E989	Injury Undetermined, Accidentally or Purposely Inflicted	179	77	256
E990–E999	Injury Resulting from Operations of War	1	0	1

Note: *** Included for interest.
Source: Statistics Canada 1996A

Appendix

Causes of Death
by Age, 1994

two

Appendix 2 ◆ Causes of Death by Age, 1994

Deaths <1

	ICD–9	Shortened Cause Name	#	%	Rate[1]
Male	XV	Perinatal Conditions	569	41.4	287.3
	XIV	Congenital Anomalies	411	29.9	207.5
	XVI	Ill-Defined – most from Sudden Infant Death Syndrome	213	15.5	107.5
	E XVII	External Causes	31	2.3	15.7
	VIII	Respiratory Diseases	29	2.1	14.6
		All Other	122	8.9	61.6
		Total	**1,375**	**100.0**	**694.3**
Female	XV	Perinatal Conditions	484	46.4	258.9
	XIV	Congenital Anomalies	318	30.5	170.1
	XVI	Ill-Defined – most from Sudden Infant Death Syndrome	117	11.2	62.6
	E XVII	External Causes	33	3.2	17.7
	VII	Cardiovascular Diseases	19	1.8	10.2
		All Other	72	6.9	38.5
		Total	**1,043**	**100.0**	**557.9**

[1]Note: Deaths per 100,000.

Deaths 1–4

	ICD–9	Shortened Cause Name	#	%	Rate[1]
Male	E XVII	External Causes	113	38.7	13.6
	XIV	Congenital Anomalies	45	15.4	5.4
	II	Cancer	25	8.6	3.0
	VI	Nervous System Diseases	24	8.2	2.9
	VII	Cardiovascular Diseases	16	5.5	1.9
		All Other	69	23.6	8.3
		Total	**292**	**100.0**	**35.2**
Female	E XVII	External Causes	82	36.4	10.4
	XIV	Congenital Anomalies	31	13.8	3.9
	II	Cancer	23	10.2	2.9
	VI	Nervous System Diseases	19	8.4	2.4
	XVI	Ill–Defined	14	6.2	1.8
		All Other	56	24.9	7.1
		Total	**225**	**100.0**	**28.5**

[1]Note: Deaths per 100,000.

Appendix 2 ◆ Causes of Death by Age, 1994 (continued)

Deaths 5–14

	ICD–9	Shortened Cause Name	#	%	Rate[1]
Male	E XVII	External Causes	213	49.4	10.5
	II	Cancer	72	16.7	3.6
	VI	Nervous System Diseases	29	6.7	1.4
	XIV	Congenital Anomalies	23	5.3	1.1
	VII	Cardiovascular Diseases	21	4.9	1.0
		All Other	73	16.9	3.6
		Total	**431**	**100.0**	**21.3**
Female	E XVII	External Causes	122	41.4	6.3
	II	Cancer	57	19.3	2.9
	VI	Nervous System Diseases	25	8.5	1.3
	VII	Cardiovascular Diseases	23	7.8	1.2
	XIV	Congenital Anomalies	16	5.4	0.8
		All Other	52	17.6	2.7
		Total	**295**	**100.0**	**15.2**

[1]Note: Deaths per 100,000.

Deaths 15–24

	ICD–9	Shortened Cause Name	#	%	Rate[1]
Male	E XVII	External Causes	1,487	77.8	72.6
	II	Cancer	102	5.3	5.0
	XVI	Ill-Defined	95	5.0	4.6
	VII	Cardiovascular Diseases	57	3.0	2.8
	VI	Nervous System Diseases	55	2.9	2.7
		All Other	116	6.1	5.7
		Total	**1,912**	**100.0**	**93.3**
Female	E XVII	External Causes	388	60.4	19.7
	II	Cancer	68	10.6	3.4
	XVI	Ill-Defined	32	5.0	1.6
	VI	Nervous System Diseases	31	4.8	1.6
	VII	Cardiovascular Diseases	29	4.5	1.5
		All Other	94	14.6	4.8
		Total	**642**	**100.0**	**32.6**

[1]Note: Deaths per 100,000.

Appendix 2 ◆ Causes of Death by Age, 1994 (continued)

Deaths 25–34

	ICD–9	Shortened Cause Name	#	%	Rate[1]
Male	E XVII	External Causes	1,680	56.2	66.6
	I	Infectious Diseases	454	15.2	18.0
	II	Cancer	237	7.9	9.4
	VII	Cardiovascular Diseases	180	6.0	7.1
	XVI	Ill-Defined	143	4.8	5.7
		All Other	293	9.8	11.6
		Total	**2,987**	**100.0**	**118.4**
Female	E XVII	External Causes	431	39.7	17.5
	II	Cancer	257	23.7	10.4
	VII	Cardiovascular Diseases	109	10.0	4.4
	XVI	Ill-Defined	56	5.2	2.3
	I	Infectious Diseases	49	4.5	2.0
		All Other	184	16.9	7.5
		Total	**1,086**	**100.0**	**44.1**

[1]Note: Deaths per 100,000.

Deaths 35–44

	ICD–9	Shortened Cause Name	#	%	Rate[1]
Male	E XVII	External Causes	1,684	35.6	69.9
	II	Cancer	806	17.0	33.4
	VII	Cardiovascular Diseases	764	16.2	31.7
	I	Infectious Diseases	692	14.6	28.7
	XVI	Ill-Defined	174	3.7	7.2
		All Other	609	12.9	25.3
		Total	**4,729**	**100.0**	**196.3**
Female	II	Cancer	1,080	46.1	45.1
	E XVII	External Causes	476	20.3	19.9
	VII	Cardiovascular Diseases	294	12.5	12.3
	VI	Nervous System Diseases	89	3.8	3.7
	XVI	Ill-Defined	83	3.5	3.5
		All Other	323	13.8	13.5
		Total	**2,345**	**100.0**	**97.9**

[1]Note: Deaths per 100,000.

Appendix 2 ◆ Causes of Death by Age, 1994 (continued)

Deaths 45–54

	ICD–9	Shortened Cause Name	#	%	Rate[1]
Male	II	Cancer	2,255	32.2	127.6
	VII	Cardiovascular Diseases	2,065	29.5	116.8
	E XVII	External Causes	1,087	15.5	61.5
	IX	Digestive Diseases	376	5.4	21.3
	I	Infectious Diseases	343	4.9	19.4
		All Other	875	12.5	49.5
		Total	**7,001**	**100.0**	**396.0**
Female	II	Cancer	2,546	58.2	145.4
	VII	Cardiovascular Diseases	676	15.5	38.6
	E XVII	External Causes	361	8.3	20.6
	IX	Digestive Diseases	199	4.6	11.4
	III	Endocrine & Others	111	2.5	6.3
		All Other	478	10.9	27.3
		Total	**4,371**	**100.0**	**249.6**

[1]Note: Deaths per 100,000.

Deaths 55–64

	ICD–9	Shortened Cause Name	#	%	Rate[1]
Male	II	Cancer	5,904	41.2	480.6
	VII	Cardiovascular Diseases	4,901	34.2	399.0
	E XVII	External Causes	792	5.5	64.5
	VIII	Respiratory Diseases	676	4.7	55.0
	IX	Digestive Diseases	659	4.6	53.6
		All Other	1,390	9.7	113.2
		Total	**14,322**	**100.0**	**1,165.9**
Female	II	Cancer	4,531	54.5	360.6
	VII	Cardiovascular Diseases	1,890	22.8	150.4
	VIII	Respiratory Diseases	390	4.7	31.0
	E XVII	External Causes	319	3.8	25.4
	IX	Digestive Diseases	311	3.7	24.7
		All Other	866	10.4	68.9
		Total	**8,307**	**100.0**	**661.1**

[1]Note: Deaths per 100,000.

Appendix 2 ◆ Causes of Death by Age, 1994 (continued)

Deaths 65–74

	ICD–9	Shortened Cause Name	#	%	Rate[1]
Male	VII	Cardiovascular Diseases	10,564	38.0	1,128.7
	II	Cancer	10,376	37.3	1,108.6
	VIII	Respiratory Diseases	2,333	8.4	249.3
	IX	Digestive Diseases	1,068	3.8	114.1
	III	Endocrine & Others	889	3.2	95.0
		All Other	2,595	9.3	277.3
		Total	**27,825**	**100.0**	**2,972.8**
Female	II	Cancer	7,519	40.7	669.2
	VII	Cardiovascular Diseases	6,183	33.5	550.3
	VIII	Respiratory Diseases	1,395	7.6	124.2
	IX	Digestive Diseases	733	4.0	65.2
	III	Endocrine & Others	710	3.8	63.2
		All Other	1,924	10.4	171.2
		Total	**18,464**	**100.0**	**1,643.3**

[1]Note: Deaths per 100,000.

Deaths 75–84

	ICD–9	Shortened Cause Name	#	%	Rate[1]
Male	VII	Cardiovascular Diseases	13,515	42.7	3,157.0
	II	Cancer	8,704	27.5	2,033.2
	VIII	Respiratory Diseases	3,943	12.5	921.0
	IX	Digestive Diseases	968	3.1	226.1
	III	Endocrine & Others	960	3.0	224.2
		All Other	3,549	11.2	829.0
		Total	**31,639**	**100.0**	**7,390.6**
Female	VII	Cardiovascular Diseases	13,272	45.2	2,022.5
	II	Cancer	7,145	24.3	1,088.8
	VIII	Respiratory Diseases	2,812	9.6	428.5
	III	Endocrine & Others	1,151	3.9	175.4
	IX	Digestive Diseases	1,117	3.8	170.2
		All Other	3,892	13.2	593.1
		Total	**29,389**	**100.0**	**4,478.5**

[1]Note: Deaths per 100,000.

Appendix 2 ◆ Causes of Death by Age, 1994 (continued)

Deaths 85+

	ICD–9	Shortened Cause Name	#	%	Rate[1]
Male	VII	Cardiovascular Diseases	7,774	45.1	7,822.3
	II	Cancer	3,008	17.5	3,026.7
	VIII	Respiratory Diseases	2,751	16.0	2,768.1
	IX	Digestive Diseases	585	3.4	588.6
	V	Mental Disorders	573	3.3	576.6
		All Other	2,532	14.7	2,547.7
		Total	**17,223**	**100.0**	**17,330**
Female	VII	Cardiovascular Diseases	16,181	51.9	7,087.9
	II	Cancer	3,586	11.5	1,570.8
	VIII	Respiratory Diseases	3,423	11.0	1,499.4
	V	Mental Disorders	1,654	5.3	724.5
	IX	Digestive Diseases	1,281	4.1	561.1
		All Other	5,038	16.2	2,206.9
		Total	**31,163**	**100.0**	**13,651**

[1]Note: Deaths per 100,000.

All Ages

	ICD–9	Shortened Cause Name	#	%	Rate[1]
Male	VII	Cardiovascular Diseases	39,885	36.3	275.2
	II	Cancer	31,496	28.7	217.3
	VIII	Respiratory Diseases	10,087	9.2	69.6
	E XVII	External Causes	9,046	8.2	62.4
	IX	Digestive Diseases	3,912	3.6	27.0
		All Other	15,316	14.0	105.7
		Total	**109,742**	**100.0**	**757.2**
Female	VII	Cardiovascular Diseases	38,688	39.7	262.2
	II	Cancer	26,815	27.5	181.7
	VIII	Respiratory Diseases	8,255	8.5	55.9
	E XVII	External Causes	4,150	4.3	28.1
	IX	Digestive Diseases	3,767	3.9	25.5
		All Other	15,660	16.1	106.1
		Total	**97,335**	**100.0**	**659.6**

[1]Note: Deaths per 100,000.

Appendix three

Cause of Death, 1991–1994

Appendix 3 ◆ Cause of Death, 1991–1994

Table 1 Males

Name	1991	1992	1993	1994
Infectious diseases	1,869	1,985	2,266	2,300
Cancer	29,670	30,054	30,483	31,014
– Oesophagus and stomach	1,950	2,103	2,006	2,074
– Intestine and rectum	3,049	3,197	3,146	3,252
– Pancreas	1,329	1,384	1,403	1,406
– Trachea, bronchus and lung	9,693	9,748	9,983	9,898
– Breast	34	35	42	31
– Uterus, ovary and adnexa	0	0	0	0
– Prostate	3,426	3,494	3,582	3,624
– Urinary system	1,549	1,528	1,630	1,641
– Lymphatic tissue and leukemia	2,702	2,596	2,676	2,797
– Other	5,938	5,969	6,015	6,291
Diabetes mellitus	2,005	2,119	2,339	2,509
Nervous system diseases	2,335	2,443	2,586	2,643
Cardiovascular diseases	39,127	39,290	40,513	39,885
– Ischaemic heart disease	24,499	24,490	25,101	24,514
– Cardiac dysrhythmias and heart failure	2,983	3,042	3,174	3,191
– Stroke	6,035	6,052	6,478	6,442
– Arteries and capillaries	2,630	2,689	2,727	2,623
– Other	2,980	3,017	3,033	3,115
Respiratory diseases	9,638	9,411	9,971	10,087
– Pneumonia and influenza	3,277	3,206	3,288	3,447
– Chronic bronchitis, emphysema and asthma	1,405	1,246	1,258	1,188
– Other chronic airways obstruction	3,850	3,824	4,257	4,296
– Other	1,106	1,135	1,168	1,156
Chronic liver disease and cirrhosis	1,498	1,419	1,469	1,489
Congenital anomalies	654	674	603	630
Certain perinatal causes	571	556	615	572
External Causes	9,150	9,054	9,293	9,046
– Motor vehicle accidents	2,522	2,389	2,445	2,246
– Accidental falls	942	985	1,023	1,055
– Suicide	2,875	2,923	3,014	2,969
– Homicide	394	403	358	327
– Other	2,417	2,354	2,453	2,449
All other causes	8,921	8,860	9,269	9,567
All causes	**105,438**	**105,865**	**109,407**	**109,742**

Appendix 3 ◆ Cause of Death, 1991–1994 (continued)

Table 2 Females

Name	1991	1992	1993	1994
Infectious diseases	755	759	858	897
Cancer	24,294	24,786	25,709	26,310
– Oesophagus and stomach	1,095	1,114	1,116	1,111
– Intestine and rectum	2,783	2,831	2,907	2,890
– Pancreas	1,293	1,325	1,407	1,458
– Trachea, bronchus and lung	4,562	4,677	5,130	5,261
– Breast	4,653	4,830	4,779	4,995
– Uterus, ovary and adnexa	2,213	2,184	2,289	2,334
– Prostate	0	0	0	0
– Urinary system	770	784	843	878
– Lymphatic tissue and leukemia	2,171	2,278	2,336	2,304
– Other	4,754	4,763	4,902	5,079
Diabetes mellitus	2,291	2,354	2,682	2,656
Nervous system diseases	2,711	2,825	3,153	3,331
Cardiovascular diseases	36,910	36,921	38,381	38,688
– Ischaemic heart disease	19,496	19,079	19,667	19,661
– Cardiac dysrhythmias and heart failure	3,655	3,766	3,898	4,174
– Stroke	8,159	8,419	8,951	8,864
– Arteries and capillaries	2,397	2,434	2,494	2,467
– Other	3,203	3,223	3,371	3,522
Respiratory diseases	7,167	7,252	8,082	8,255
– Pneumonia and influenza	3,502	3,444	3,759	3,855
– Chronic bronchitis, emphysema and asthma	812	795	859	857
– Other chronic airways obstruction	1,934	2,095	2,374	2,432
– Other	919	918	1,090	1,111
Chronic liver disease and cirrhosis	733	703	768	719
Congenital anomalies	554	542	525	527
Certain perinatal causes	442	425	440	487
External Causes	4,087	4,062	4,277	4,150
– Motor vehicle accidents	1,090	1,067	1,128	949
– Accidental falls	1,112	1,153	1,215	1,292
– Suicide	718	786	789	780
– Homicide	228	194	168	171
– Other	939	862	977	958
All other causes	10,186	10,041	10,630	11,315
All causes	**90,130**	**90,670**	**95,505**	**97,335**

Table 3 Both

Name	1991	1992	1993	1994
Infectious diseases	2,624	2,744	3,124	3,197
Cancer	53,964	54,840	56,192	57,324
– Oesophagus and stomach	3,045	3,217	3,122	3,185
– Intestine and rectum	5,832	6,028	6,053	6,142
– Pancreas	2,622	2,709	2,810	2,864
– Trachea, bronchus and lung	14,255	14,425	15,113	15,159
– Breast	4,687	4,865	4,821	5,026
– Uterus, ovary and adnexa	2,213	2,184	2,289	2,334
– Prostate	3,426	3,494	3,582	3,624
– Urinary system	2,319	2,312	2,473	2,519
– Lymphatic tissue and leukemia	4,873	4,874	5,012	5,101
– Other	10,692	10,732	10,917	11,370
Diabetes mellitus	4,296	4,473	5,021	5,165
Nervous system diseases	5,046	5,268	5,739	5,974
Cardiovascular diseases	76,037	76,211	78,894	78,573
– Ischaemic heart disease	43,995	43,569	44,768	44,175
– Cardiac dysrhythmias and heart failure	6,638	6,808	7,072	7,365
– Stroke	14,194	14,471	15,429	15,306
– Arteries and capillaries	5,027	5,123	5,221	5,090
– Other	6,183	6,240	6,404	6,637
Respiratory diseases	16,805	16,663	18,053	18,342
– Pneumonia and influenza	6,779	6,650	7,047	7,302
– Chronic bronchitis, emphysema and asthma	2,217	2,041	2,117	2,045
– Other chronic airways obstruction	5,784	5,919	6,631	6,728
– Other	2,025	2,053	2,258	2,267
Chronic liver disease and cirrhosis	2,231	2,122	2,237	2,208
Congenital anomalies	1,208	1,216	1,128	1,157
Certain perinatal causes	1,013	981	1,055	1,059
External Causes	13,237	13,116	13,570	13,196
– Motor vehicle accidents	3,612	3,456	3,573	3,195
– Accidental falls	2,054	2,138	2,238	2,347
– Suicide	3,593	3,709	3,803	3,749
– Homicide	622	597	526	498
– Other	3,356	3,216	3,430	3,407
All other causes	19,107	18,901	19,899	20,882
All causes	**195,568**	**196,535**	**204,912**	**207,077**

Source: Statistics Canada 1994D, 1995A, 1996B, 1996C

Appendix

Morbidity and Mortality Risk Factors

four

Appendix 4 ◆ Morbidity and Mortality Risk Factors

Table 1 Human Biology

Disease	Heredity	Ethnic Group	Blood Group	Reprod. History	Pre-Disposing Conditions Blood Pressure	Choles-terol	Infection	Ulcer	Trauma
Cancer									
Esophagus									
Stomach		+	+						
Rectum	+	+						?	
Pancreas									
Lung	?								
Melanoma	+	+							
Breast	+							+	
Cervix		+		+			?		
Ovary				+					
Prostate		+		+			?		
Bladder							+	+	
Eye	+								?
Brain	?	?	+						
Thyroid									
Hodgkin's	+						+		
Leukemia	+	?	?				?		
Non Cancer*									
Tuberculosis		+							
Diabetes Mellitus	+	+	+				?		
Multiple Sclerosis	+	+	+				?		
Epilepsy	+						+		+
Cataract	+						+		+
Hypertensive	+	+					+		
Ischemic Heart	+	+			+	+			
Stroke	+				+	+			
Cirrhosis of Liver	+						+		
Arthritis	+		+						+
Congenital Anomaly	+			+			+		
Fracture of Skull/Spine								+	
Fracture of Femur								+	
Internal Injury								+	
Burns									

*Selected

Appendix 4 ◆ Morbidity and Mortality Risk Factors (continued)

Table 2 Environment

Disease	Socio-Economic	Occupation	Housing	Pollution Air	Pollution Water	Pollution Food	Weather/UVR
Cancer							
Esophagus		?					
Stomach	+				?	?	
Rectum	+	?					
Pancreas							
Lung		+		+			
Melanoma		?					+
Breast	+						
Cervix	+						
Ovary							
Prostate		+					
Bladder		+					
Eye							?
Brain		?			?		
Thyroid							
Hodgkin's		?					
Leukemia		+					
Non Cancer*							
Tuberculosis	+		+				
Diabetes Mellitus							
Multiple Sclerosis							
Epilepsy							
Cataract							
Hypertensive	+	+					
Ischemic Heart					+		+
Stroke							
Cirrhosis of Liver		+					
Arthritis		+					
Congenital Anomaly							
Fracture of Skull/Spine		+					+
Fracture of Femur			+				+
Internal Injury		+					
Burns		+	+				

*Selected

Appendix 1 ◆ Morbidity and Mortality Risk Factors (continued)

Table 3 Lifestyle

Disease	Tobacco	Alcohol	Diet / Obesity	Physical Activity	Promiscuity	Car / Motorcycle	Stress
Cancer							
Esophagus	+	+	+				
Stomach	?	?	+				
Rectum		?	+				
Pancreas							
Lung	+						
Melanoma							
Breast			+				
Cervix					+		
Ovary							
Prostate			?		?		
Bladder	+		?				
Eye							
Brain							
Thyroid			+				
Hodgkin's							
Leukemia							
Non Cancer*							
Tuberculosis	?						
Diabetes Mellitus		+	+				
Multiple Sclerosis			?				
Epilepsy							
Cataract							
Hypertensive		+	+	+			+
Ischemic Heart	+	+	+	+			+
Stroke			+				
Cirrhosis of Liver		+					
Arthritis							
Congenital Anomaly							
Fracture of Skull/Spine		+		+		+	
Fracture of Femur			+	+			
Internal Injury		+		+		+	
Burns	+	+					

Selected

Appendix 4 ◆ Morbidity and Mortality Risk Factors (continued)

Table 4 Health Care

Disease	Early Detection	Drugs	X-Rays
Cancer			
Esophagus			
Stomach			
Rectum	+		
Pancreas			
Lung			
Melanoma		?	
Breast	+	?	+
Cervix	+		
Ovary			
Prostate			
Bladder			+
Eye			
Brain			+
Thyroid			+
Hodgkin's			
Leukemia			
Non Cancer*			
Tuberculosis	+		
Diabetes Mellitus			
Multiple Sclerosis			
Epilepsy			
Cataract			
Hypertensive	+	+	
Ischemic Heart			
Stroke			
Cirrhosis of Liver		+	
Arthritis			
Congenital Anomaly			
Fracture of Skull/Spine			
Fracture of Femur		+	
Internal Injury			
Burns			

*Selected

Adapted from Moore 1985, Table 2

Glossary

Age-standardization. A procedure for adjusting rates designed to minimize the effects of differences in population age composition when comparing rates for different populations (Last 1995).

Carcinogen. An agent that can cause cancer (Last 1995).

Cause of Death. All those diseases, morbid conditions, or injuries that either resulted in or contributed to death and the circumstances or the accident or violence that produced any such injuries (Last 1995).

Canadian Environmental Protection Act (CEPA). Authorizes the Ministers of Environment and Health to investigate a wide variety of substances that may contaminate the environment and cause adverse effects on the environment and/or on human health (Meek et al. 1994).

Death Certificate. A vital record signed by a licensed physician or by another designated health worker that includes cause of death, decedent's name, sex, birth date, places of residence, and of death, and whether the deceased had been medically attended before death (Last 1995).

Death Rate. An estimate of the proportion of a population that dies during a specified period. The numerator is the number of persons dying during the period; the denominator is the number in the population, usually estimated as the midyear population (synonyms: crude death rate, mortality rate) (Last 1995).

Epidemiology. The study of the distribution and determinants of health-related states or events in specified populations, and the application of this study to control of health problems (Last 1995).

Evidence. Information or knowledge that proves or disproves something.

Exposure/Potency Index (EPI). The estimated daily intake of a CEPA Group I or II carcinogen divided by a quantitative estimate of the carcinogenic or mutagenic potency of the compound (Meek et al. 1994).

Extrapolation. Predicting the value of a variate outside the range of observations (Last 1995).

Hazard. A factor or exposure with the capability or potential to adversely affect health.

Human Exposure dose/Rodent Potency dose (HERP). An approach based on estimates of human exposure and potency in rodent carcinogen bioassays that can be used to rank relative priorities of concern with regard to carcinogens (Ames et al. 1987).

Inference. The process of applying reasoning; reaching conclusions or judgements based on premises or evidence.

International Classification of Disease (ICD). The classification of specific conditions and groups of conditions determined by an internationally representative group of experts who advise the World Health Organization (Last 1995).

Integrated Risk Information System (IRIS). An electronic database containing information on animal toxicology and human health effects that may result from exposure to various chemicals in the environment. The database is prepared and maintained by the US Environmental Protection Agency.

Life Expectancy. The average number of years an individual of a given age is expected to live if current mortality rates continue to apply (Last 1995).

Loss of Life Expectancy (LLE). A measure of the relative impact of various diseases and lethal forces, calculated using the age at death relative to a specified average life expectancy.

Maximum Tolerated Dose (MTD). The maximum possible dose that does not produce non-tumour effects, affect the longevity of the animals, or reduce the animals' weight by more than 10% compared with the controls.

No Observed Adverse Effect Level (NOAEL). The highest level of exposure in toxicological experiments that can be judged to cause no significant adverse effect.

Potential Years of Life Lost (PYLL). A measure of the relative impact of various diseases and lethal forces that are factors in the age at death. The PYLL emphasizes youthful or early deaths.

Population Attributable Risk (PAR). The incidence of a disease in a population that is associated with (attributable to) exposure to a specified risk factor (Last 1995).

Reference Dose (RfD). The value derived after applying uncertainty factors to reduce the NOAEL (synonym: Tolerable Daily Intake).

Relative Risk (RR). The ratio of the risk of disease or death among the exposed to the risk among the unexposed (synonyms: risk ratio, rate ratio) (Last 1995).

Risk Assessment. The process of estimating risk to health attributable to various hazards, typically consisting of: hazard identification, dose-response assessment, exposure assessment, and risk characterization.

Risk Factor. An aspect of personal behaviour or lifestyle, an environmental exposure, or an inborn or inherited characteristic, which on the basis of epidemiologic evidence is known to be associated with health-related condition(s) (Last 1995).

Risk. A term with many meanings in common usage, most involving some degree of danger and chance. For this book, risk means the likelihood of an adverse effect occurring within a specified time-frame (e.g., the chance that an individual will die in any given year or at any given age).

Tolerable Daily Intake (TDI). See Reference Dose.

Toxicology. The study of the adverse effects of specific chemicals on living organisms (Amdur et al. 1991).

Underlying Cause of Death (UCD). The disease or injury that initiated the train of events leading directly to death, or the circumstances of the accident or violence that produced the fatal injury (Last 1995).

Uncertainty. A condition of being unsure, which is the result of variability and/or inadequate knowledge of the item under consideration.

References

ACES. 1992. *A Standard for N-nitrosodimethylamine (NDMA)*. Advisory Committee on Environmental Standards. Ontario Ministry of Environment.

Alderson, M. R. 1988. *Mortality, Morbidity and Health Statistics*. New York: Stockton Press.

Amdur, M. O., J. Doull, and C. D. Klaassen. 1991. *Casarett and Doull's Toxicology*. 4th ed. New York: McGraw-Hill.

Ames, B. N. 1989. Mutagenesis and Carcinogenesis: Endogenous and Exogenous Factors. *Environmental and Molecular Mutagenesis* 14 (Supp. 16): 66–77.

Ames, B. N., R. Magaw, and L. S. Gold. 1987. Ranking Possible Carcinogenic Hazards. *Science* 236: 271–280.

Ames, B. N., L. S. Gold, and W. C. Willett. 1995. The Causes and Prevention of Cancer. *Proceedings of the National Academy of Sciences. USA* 92: 5258–5265.

Barrett, H. R. 1992. *Population Geography*. Harlow: Oliver & Boyd.

Beaglehole, R., R. Bonita, and T. Kjellstrom. 1993. *Basic Epidemiology*. Geneva: World Health Organization.

Bender, R. 1995. Impact of New Population Estimates on Health and Vital Statistics. *Health Reports* 7(1): 7–18.

Berger, B. 1994. *Beating Murphy's Law*. New York: Delta Trade Paperbacks.

Blumenthal, S. J., and D. J. Kupfer. 1990. Epilogue in *Suicide Over the Life Cycle*. S. J. Blumenthal and D. J. Kupfer. Washington, DC: American Psychiatric Press, 735–737.

Byers, T. 1995. Body Weight and Mortality. *New England Journal of Medicine* 333(11): 723–724.

CDC. 1994. *Addressing Emerging Infectious Disease Threats: A Prevention Strategy for the United States*. Atlanta, Ga.: Centers for Disease Control and Prevention.

Cherry, W., R. Bennett, and J. Shortreed. 1991. *Benchmark Risks for Use in Risk Assessment*. Final Report. Waterloo: Institute for Risk Research, University of Waterloo.

Cohen, B. L. 1991. Catalog of Risks Extended and Updated. *Health Physics* 61(3): 317–335.

Cohen, B. L., and I.–S. Lee. 1979. A Catalog of Risks. *Health Physics* 36: 707–722.

Colombo, J. R. 1996. *Canadian Global Almanac*. Toronto: Macmillan Canada.

DeSpelder, L. A., and A. L. Strickland. 1992. *The Last Dance: Encountering Death and Dying*. Mountain View, Calif.: Mayfield Publishing.

Doll, R., and R. Peto. 1981. The Causes of Cancer: Quantitative Estimates of Avoidable Risks of Cancer in the United States Today. *Journal of the National Cancer Institute* 66(6): 1192–1308.

Dominion Bureau of Statistics. 1933. *Vital Statistics, 1930*. Catalogue 84–202. Ottawa.

Dominion Bureau of Statistics. 1937. *Vital Statistics, 1935.* Catalogue 84–202. Ottawa.

Dominion Bureau of Statistics. 1942. *Vital Statistics, 1940.* Catalogue 84–202. Ottawa.

Dominion Bureau of Statistics. 1948. *Vital Statistics, 1945.* Catalogue 84–202. Ottawa.

Dominion Bureau of Statistics. 1953. *Vital Statistics, 1950.* Catalogue 84–202. Ottawa.

Dominion Bureau of Statistics. 1956. *Vital Statistics, 1955.* Catalogue 84–202. Ottawa.

Dominion Bureau of Statistics. 1962. *Vital Statistics, 1960.* Catalogue 84–202. Ottawa.

Dominion Bureau of Statistics. 1967. *Vital Statistics, 1965.* Catalogue 84–202. Ottawa.

Dominion Bureau of Statistics. 1968. *Population 1921–66: Revised Annual Estimates of Population, by Sex and Age, Canada and the Provinces.* Catalogue 91–511. Ottawa.

Ellison, L. F., Y. Mao, and L. Gibbons. 1995. Projected Smoking-Attributable Mortality in Canada, 1991–2000. *Chronic Diseases in Canada* 16(2): 84–89.

Evans, A. S. 1976. Causation and Disease: The Henle-Koch Postulates Revisited. *Yale Journal of Biology and Medicine* 49: 175–195.

Finkel, A. M. 1990. *Confronting Uncertainty in Risk Management.* Washington, DC: Resources for the Future.

Food Safety Council. 1980. Quantitative Risk Assessment. *Food and Cosmetics Toxicology* 18: 711–734.

Fuchs, C. S., M. J. Stampfer, G. Colditz, A. E. L. Giovannucci, J. E. Manson, et al. 1995. Alcohol Consumption and Mortality among Women. *New England Journal of Medicine* 332(19): 1245–1250.

Gordon, J. E. 1949. The Epidemiology of Accidents. *American Journal of Public Health* 39: 504–515.

Gough, M. 1989. Estimating Cancer Mortality. *Environmental Science & Technology* 23(8): 925–930.

Graham, J. D., B.–H. Chang, and J. S. Evans. 1992. Poorer is Riskier. *Risk Analysis* 12(3): 333–337.

Halperin, K. 1993. A Comparative Analysis of Six Methods for Calculating Travel Fatality Risk. *Risk-Issues in Health & Safety* 4: 15–33.

Hart, R.W., A. Neuman, and R.T. Robertson (eds.). 1995. *Dietary Restriction - Implications for the Design and Interpretation of Toxicity and Carcinogenicity Studies.* Washington, D.C.: International Life Sciences Institute Press.

Hatch, T. 1962. Changing Objectives in Occupational Health. *Industrial Hygiene Journal* (Jan.–Feb.): 1–7.

Hayes, O. 1994. Fact Sheet: Suicide — Focus on Canadian Youth (ICD-9 E950-9). *Chronic Diseases in Canada* 15(4): 132–134.

Health and Welfare Canada. 1980. *Mortality by Income Level in Urban Canada.* Ottawa.

Health and Welfare Canada. 1991. *Carcinogen Assessment.* Ottawa.

Health Canada. 1993. *Focus On: Canadians and Tobacco.* Ottawa.

Health Canada. 1995. *Canada's Guide to Healthy Eating.* Ottawa.

Heart and Stroke Foundation of Canada 1995. *Cardiovascular Disease in Canada*. Ottawa.

Henderson, Michael. 1987. *Living with Risk*. Chichester: British Medical Association.

Higginson, J. 1992. The Epidemiological Approach to the Causes of Human Cancer and the Implications for Cancer Policy Control. *Development of Environmental Health Status Indicators*. Waterloo: R. S. McColl, Institute for Risk Research, University of Waterloo, 147–158.

Higginson, J., and C. S. Muir. 1979. Environmental Carcinogenesis: Misconceptions and Limitations to Cancer Control. *Journal of the National Cancer Institute* 63(6): 1291–1298.

Hill, S. A. B. 1965. The Environment and Disease: Association or Causation? *Proceedings of the Royal Society of Medicine* (Jan. 14): 295–300.

Hirayama, T. 1990. *Life-Style and Mortality: A Large-Scale Census-Based Cohort Study in Japan*. New York: S. Karger AG.

Hoffman, F. O. and J. S. Hammonds. 1994. Propagation of Uncertainty in Risk Assessments: The Need to Distinguish between Uncertainty Due to Lack of Knowledge and Uncertainty Due to Variability. *Risk Analysis* 14(5): 707–712.

Howe, G. R., and J. P. Lindsay. 1983. A Follow-Up Study of a Ten-Percent Sample of the Canadian Labor Force. 1. Cancer Mortality in Males, 1965–1973. *Journal of the National Cancer Institute* 70(1): 37–44.

Hrudey, S. E. 1995. Major Concerns with Quantitative Cancer Risk Assessment for Environmental Risk Management. *Transactions of the Institution of Chemical Engineers* 73,B: S24–S26.

Hrudey, S. E. 1997. Current Needs in Environmental Risk Management. *Environmental Reviews* 5:7–15.

Hrudey, S. E., and D. Krewski. 1995. Is There a Safe Level of Exposure to a Carcinogen? *Environmental Science & Technology* 29(8): 370A–375A.

Hrudey, S. E., W. Chen, and C. G. Rousseaux. 1996. *Bioavailability in Environmental Risk Assessment*. Boca Raton, Fl.: CRC/Lewis Publishers.

Illing, E. M. M., and M. J. Kaiserman. 1995. Mortality Attributable to Tobacco Use in Canada and its Regions, 1991. *Canadian Journal of Public Health* 86(4): 257–265.

Jin, R. L., C. P. Shah, and T. Svoboda, J. 1995. The Impact of Unemployment on Health: A Review of the Evidence. *Canadian Medical Association Journal* 153(5): 529–540.

Kannel, W.B. and T. Gordon (eds.). 1976. *The Framingham Study: An Epidemiological Investigation of Heart Disease*. Washington, D.C.: U.S. Government Printing Office.

Kaplan, S., and B. J. Garrick. 1981. On the Quantitative Definition of Risk. *Risk Analysis* 1(1): 11–27.

Keeney, R. L. 1990. Mortality Risks Induced by Economic Expenditures. *Risk Analysis* 10(1): 147–159

Kleindorfer, P. R., H. C. Kunreuther, and P. J. H. Schoemaker. 1993. *Decision Sciences: An Integrative Perspective*, Cambridge, UK: Cambridge University Press.

Koshland Jr, D. E. 1994. Molecule of the Year: The DNA Repair Enzyme. *Science* 266: 1925.

Krewski D., D.W. Gaylor, A.P. Soms, and M. Szszykowicz. 1993. An Overview of the Report: Correlation Between Carcinogenic Potency and Maximum Tolerated Dose: Implications for Risk Assessment. *Risk Analysis* 13 (4): 383–398.

Lalonde, M. 1974. *A New Perspective on the Health of Canadians*. Ottawa: Department of Health and Welfare.

Last, J. M., ed. 1995. *A Dictionary of Epidemiology*. 3rd ed. New York: Oxford University Press.

Laudan, L. 1994. *The Book of Risks*. New York: John Wiley & Sons.

Letourneau, E. G., D. Krewski, N. W. Choi, M. J. Goddard, R. G. McGregor, et al. 1994. Case-Control Study of Residential Radon and Lung Cancer in Winnipeg, Manitoba, Canada. *American Journal of Epidemiology* 140(4): 310–322.

Lilienfeld, D. E., and P. D. Stolley. 1994. *Foundations of Epidemiology*. 3rd ed. New York: Oxford University Press.

Lindahl, B. I. B., E. Glattre, R. Lahti, G. Magnusson, and J. Mosbech. 1990. The WHO Principles for Registering Causes of Death: Suggestions for Improvement. *Journal of Clinical Epidemiology* 43(5): 467–474.

Lindsay, C. 1996. *Risk Communication: A Cross-Cultural Dialogue*. Master's Thesis, Department of Anthropology, University of Alberta.

Lipfert, F. W., and R. E. Wyzga. 1995. Air Pollution and Mortality: Issues and Uncertainties. *Journal of the Air & Waste Management Association* 45: 945–966.

Macneill, I. B., J. M. Elwood, D. Miller, and Y. Mao. 1995. Trends in Mortality from Melanoma in Canada and Prediction of Future Rates. *Statistics in Medicine* 14: 821–839.

Madigan, M. P., R. Ziegler, B. Jacques, C. Byrne, and R. N. Hoover. 1995. Proportion of Breast Cancer Cases in the United States Explained by Well-Established Risk Factors. *Journal of the National Cancer Institute* 87(22): 1681–1685.

Manson, J. E., W. C. Willett, M. J. Stampfer, G. A. Colditz, D. J. Hunter, et al. 1995. Body Weight and Mortality among Women. *New England Journal of Medicine* 333(11): 677–685.

McMichael, A. J. 1991. Setting Environmental Exposure Standards: Current Concepts and Controversies. *International Journal of Environmental Health Research* 1: 2–13.

McNeil, B. J., S. G. Parker, H. C. Sox and A. Tversky. 1982. On the Elicitation of Preferences for Alternative Therapies. *New England Journal of Medicine* 306: 1259–1262.

Meek, M. E., R. Newhook, R. G. Liteplo, and V. C. Armstrong. 1994. Approach to Assessment of Risk to Human Health for Priority Substances under the Canadian Environmental Protection Act. *Environmental Carcinogenesis & Ecotoxicology Reviews* C12(2): 105–134.

Meek, M. E. and Long. 1996. *Health-Based Tolerable Daily Intakes/Concentrations and Tumorigenic Doses/ Concentrations for Priority Substances*. Ottawa: Health Canada.

Messite, J., and S. D. Stellman. 1996. Accuracy of the Death Certificate Completion. *Journal of the American Medical Association* 275(10): 794–796.

Millar, W. J. 1995. Accidents in Canada, 1988 and 1993. *Health Reports* 7(2): 7–16.

Miller, A. B. 1992. Planning Cancer Control Strategies. *Chronic Diseases in Canada* 13 (Supp. 1): S1–S40.

Miller, A. B. 1995. Perspectives on Cancer Prevention. *Risk Analysis* 15(6): 655–660.

Moore, K. G. 1985. *Hospital Morbidity and Mortality in Canada. An Epidemiological Interpretation.* Edmonton: Alberta Department of Hospitals and Medical Care.

Nam, C. B. 1990. Mortality Differential from a Multiple-Cause-of-Death Perspective. *Measurement and Analysis of Mortality.* J. Vallin, S. D'Souza, and A. Palloni. New York: Oxford University Press, 328–342.

National Cancer Institute of Canada. 1996. *Canadian Cancer Statistics 1996.* Toronto.

National Cancer Institute of Canada. 1997. *Canadian Cancer Statistics 1997.* Toronto.

Nelson, N. 1988. Toxicology and Epidemiology: Strengths and Limitations. *Epidemiology and Health Risk Assessment.* L. Gordis. New York: Oxford University Press, 37–48.

Northridge, M. E. 1995. Annotation: Public Health Methods-Attributable Risk as a Link Between Causality and Public Health Action. *American Journal of Public Health* 85(9): 9–10.

Nuland, R. 1993. *How We Die.* New York: Vintage Books.

Peto, R., A. D. Lopez, J. Boreham, M. Thun, and C. Heath Jr. 1992. Mortality from Tobacco in Developed Countries: Indirect Estimation from National Vital Statistics. *The Lancet* 339 (May 23): 1268–1278.

Rasmussen, N. C. 1981. The Application of Probabilistic Risk Assessment Techniques to Energy Technologies. *Annual Review of Energy* 6: 123–138.

Reichhardt, T. 1995. Weighing the Health Risks of Airborne Particulates. *Environmental Science & Technology* 29(8): 360A–364A.

Renn, O. 1992. Concepts of Risk: A Classification. *Social Theories of Risk.* S. Krimsky and D. Golding. Wesport, Conn.: Praegar, 52–79.

Rhomberg, L. 1995. What Constitutes "Dose"? (Definitions). *Low-Dose Extrapolation of Cancer Risks: Issues and Perspectives.* S. Olin, W. Farland, C. Park, et al. Washington, DC: International Life Sciences Institute, 185–198.

Riley, R., and P. Paddon. 1989. Accidents in Canada: Mortality and Hospitalization. *Health Reports* 1(1): 23–50.

Rowe, W. 1977. *An Anatomy of Risk.* New York: John Wiley & Sons.

Rowland, A. J., and P. Cooper. 1983. *Environment and Health.* London: Edward Arnold.

Shah, C. P. 1994. *Public Health and Preventive Medicine in Canada.* 3rd ed. Toronto: University of Toronto Press.

Shlyakhter, A., C. B. Shlyakhter, and R. Wilson. 1993. Estimating Uncertainty in Physical Measurements, Observational and Environmental Studies: Lessons from Trends in Nuclear Data. *1993 IEEE*: 310–317.

Siemiatycki, J. 1992. Review of Findings from a Registry-Like Database Designed to Discover Occupational Carcinogens. *Development of Environmental Health Status Indicators*. Waterloo: R. S. McColl, Institute for Risk Research, University of Waterloo,159–168.

Siemiatycki, J., R. Dewar, L. Nadon, and M. Gerin. 1994. Occupational Risk Factors for Bladder Cancer: Results from a Case-Control Study in Montreal, Quebec, Canada. *American Journal of Epidemiology* 140(12): 1061–1080.

Single, E., L. Robson, X. Xie, et al. 1996. *The Costs of Substance Abuse in Canada*. Canadian Center on Substance Abuse.

Slovic, P. 1997. Trust, Emotion, Sex, Politics and Science: Surveying the Risk Assessment Battlefield. *Environment and Ethics in Management*, M. Bazerman, D. Messick, A. Tenbrunsel, and K. Wade–Benzoni, eds. San Francisco: New Lexington, 277–313.

Slovic, P., B. Fischhoff, and S. Lichtenstein. 1979. Rating the Risks. *Environment* 21(3): 14–39.

Society of Actuaries. 1980. *Blood Pressure Study, 1979*. Society of Actuaries and Association of Life Insurance Medical Directors of America.

St. Leger, A. S., A. L. Cochrane, and F. Moore. 1979. Factors Associated with Cardiac Mortality in Developed Countries with Particular Reference to the Consumption of Wine. *The Lancet* (May 12): 1017–1020.

Statistics Canada. 1970. *Estimates of Population by Sex and Age for Canada and the Province*. Catalogue 91–202. Ottawa.

Statistics Canada. 1972. *Vital Statistics, 1970*. Catalogue 84–202. Ottawa.

Statistics Canada. 1975. *Estimates of Population by Sex and Age for Canada and the Provinces, 1975*. Catalogue 91–202. Ottawa.

Statistics Canada. 1978. *Vital Statistics*. Vol. III, *Deaths, 1975*. Catalogue 84–206. Ottawa.

Statistics Canada. 1980. *Estimates of Population by Sex and Age for Canada and the Provinces, 1980*. Catalogue 91–202. Ottawa.

Statistics Canada. 1983. *Vital Statistics*. Vol. III, *Mortality Summary List of Causes, 1980*. Catalogue 84–206. Ottawa.

Statistics Canada. 1985. *Postcensal Annual Estimates of Population by Marital Status, Age, Sex and Components of Growth for Canada, Provinces and Territories, June 1, 1985*. Catalogue 91–210. Ottawa.

Statistics Canada. 1987. *Vital Statistics*. Vol. III, *Mortality Summary List of Causes, 1985*. Catalogue 84–206. Ottawa.

Statistics Canada. 1990. *Postcensal Annual Estimates of Population by Marital Status, Age, Sex and Components of Growth for Canada, Provinces and Territories, June 1, 1990*. Catalogue 91–210. Ottawa.

Statistics Canada. 1994A. *Employment, Earnings, and Hours. Catalogue* 72–002. Ottawa.

Statistics Canada. 1994B. *Mortality — Summary List of Causes, 1990.* Rev. Vol. 4. Health Reports, No. 1. Supp. No. 12. Catalogue 82-003S12. Ottawa.

Statistics Canada. 1994C. *Selected Mortality Statistics, Canada, 1921–1990.* Catalogue 84–548. Ottawa.

Statistics Canada 1994D. *Mortality — Summary List of Causes, 1991.* Catalogue 84 209. Ottawa.

Statistics Canada. 1995A. *Mortality — Summary List of Causes, 1992.* Catalogue 84–209. Ottawa.

Statistics Canada. 1995B. *National Population Health Survey Overview 1994–95.* Catalogue 82–567. Ottawa.

Statistics Canada. 1995C. *Quarterly Demographic Statistics, April–June 1995.* Ottawa.

Statistics Canada. 1995D. *Work Injuries 1992–1994.* Catalogue 72–208. Ottawa.

Statistics Canada. 1996A. *Causes of Death, 1994.* Catalogue 84–208. Ottawa.

Statistics Canada. 1996B. *Mortality — Summary List of Causes, 1994.* Catalogue 84–209–XPB. Ottawa.

Statistics Canada. 1996C. *Mortality — Summary List of Causes, 1993.* Catalogue 84–209–XPB. Ottawa.

Stedman's Medical Dictionary. 1995. *Stedman's Medical Dictionary.* 26th ed. Baltimore: Williams & Wilkins.

Stewart, P. J., J. Potter, C. Dulberg, P. Niday, C. Nimrod, et al. 1995. Change in Smoking Prevalence among Pregnant Women 1982–93. *Canadian Journal of Public Health* 86(1): 37–41.

Swales, J., and D. de Bono. 1993. *Cardiovascular Risk Factors.* New York: Gower Medical Publishing.

Taubes, G. 1995. Epidemiology Faces Its Limits. *Science* 269: 164–169.

Taylor, E. 1992. New International Disease Classification. *Health Reports* 4(3): 331–333.

Thomas, S. P. 1996. Analysis of Health Risk Evidence and Inference in Canada. Master's Thesis, University of Alberta.

Transport Canada. 1994. *Traffic Collision Statistics in Canada, 1992.* Transport Canada. TP11743–92(E).

Transport Canada. 1995A. *Alcohol Use among Drivers and Pedestrians Fatally Injured in Motor Vehicle Accidents: Canada, 1993.* Transport Canada. TP11759–93(E).

Transport Canada. 1995B. *Canadian Motor Vehicle Traffic Collision Statistics.* Transport Canada. TP 3322.

Trefil, J. S. 1984. Odds Are Against Your Breaking That Law of Averages. *Smithsonian* (Sept.): 66–75.

Urquhart, J., and K. Heilmann. 1984. *Risk Watch.* New York: Facts on File Publications.

US EPA. 1986. Guidelines for Carcinogen Risk Assessment. *Federal Register* 51(185): 33992–34003.

US EPA. 1993. *Respiratory Health Effects of Passive Smoking: Lung Cancer and Other Disorders.* Washington, DC.

US EPA. 1996. IRIS (Integrated Risk Information System). CD-ROM.

US NRC. 1983. *Risk Assessment in the Federal Government.* Washington, DC: National Academy Press.

US NRC. 1989. *Diet and Health*. Washington, DC: National Academy Press.

US NRC. 1994. *Science and Judgment in Risk Assessment*. Washington, DC: National Academy Press.

US NRC. 1996. *Understanding Risk*. Washington, DC: National Academy Press.

Vainio, H., and J. Wilbourn. 1993. Cancer Etiology: Agents Causally Associated with Human Cancer. *Parmacol-Toxicol* 72 (Supp. 1): 4–11.

Villeneuve, P. J. and Y. Mao. 1994. Lifetime Probability of Developing Lung Cancer, by Smoking Status, Canada. *Canadian Journal of Public Health* 85(6): 385–388.

WHO. 1975. *International Classification of Diseases, 1975 Revision*. Vol. 1. Geneva: World Health Organization.

WHO. 1979. *Medical Certification of Cause of Death*. Geneva: World Health Organization.

WHO. 1994. *Cardiovascular Disease Risk Factors: New Areas for Research*. Geneva: World Health Organization.

Wilkins, K. 1989. The Major Causes of Death among Young Adults: Trends from 1926 to 1985. *Chronic Diseases in Canada* 10(1): 3–7.

Wilkins, K. 1994. Comment on "Speaking for the Dead to Protect the Living: The Role of the Coroner in Ontario." *Health Reports* 6(3): 353.

Wilkins, K. 1995. Causes of Death: How the Sexes Differ. *Health Reports* 7(2): 33–43.

Wilkins, K., and E. Mark. 1992. Potential Years of Life Lost, Canada, 1990. *Chronic Diseases in Canada* 13(6): 111–115.

Wilkins, R., O. Adams, and A. Brancker. 1989. Changes in Mortality by Income in Urban Canada from 1971 to 1986. *Health Reports* 1(2): 137–174.

Wilkins, R., G. J. Sherman, and P. A. F. Best. 1991. Birth Outcomes and Infant Mortality by Income in Urban Canada, 1986. *Health Reports* 3(1): 7–31.

Willett, W. C. 1994. Diet and Health: What Should We Eat? *Science* 264: 532–537.

Wilson, R., and E. Crouch. 1982. *Risk/Benefit Analysis*. Cambridge: Ballinger Publishing Company.

Wynder, E. L., and G. B. Gori. 1977. Contribution of the Environment to Cancer Incidence: An Epidemiologic Exercise. *Journal of the National Cancer Institute* 58(4): 825–832.

Young, J. G., and J. M. Wagner. 1994. Speaking for the Dead to Protect the Living: The Role of the Coroner in Ontario. *Health Reports* 6(3): 339–352.